Hi-De-Ho

Hi-De-Ho

The Life of Cab Calloway

ALYN SHIPTON

OXFORD
UNIVERSITY PRESS
2010

OXFORD
UNIVERSITY PRESS

Oxford University Press, Inc., publishes works that further
Oxford University's objective of excellence
in research, scholarship, and education.

Oxford   New York
Auckland   Cape Town   Dar es Salaam   Hong Kong   Karachi
Kuala Lumpur   Madrid   Melbourne   Mexico City   Nairobi
New Delhi   Shanghai   Taipei   Toronto

With offices in
Argentina   Austria   Brazil   Chile   Czech Republic   France   Greece
Guatemala   Hungary   Italy   Japan   Poland   Portugal   Singapore
South Korea   Switzerland   Thailand   Turkey   Ukraine   Vietnam

Copyright © 2010 by Oxford University Press, Inc.

Published by Oxford University Press, Inc.
198 Madison Avenue, New York, New York 10016

www.oup.com

Oxford is a registered trademark of Oxford University Press

Library of Congress Cataloging-in-Publication Data
Shipton, Alyn.
Hi-de-ho : the life of Cab Calloway / by Alyn Shipton.
    p.   cm.
Includes bibliographical references and index.
ISBN 978-0-19-514153-5
1. Calloway, Cab, 1907–1994.
2. Jazz musicians—Biography. I. Title.
ML410.C265S55   2010
781.65092—dc22
[B]
2010007435

1 3 5 7 9 8 6 4 2

Printed in the United States of America
on acid-free paper

Contents

Introduction and Acknowledgments

C lad in white tie and tails, dancing energetically, waving an oversized baton, and singing "Minnie the Moocher," Cab Calloway is one of the most iconic figures in popular music. He was the first great African American vocalist in jazz who specialized in singing without also doubling on an instrument, and he was also a conductor and bandleader who assembled a series of remarkably consistent hard-swinging ensembles. By always striving to hire the best musicians and arrangers, he took the art of big band playing forward consistently from the start of the 1930s to the end of the 1940s. The tenor saxophonist Chu Berry made some of his finest records in the Calloway band, as did trumpeter Jonah Jones, saxophonists Ike Quebec and Eddie Barefield, and drummer Cozy Cole. At its peak in the late 1930s and early 1940s, Calloway's was the highest earning African American orchestra and, by virtue of its biggest hit "Minnie the Moocher," also one of the few to have broken through to the general public with a million-selling record. People loved Cab and his antics for what he was, irrespective of color. In later life, Cab transformed into an elegant and sophisticated star of the musical theater, but from the 1930s to the 1990s, he never forgot how to "hi-de-ho," and win over a crowd.

Before I began work on this book I had only a scant awareness of the full and impressive range of Calloway's achievements. In the mid-1980s, I was working in New Orleans with the guitarist Danny Barker on the first of two volumes of his memoirs. I knew Danny through his work in the city, and his long association with the New Orleans Jazz Museum. As a player, he was not only a revivalist of traditional styles but also someone who had been an eyewitness to the very earliest days of jazz. I knew that he had played with the likes of Lee Collins and Little Brother Montgomery. Probably because my opinions had been formed by the kinds of critics who did not take Cab Calloway seriously as a jazz musician, dismissing his singing as "commercial" and considering only the intermittent snatches of instrumental music in his copious catalogue of vocal recordings, I knew very little about Danny's many years in the Calloway orchestra.

Danny changed all that. Sitting in the humid Louisiana dusk on his porch, with the sounds of the South all round us, the wail of freight trains rumbling away to our left, a distant roar of traffic from the freeway to the right, we listened to many of the great recordings he had made with Cab Calloway. Danny patiently explained to me about the wonderful rhythm section in which he had the privilege to work. He still revered Cab for what he had achieved in terms of African American entertainment. Although the manner of Danny's departure still rankled with him, his admiration for Cab and the band was utterly sincere. I realized that this was a band I had to listen to and discover more about.

Later I met and worked with Doc Cheatham on a book about his life, and discovered plenty about an earlier era of Cab's career. Soon, through Doc, I had encountered Milt Hinton, Jonah Jones, and other musicians who had known and worked with Cab. I found myself intrigued by how such a great orchestra as his seemed to have been overlooked by most jazz writers, with the honorable exception of Gunther Schuller. As I began work on *Groovin' High*, my biography of Dizzy Gillespie, in the mid-1990s, I listened to every record the band had made from 1939 to 1941 and started the groundwork for the research on this book.

First and foremost, therefore, I have to thank Danny Barker and Doc Cheatham for getting me started. Mark Tucker also gave my enquiries a boost when we worked together on the British publication of his edition of Garvin Bushell's memoirs.

I am most grateful to the trustees of the Peter Whittingham Award, at the Musicians' Benevolent Fund in London, who awarded me a grant in 1996 to finish Danny Barker's second volume of memoirs, which involved several days of work on the Cab Calloway papers at Boston University. Karen Mix, who was then the librarian of the Calloway archive at the Mugar Memorial Library, was a great help. Later in the same visit to the United States, I was able to consult papers pertaining to *Porgy and Bess* and *Hello, Dolly!* at the Amistad Research Center, Tulane University, New Orleans, where Rebecca Hankins was an enthusiastic guide to the collections.

I have also been greatly helped in my research by the efforts of others. Principally, as in so many of my books, by the selfless Howard Rye, who has given up time to answer queries, to track down obscure references, and to comment on a draft manuscript. He and Josephine Beaton kindly shared the fruits of their research into A.F.M. transfers. Franz Hoffman's work on the black press has also been invaluable, as has Ken Vail's research into Dizzy Gillespie's time in the band. Mark Cantor has generously answered questions on films and soundies. My old friend Steve Voce helpfully supplied transcripts of his 1958 interview with Cab. In Chicago Robert Helfer searched the records of Crane College alumni.

Shortly after Cab Calloway's death, BBC Radio 3 commissioned me to make a six-part documentary series in tribute to him, and my thanks go to my producer Derek Drescher for setting up many of the 1995 interviews about Cab. Working on a documentary about Blue Note records in 1997 for Radio 3's Brian Morton also brought me back in touch with many of Cab's colleagues, including Jonah Jones. As Cab's centenary approached, BBC Radio 2 asked me to write and research a new series on Cab to be presented by Clarke Peters. Clarke, my producer Terry Carter, and I had great fun looking into further details of Cab's life. Through this project, I came to meet Christopher Calloway Brooks, Cab's grandson, who has become a firm friend and a tremendous source of ideas, materials, and enthusiasm. He has been my sternest and most constructive critic. Equally, his mother, Camay Calloway Murphy, Cab's eldest daughter, was not only the most charming of interviewees but a great help as well in sorting out the early days of Calloway family history. In this respect I must also mention the support of Jean-François Pitet in Paris, whose Hi-De-Ho Blog is a masterly collection of Calloway resources. Gail Levin has also shared information concerning a television documentary she was making for the European Arte Channel. Thanks to Jimmy McHugh III, Lee Newman, and Guy Thomas for help in providing materials from the Jimmy McHugh archives, notably original Cotton Club programs.

Thanks to John Stedman at JSP Records, to all the staff at Discovery Records, to Alan Price at Proper Records, and to the BBC Gramophone Library for help in tracking down sound recordings. My gratitude also goes to Paul Pace, formerly of Ray's Jazz Shop in London, for additional help with records.

I would like to acknowledge all the musicians, enthusiasts, and friends of Cab who have talked to me for this project: Danny Barker, Alan Barnes, Doc Cheatham, Alan Cohen, Stanton Davis, Elizabeth Forbes, Milt Hinton, Danny Holgate, Illinois Jacquet, Jonah Jones, Gene Lees, Dan Morgenstern, Snub Mosley, Zane Paul, Julian Presley, Stan Scotland, and Clark Terry.

Peter Symes has helped me with the pictures for several books and he has come up trumps again in the research for this one, with the help of Frank Driggs. I am also grateful to the estates of Danny Barker and Doc Cheatham for the use of their photos, and to my friend Robert Gore for the picture of Cab's band en route to Britain.

At Oxford, first of all, the late Sheldon Meyer started it off; Maribeth Payne nudged it along a bit further; and Suzanne Ryan has gone beyond the call of duty to ensure that the book was eventually finished. Thanks, too, to Madelyn Sutton and Christine Dahlin for their calm efficiency.

Above all, thanks to Cab Calloway himself, for a treasury of music that is as vibrant and lively today as during the sixty-odd years in which it was recorded.

Hi-De-Ho

Chapter 1

Baltimore Buzz
1907–1927

. . . .

Cypress Street in Rochester, New York, is a long tree-lined boulevard with wide grass verges on each side, and well-appointed one- and two-story wooden houses standing back from the road. Starting a couple of blocks inland from the east bank of the Genesee River, close by the city's central loop, all the streets in this verdant area known as South Wedge are named after trees. Not far from the intersection with Poplar stood 18 Cypress Street, where Cabell Calloway was born on Christmas Day, 1907. The original wooden-framed house is now long gone, torn down in the 1970s for the construction of one of the street's few apartment buildings, but the surrounding homes still stand much as they did over a century ago, and the overall appearance of the neighborhood has hardly changed since the Calloway family lived there.

When he was christened Cabell, the new baby boy became the third successive generation of Calloway males to take the name, but he quickly became known, as he would be for the rest of his life, as Cab. His grandfather, born in 1846, was still head of the family, and lived in Baltimore, Maryland, but the child's father had moved from there to Rochester the previous year. According to family legend, Cabell II, the baby's father, had studied at Lincoln University in Pennsylvania, the first institution in the United States to award degrees to African Americans, and he then worked as a clerk for a legal firm in Baltimore before making his way into the real estate business.[1] That venture was not a success, and this—probably coupled with the disastrous effects on the property market of the great Baltimore fire of February 1904, which razed huge tracts of buildings in and around the downtown business district—was why he and his young family, with daughters Blanche and Bernice, moved away to seek their fortunes in the rapidly growing lakeside town of Rochester, at the northern end of New York State.

Cabell II's older brother Henry came along as well, and the two young men looked for work together. By the time Cab was born, his father was still down on his luck, and despite his middle-class education and his previous career was working as a porter doing what the 1910 census referred to as "shopwork." Brother Henry was a factory porter. Consequently, the boy's mother, Eulalia, as well as having produced three children in five years, worked as a music teacher to help support the family. At various points she seems to have taught in the public school system, but when young Cabell entered the world, she was teaching pupils at home.[2] In the years that followed, hers was the strong personality that held the family together.

Accounts vary as to exactly when the family moved back to Baltimore, and the fact that there were three generations of male Calloways with the same name makes the chronology a little hard to determine. However, it seems that Cabell II and his young family stayed in Rochester until at least 1912. By 1910 they had moved to 93 Henrietta Street in the more densely populated Swilburg district, a little farther from the center of town than their first home. Although this road was not quite so leafy or spaciously laid out as Cypress Street, it was only ten blocks or so from the big open space of Cobb's Hill Park, with its lakes, grassy slopes, and abundant trees, and must have been a good place to raise a young family.

Even so, Cab recounted little of his early years in Rochester. There may well have been family excursions to the nearby shores of Lake Ontario, and trips to see the dramatic gorge of the Genesee River and its big, noisy waterfalls, some of which provided the roaring sound track to the town center, but he recalled nothing of this, other than that his mother taught school and that much of the family's leisure time was taken up in church activities. From the sounds of Eulalia's pupils picking their way through their first piano pieces to the robust singing of the Presbyterian congregation, the one constant factor in the infant Cab's life was the sound of music.

The family remained in the city for the birth of Cab's younger brother Elmer in 1912,[3] but at some time during the next twelve months they came back to Baltimore, and moved in with Cabell I and Elizabeth Calloway at 1017 Druid Hill Avenue, which had been the main family home since before the turn of the century. According to Cab's autobiography, this was a three-story wooden house, in an exclusively African American neighborhood. Nowadays the 1000 block is at the less salubrious end of this long avenue, but the neighborhood remains a predominantly African American area with a tall apartment building standing high above the site of 1017, amid a sea of low-rise postwar project housing. These utilitarian brick blocks replaced what would once have been more elegant older homes, including the long-vanished Calloway house. Up at the north end of the avenue, toward Druid Hill Park itself, plenty of handsome nineteenth-century brick- and stucco-fronted homes remain, that— even though they are not all in the best state of repair—give more than a hint as to how it would have looked when Cabell II, his wife, and four children moved back there.

Baltimore was a city well provided with sturdy housing, and many miles of well-built Georgian houses, of two or three stories, survived the fire and gave the town much of its character. In the late nineteenth century, most families here, white or African American, could aspire to live in a house, rather than an apartment. With a red-brick front and light-colored marble steps, a house was something to be proud of, even if the city had lagged behind in other respects. Its first proper sewerage system, for example, was only being installed during the years when the Calloway family was up north. Built because its many springs and rivers drove plenteous water-powered flour mills, and because it had a fine deepwater harbor close to its downtown area, Baltimore offered plenty of work for all levels of society. In particular it had a sizable African American population that accounted for over 20 percent of the total inhabitants.

In the aftermath of the fire, heavy industry moved in as well, and in the first two decades of the twentieth century the city quickly found itself coping with an unprecedented influx of manual workers from the South and Southwest. Some areas that had once been quiet, well-to-do Georgian streets became so densely packed that they turned into slums, with one-time family homes being rapidly converted into numerous small boxy apartments. The area just a few blocks below where the Calloways lived, down toward West Preston Street and Pennsylvania Avenue, was rife with tuberculosis and other urban ills caused by overcrowding, poor ventilation, and inadequate sanitation. Better off African Americans moved away from this district and began to settle in formerly

whites-only streets such as Myrtle and McCulloh. This led to occasional inci-
dences of violence and mass protests from whites against "black encroachment." Yet by 1913 when the young Calloways moved back from Rochester,
these public demonstrations were largely over.

As in so many American cities, a few blocks can make a huge difference in
living conditions. Having been settled for over twenty years in the area known
as Upton, the Calloways regarded themselves as middle-class, even if behind
the respectable facade of their home they were occasionally reduced by strait-
ened finances to eating beans for every meal. "Baltimore was a rough town,
then," observed Cab's eldest daughter, Camay. "But they lived in the middle
section and his family was very much considered to be on an upper-class level
there. Their family friends were ministers, teachers, people in real estate, so
they had fine social ambitions for Cab."[4]

Grandfather Cabell I was frequently away for long periods of time. When
he was not managing his pool hall in Baltimore, he was in New York or other
far-off towns. Consequently Elizabeth Calloway, a firm Presbyterian, took over
and ruled her household with a rod of iron. Every Sunday, the whole family
would be dressed up in its best clothes for the lengthy walk beyond Druid Hill
Park to Grace Presbyterian Church, where Eulalia played the organ. At home,
Elizabeth was determined that her family would live in a manner that was well
protected from what she regarded as the less desirable elements of the bustling
street life outside. Cab recalled Grandmother Calloway's tough discipline at
mealtimes, and the sense of longing with which he watched other neighborhood children playing outdoors while he and his sisters were kept inside, under
strict orders not to run about or disturb the peace of the household.[5] However,
in this matriarchal setup, the fragile personality that had in all probability been
the underlying reason for Cabell II's failures in business came to light when,
not long after moving back to his home town, he suffered a major nervous
breakdown. Cabell II was institutionalized and on October 15, 1913, he died,
aged just thirty-five.[6]

After his death, the tensions in Elizabeth's household became unbearable.
Eulalia believed that her mother-in-law held her to blame for Cabell II's death,
and it was not long before she moved back to her own parents' house a short
distance away. Her family, the Reeds, lived in a much more relaxed manner,
less dominated by the church and formal rules. There was laughter and fun,
and the children were allowed to play with their neighbors in the yard and on
the street. Within a year, Eulalia had found a new husband, and John Fortune

became Cab's stepfather. In 1916 Eulalia bore John a son, also called John, and a daughter, Mary Camilla, followed in 1918. By January 1920 the family of eight were living in their own rented brick-fronted house on the heights close to the park at 2216 Druid Hill Avenue.[7]

John Fortune became the senior man in the Calloway family when Grandfather Cabell I died in May 1919.[8] But although Cab was later to develop a good relationship with his stepfather, or "Papa Jack" as he was known, at the start of the 1920s he displayed all the signs of a boy who lacked a strong male role model. He ran wild, played hooky from school, shot craps, and took himself to the racetrack. But he was also industrious, and hustled up any number of small jobs to make himself money. He sold papers, shone shoes, distributed race cards, and walked horses around the exercise ring. If he had any role model at this period, it was his late grandfather, whom he once described as "a kind of Sportin' Life."[9] Although the young Cab had been forbidden to visit the pool hall, Grandfather Calloway's streetwise lifestyle amid hustlers, gamblers, and pool sharks seems to have been very appealing to him.

As a teenager he came close to this exotic milieu at Pimlico Race Course, a fifteen-minute trolley ride from home, where by selling race cards to punters and shining shoes, he could blend into the excited throng at the seventy-acre site every afternoon in the racing season. Known as "Old Hilltop," Pimlico was the country's second-oldest horse-racing track, and Cab would make his way to the gentle rise at the center of the infield, which offered a commanding view of every race. (Sadly the hillock was leveled in the 1930s, removing this very atmospheric feature of the old track.) From his early teens onward, Cab was compulsively drawn to the world of horses and racing, and at every stage of his adult life he would spend as much time as possible at the track, eventually developing a deep knowledge of form, and constantly trying his luck as a gambler. As his latter-day manager and confidant Stan Scotland said:

> You wouldn't know Cab Calloway if you didn't know racehorses. I was never sure what was more important to him, his horses or his music. Whenever I had to meet him to sign a contract . . . I would have to meet him at his "office," which we knew was the racetrack. I would see him at the Governor's Room, and he had a wonderful system which I could never understand. He was an excellent handicapper. I don't think he

was ahead of the game, just like every horse player, but he really loved his horses.[10]

On his own admission Cab did not have much time for school, but despite the hustling, the hooky, and the horses, there was one aspect of his education that he was serious about, and that was music. He told the British writer Steve Voce, "It's no good trying to be a musician unless you're satisfied that you've had a full musical training. I spent a lot of time at grammar school and all my time at high school studying voice—about eight years in all."[11]

Apart from the constant, almost subliminal, input from his mother's work as a music teacher, Cab had another reason, as the 1920s began, to be involved in developing his interest in singing. His older sister Blanche, born in 1902 and already by her late teens a very good-looking and charismatic woman, was on the point of launching her career as a professional singer and actress. A newspaper report from the period singles her out for praise, commending her "voice of wide range [which] attracted considerable attention" in concerts by the choir at Grace Presbyterian Church.[12] It is clear that Cab looked up to her and admired her talent, and for her part she took a keen interest in him, no doubt spotting the green shoots of his own nascent abilities as a singer and dancer.

In 1921, Blanche left home to join the first of a series of touring cabaret troupes, with whom she was to forge a career that put her in the top echelon of African American entertainers. This was the Smarter Set Co., which had been organized in 1909 to tour the vaudeville circuit by the brothers Salem Tutt Whitney and J. Homer Tutt. The two men wrote endless short skits and sketches, in which they starred themselves, interspersed with music and dancing from their "World Famous Bronze Beauties." Their long-running touring shows included *The Mayor of Newtown*, *Darkest Americans*, *Children of the Sun*, and *Bamboula*, and these preceded the opening at the Grand Theater, Chicago, on December 5, 1921, of the pair's new revue *Up and Down*, in which Blanche Calloway was listed among the Bronze Beauties for the very first time.[13]

Within a couple of months she was off on tour with the company, and by the time the Smarter Set reached the Lafayette Theatre in New York City in March with *Up and Down*, Blanche was no longer just a chorus girl but playing bit parts in the sketches, her role as Miss Green being picked out by one critic as a high point in the otherwise "somewhat thin" plot of the show.[14] Although

Blanche Calloway was to be a better-known star than her younger brother until the late 1920s, the early stage of her career remains shrouded in obscurity. However, in the years that followed her Smarter Set debut, her progress can be spotted via the occasional review or advertisement, as she slowly but surely worked her way up through the profession, from chorus girl and bit part actress to featured singer, eventually taking a share of the headlines herself. One thing that everyone who saw her in those early years agreed on was that she was already a dazzling talent. Pianist Earl Hines, for example, who encountered her in Chicago, wrote, "Blanche Calloway . . . had a very good way of entertaining. She was wild and wiry in certain things, and very sensitive when it came to balance."[15] The trombonist Clyde Bernhardt was equally enthusiastic: "She was terrific! She was a headliner."[16]

Blanche left the Smarter Set to join Maud Mills and Eddie Rector in a Manhattan revue called *Buzzin' Around*. Then came a spell in the cast of the touring production of the best-known African American revue of the 1920s, Miller and Lyles's *Shuffle Along*. Blanche joined the cast when the impresario Walter Brooks took it on the road after a long run at Daly's Sixty-third Street Theatre in New York to play at prestigious white theaters across the country. At some point after this she was in Eddie Hunter's 1923 revue *How Come* (which also included the saxophone virtuoso Sidney Bechet) and by July that year she had fetched up in what was to be her home base for some years, Chicago. There she was given principal billing along with the tenor Ollie Powers in the revue *Ramblin' Round* at the Grand Theater, the same venue at which she had started out as a chorus girl a mere eighteen months earlier.[17]

By the fall of 1924, Blanche had become an established figure on Chicago's African American music scene. She had appeared at several more theaters and cabarets, and in September 1924 she began working at the venue that would become something of a home from home for her, as well as subsequently providing a launchpad for her brother's career, the Sunset Café. It was billed as "Chicago's Classiest Cabaret," and heading a cast of "twenty sparkling personalities" Blanche starred there in the revue *Sunset Vanities*.[18] We can get an idea of the overall sound of the show, because its backing band was led by one of Chicago's principal theater and club musical directors, Sammy Stewart, who made some records at the time. He hailed from Ohio, had brought his first band from Columbus to Chicago at the start of the 1920s, and according to several accounts was immediately paid the top rate of thirty-six hundred dollars a week for his band by the promoter Joe Glaser, later Louis Armstrong's manager, and the man who ran the music at the Sunset.

"Sammy Stewart had gathered together only musicians of class," remembered his deputy pianist, Tommy Brookins, "and he played arrangements in a style that was sophisticated for that era."[19] Although Stewart's pit orchestra at the club and at the various theaters where he played was usually eighteen men, at exactly the time that he and Blanche went into the Sunset he took a slightly smaller band into the recording studios for Paramount, and made the aforementioned records, of which the highlight is a bouncy, swinging version of "Copenhagen." From this it is possible to see why he was to earn the reputation of directing one of Chicago's finest bands, and his long association with Blanche Calloway no doubt gave her an excellent grounding in the fundamental skills she needed to become a bandleader in her own right. The show was an immediate success. One critic wrote:

> What is termed as the greatest feature of recent mention has attracted attention at the Sunset Cafe, 35th and Calumet Avenue, with the opening of the new revue "Sunset Vanities," a spicy medley of song and dance, produced by Lawrence Deas, featuring Blanche Calloway, late star of "Shuffle Along'" . . . and Sammy Stewart's famous orchestra.[20]

News of Blanche's triumphs would have constantly filtered back to her family in Baltimore. Her mother could justifiably be proud of a daughter who was starring in one of Chicago's leading cabarets, and who, in three short years, had worked her way from teenage chorus girl to mature headliner. And there was more success to come. In November 1925 Blanche made her first record for the Okeh label, accompanied by none other than the Sunset's principal attraction, Louis Armstrong, and the seemingly ubiquitous studio pianist Richard M. Jones. Sending home her first pressing of "Lazy Woman's Blues," with "Lonesome Lovesick" on the other side, Blanche would have been the talk of the neighborhood. The latter song, in particular, shows her talent for acting a role as she sang, and her keening, swooping voice, with Armstrong's cornet weaving mournful arabesques behind it, neatly conjures up the lovesick woman portrayed in the lyric. This disc must have acted as an inspirational spur to the young Cab, who now, on the eve of his eighteenth birthday, nurtured musical ambitions of his own.

However, such ambitions had been a long time in coming. The period between Blanche's departure from the family home and the arrival of her first record four years later had not been an easy time for Cab. Eulalia focused her attention on him almost as soon as Blanche had left home, and she turned the full force of her disapproval toward the way of life he had fallen into, and in particular his friends and his hustling. Although she was happy to accept his financial contributions to the household budget from his paper selling or shoe shining, in the weeks immediately after Blanche left, Eulalia was unable to cajole her son into a return to churchgoing, or to better attendance at school. His relationship with John Fortune remained awkward, even though "Papa Jack" was beginning to prosper as one of Baltimore's first African American insurance agents, and was therefore providing a better standard of living for his family than when he had been working as a chauffeur and a shopkeeper at the time he set up home with Eulalia. What had begun on Cab's part as resentment of his stepfather settled into an uneasy truce, and Fortune made it clear that help and support was there for the taking if Cab wanted it. Until things came to a head in late 1921, Cab chose to ignore Fortune's support and continue with an increasingly wayward adolescence.

In the end—desperate to stop her son from wasting his opportunities in life—Eulalia turned to her uncle, her mother's brother the Reverend William Credit, for help. In the academic year 1904–5, Credit had founded one of the several industrial and agricultural schools for African Americans that were beginning to revolutionize education for the black community in the early twentieth century, and by 1921 a couple of his other great-nephews were also students there.[21] Several jazz musicians of Cab's generation were to owe their start to just such institutions. Dizzy Gillespie, for example, attended the Laurinburg Institute in North Carolina. The pianist Teddy Wilson went to Tuskegee College in Alabama, where both his parents were teachers. Cab was to be sent to Credit's Industrial and Agricultural School, which was six miles outside Downingtown, Pennsylvania, on the Horseshoe Turnpike, leading to the picturesquely named East Brandywine Township.

The principle on which all these schools operated was the same. They offered pupils the opportunity to acquire basic literacy and numeracy, and encouraged them to learn practical skills as well. Offering a curious mixture of academic opportunity and the strict discipline of a reformatory, these institutions were usually built well away from other settlements, and on a large enough site to be self-sufficient. Every aspect of running the school made use of the labor of the pupils themselves. Teddy Wilson wrote of his experience at Tuskegee:

> Many pupils used to scrape together their school fees from the work they did, which included raising food on the school farm. For those who had no money at all there was the possibility of a scholarship. This was a trade school where all students, besides an academic education, had to learn a trade. You had a selection of twenty-two.[22]

The Downingtown School was very similar, according to one of the first reports of the institution and how it operated:

> The Downingtown Industrial School, Downingtown, is a new institution, started in 1905, and grew out of the work of the Rev. Dr. William A. Creditt [sic] pastor of the First African (Cherry Memorial) Baptist Church, and its purpose is to meet the increasing need of Negro youth for industrial as well as literary training. It also acts as a preparatory school for Lincoln University. The enrollment for the year 1906–7 was 65. Its largest building, Pennsylvania Hall, was erected entirely by Negro mechanics. A full industrial course is to be offered. The teachers are all Negroes. The chief source of income is voluntary contributions. There is no endowment.[23]

Nine years after that was written, Cab, welcomed by his cousins, quickly settled in to the routine at Downingtown. There were two or three days a week of academic lessons, and the remainder of the time was spent farming, learning woodwork, and helping to install a water and sanitation system for a newly built dormitory, initially by digging trenches for the pipelines. There were seasonal food shortages, when the farm was not producing enough to feed the community, which had now grown to around two hundred pupils and staff, but everybody suffered together. In later life Cab was to say that Downingtown taught him the qualities of self-reliance and teamwork, both of which were to stand him in very good stead in the music business.

In the spring of 1922, after a year at the school, Cab scraped together what he had saved from his earnings from the farm, packed his bag, and crept out, determined to return to Baltimore. Having hiked his way the six miles into town, he found that he could not afford the fare from Downingtown, so he walked on another ten miles further south to West Chester, Pennsylvania, where a commuter railroad ran into Philadelphia. He caught a train there and eventually made his way home.[24] He was chastened by the experience of Downingtown, and determined to try harder at school, so that his family did not force him to return there, but he had not been in Baltimore for long when his old gang clustered back around him, and with them came their streetwise habits.

What saved him from returning completely to his old way of life was that his family decided to move away from Druid Hill. They settled five miles or so to the northeast in a new development being built by another African American insurance man, Harry O. Wilson, who named the area's central open space Wilson Park, by which name it is still known today. John Fortune rented a sizable and attractive house there, and Cab quickly assumed the ethos of this new neighborhood, which was about striving to better oneself. Boys here did not play hooky. School was to be valued, and so, too, was the idea of playing competitive sports. For the first time in his life, at the age of nearly fifteen, Cab applied himself to improving his academic work and to playing baseball. He also began attending church again, where he had the chance to immerse himself in the sounds of gospel music, although in later life he was keener to remember the long afternoons after worship where the men gathered in the surrounding country to shoot dice and put the world to rights. The rekindled interest in music led his mother to arrange voice lessons for Cab with an old family friend, Ruth Macabee. Every Wednesday evening Cab had his lesson, and the perfect diction and remarkable voice control that he was to develop as an adult both had their roots in these classes, where Cab learned breath control, how to use the diaphragm, and how to project his voice, as well as how to extend his natural range.[25]

The move to Wilson Park was not long-term. The family was back by the summer of 1924 to 1306 Madison Avenue, just a couple of blocks away from its old home in Baltimore. Parallel to Druid Hill Avenue, this was a street of tall, elegant town houses, although the 1300 block is now the site of the recently built Renaissance Academy, creating something of a gap among the original rows of homes. Enough remains of the street's original skyline, however, to evoke the atmosphere of 1920s Baltimore, and it was from here that Cab traveled each day to Frederick Douglass High School. In the evenings, he continued a part-time job he had begun while living in Wilson Park, working as a busboy or order checker at the Century Roof, a fashionable supper club.

Cab's mother now nurtured an ambition for her reformed son to follow his father into the study of the law, so there was considerable family pressure on him to work at his books. Nevertheless, formal study often took a back seat in his life because Cab was now seriously playing a new sport, basketball, or working in the restaurant, or—increasingly as time went on—singing and playing the drums with some high school friends in a jazz band. He also carried on with his voice lessons, transferring to a new teacher, Llewelyn Wilson.

As Cab's daughter Camay observed, all this activity, and his considerable earnings from hustling up his various jobs, made for rather an exceptional pupil:

> When he was in high school he was a show-off. Because he was playing basketball, [and] he was very handsome, all the girls were around him, and before he left school, he got a car, because he had all these little jobs. He played the drums, but he also walked horses, sold newspapers, he was hustling, selling different things around town, so this meant he had enough money to buy a car. He told me how he parked it one day right in front of the school, when they were having this big assembly. As it began, the principal got up and asked if the teacher who had parked out front would kindly go out and move his car, because it was in a restricted area. There was silence in the auditorium, then my father stands up and the whole auditorium erupts, with kids shouting "Go Cab go!" as he walks his very hip walk up the aisle to go out and move *his* car.[26]

As it turned out, Cab had bought the car on an installment plan and in due course he failed to earn sufficient money to keep up the payments, but this brief moment of glory was one he loved to remember in later life. He also recalled that at this point in his school career he faced the choice at Douglass High between opting for a career in sports or one in music, the twin routes by which African Americans of the time could achieve some measure of fame and fortune. The Douglass basketball team, on which Calloway played guard, was one of the most successful in interschool competitions, and according to Cab, he was consequently recruited to play for a local semiprofessional team, the Baltimore Athenians. This brought Cab into Colored Intercollegiate Athletic Association games all around the Chesapeake Bay region, against the likes of such successful and well-known teams as Howard University from

Washington, D.C.—indeed these were widely regarded as the two top teams in the association. At the end of the 1925 season, the Athenians narrowly beat Howard 27–24, although the university gained its revenge in the final game of 1926, beating the Athenians 25–18.[27]

Athletic and streetwise, Cab was no doubt a popular player in school and semipro games, but in the surviving reports from the 1925–26 season, his name does not appear alongside such regulars of the Baltimore Athenians lineup as the high-scoring stars: Poles, Baskerville, Wheatley, Kriller, Veney, and Brown.[28] Nevertheless Cab remained keen on playing basketball at a high level in the years that followed, although by the second half of 1926 he had begun to favor his musical career over sports.

During the mid-1920s Prohibition was at its height, yet in Baltimore, as in Chicago, New York, Kansas City, and other major urban centers, there were plenty of nightclubs and cabarets where drinks could be procured and entertainment was on offer. In interviews and in his autobiography, Cab recalled singing at several such venues, the Gaiety, Bailey's and the Arabian Tent. He began by sitting in with the house piano player, often just putting across his specialty song "Muddy Waters," but gradually he added to his repertoire to the point where he could hold his own for an entire set. After bluffing to a local group that he was a drummer, he began playing drums and singing regularly at a roadhouse just out of town, and before long he ended up both leading the band and bringing it to perform at various of the downtown clubs. As well as leading his own group and playing drums—modeling his playing visually, if not aurally, after the renowned drummer Chick Webb—Cab went on to sing with Baltimore's leading big band, the ten-piece orchestra led at the Arabian Tent Club by the pianist Jimmy Jones.[29] The years of voice lessons paid off. Although his teachers would have been horrified to learn that Cab was singing, unamplified, over raucous jazz bands in some of Baltimore's most notorious speakeasies, he had the vocal skill, the projection, and the timing to make a success of his appearances there, and also in variety shows at the Regent Theatre, giving him a taste for starring on stage in front of an appreciative audience. Such an apprenticeship was ultimately to prove far more valuable to Cab than his daytime studies at Frederick Douglass High School, although in 1926 his mother still nurtured plans for him to study law at a university.

Her plans were further complicated by the fact that at the age of eighteen, Cab fell seriously in love. His girlfriend was Zelma Proctor, who was also a senior at the same high school. In the late spring of 1926, she became pregnant.

Zelma was quite sure of two things. She wanted to have the baby, and she did not want to marry Cab. She was remarkably level headed to realize that, however much she loved Cab, it was folly to marry a man who it was evident would soon be making his career in the notoriously fickle world of show business. Zelma already lived separately from her parents, lodging with an aunt in Baltimore. She resolved to move to New York to have the baby, where she could stay with another aunt, in order to bring up the child.

Cab, it seems, after initially assuming he would have to do the "proper thing" and marry her, quickly realized the wisdom of Zelma's plan, and replaced romantic idealism with a strain of practicality. He tried to help her on her way by driving her as far as Atlantic City, the entertainment capital of the East Coast in the mid-1920s, where he hustled up enough money to set her up in New York by sitting in and singing at every nightclub he could. She then made her way to her aunt's house, and he went back to Baltimore. Their daughter, Camay Proctor, was born on January 15, 1927.

In Cab's own account of his life, he relates how he returned to Baltimore to continue his senior year at school. In fact it seems that he had already left full-time education, almost certainly without graduating from high school. The evidence suggests that although he presented himself in interviews and in his autobiography as quite emotionally detached from the experience of becoming a father, he was prompted by Camay's birth to find a way into show business in order to start earning enough money to help support his daughter. Within a month of Camay's birth, Cab was appearing on stage at the Lafayette Theatre in New York with the revue *Plantation Days*, as a member of a touring company that starred his sister Blanche.[30]

This show was one of the most famous African American touring revues of that decade, second only to *Shuffle Along* in terms of its longevity. Back in 1923 when Blanche was appearing in *How Come*, a *Plantation Days* touring company was winding its way from Washington State through Montana and Utah, playing the Pantages circuit. Another version of the show went to London, featuring the great pianist James P. Johnson among its cast, and throughout 1924–25 another touring production under the *Plantation Days* title—billed as a "snappy girly musical revue"—traveled the length and breadth of the United States.[31] All through that tour, the show enhanced its reputation among black and white audiences alike, with a string of positive and laudatory reviews:

A gem of purest humor . . . the peppiest, dancingest, singingest, speediest show of the year is the all Negro "Plantation Days" . . . these dusky entertainers go about their task of pleasing the audience with a vim and spirit that puts the show over from the first number. Names are hard things to find in the program. There are eight dancing girls who do a bit that would make the Tiller Girls—at least those who have crossed the Mississippi River—envious; half a dozen dancers in the company shuffle their feet in a manner to drill the toes of many hoofers.[32]

In the *Chicago Tribune*, the critic Ashton Stevens called *Plantation Days* the "fastest and best show I have seen in years," and another reviewer for the Chicago press hailed what he called the "peppiest thing on stage today" as making " 'Shuffle Along' look like a funeral procession."[33]

Blanche Calloway first joined the cast in November 1925, when the show returned to the aptly named Plantation Café in Chicago. It seems from contemporary reports that this was a cut-down version of the full stage revue, designed to run in the more informal setting of a nightclub, and intended to help restore the venue's fortunes.

This black and tan resort in the heart of the colored [district] once catered to a vast number of whites, who were the main support of the place. It has recently become inhabited with undesirable characters whose actions have driven off practically all the white trade this café once enjoyed. White people are now given no protection when entering this café. Four white couples and approximately twenty colored people were present when this reviewer witnessed this "Plantation Revue." The show is presented in sections with the first one appearing around 11. . . . The Five Crackerjacks are the feature . . . suggestive in their maneuvers . . . Blanche Calloway, good prima donna, but also misplaced . . . an octet of the choristers intervene during numbers supplying some good stepping. Part of the original "Plantation Days," originally in for an indefinite run but will pull out after four weeks.[34]

Blanche did not stay with the company through the early part of 1926. Indeed at the very time that Cab was becoming involved with Zelma Proctor, Blanche set up home with the man who was to be her manager, agent, and common-law husband during the 1920s, Henry Waddy.[35] He was a fast-living man after Cab's own heart, with a penchant for racehorses and gambling. Waddy and Blanche initially settled in New York, and Blanche spent much of the spring of 1926 there, starring at Ciro's nightclub. By the time she returned to headline at the Sunset in Chicago in May, she was billing herself as "former star of the original 'Shuffle Along' and 'Plantation Days,' " but when a full-scale revival of *Plantation Days* was set up to begin a national tour in Chicago that October, Blanche once again joined the cast.

Exactly when Cab became part of the show is not documented. His own account suggests that the touring production came to Baltimore in the "summer" of 1927 and he joined at that time as a member of a close-harmony quartet when another player left the cast.[36] However by the summer, he had already been in Chicago for several months, so he came into the company somewhat earlier, certainly by the time it came south to New York in February 1927 after touring through Missouri and Illinois. During its stay at the Lafayette in New York City, Cab would have had plenty of time to see Zelma and Camay, who had been born at the nearby Harlem Hospital. He was periodically to send money to Zelma to support her from this point onward, and although he and Zelma never married, they remained very close friends throughout their lives, and Camay was welcomed into the Calloway family.

In due course, as a member of the male voice Hollywood Four, Cab left New York for a short tour with *Plantation Days*, and in April the revue wound up once more in Chicago from where it had set forth six months earlier, playing at the Grand Theater. With an eye to her career after the show finally folded, Blanche used her return to Chicago to start doubling between the Grand and Sammy Stewart's new revue at the Metropolitan Theater. No doubt she and the ever-hustling Henry Waddy (whom Cab knew as "Watty") intro-duced her energetic and charismatic younger brother to Stewart, because on April 30, 1927, Cab achieved his first billing in his own right as " 'Cab' Calloway, Tenor Robusto, assisted by Sammy Stewart and His Syncopators" at the Metropolitan.[37]

According to Cab, his mother and sister both insisted that as soon as he arrived in Chicago he was to enroll at Crane Junior College to pursue his stud-ies, with the aim of specializing in the law. His cousin William Credit, whom he had known at Downingtown, was already a student there, so he quickly got to meet a group of students of about his own age. In various memoirs, he also recalled playing basketball for Crane, but a search of the 1928–29 yearbook shows no mention of anyone named Calloway, either among the students or in the many photographs of teams and sporting events. It seems that if Cab had a career at Crane it was extremely brief.[38] Instead of legal training, he threw himself into the world of professional entertaining, and started putting in the hours of experience that would take him to the very top of his profession as a singer and dancer.

Chapter 2

Chicago High Life
1927–1930

....

The Sunset Café at 315 East Thirty-fifth Street on the corner of Calumet Avenue in Chicago started life in 1909 as an automobile garage, but in 1921 the local architect Alfred Schwartz remodeled it into a sizable nightclub. His scheme created a big stage at the back of the room, in front of which was a dance floor surrounded by plenty of tables, catering to around 250 patrons. The whole place was decorated with elaborate murals depicting the jazz age, showing both dancers and musicians. One of these paintings survives today, albeit partly out of public view, in what is presently a hardware store.[1] Despite the club being located in a predominantly African American area, audiences were mixed race, and the entertainers were in very close contact with their public. Singing, comedy routines, and dancing were presented on an open space at floor level in front of the stage—literally a "floor show." The Sunset was owned by local businessmen Edward Fox and Sam Rifas, and managed by the Glaser family in cahoots with Al Capone's mob, but despite its gangland connections it was not immune from police raids. When the pianist Earl Hines worked there, he wryly recalled, these happened so frequently that, on first sight of the police, he would run briskly to the door to ensure getting his regular seat on the paddy wagon rather than having to stand all the way to the station.[2] This lively milieu was to be the club where Cab Calloway transformed himself from an unknown member of a close-harmony singing group into a star in his own right.

He arrived there in July 1927 relatively soon after *Plantation Days* finished its run at the Grand Theater. In his autobiography, Cab recalled first working as a singer at a quite different club, the Dreamland Café, once he had left the show and begun working his way up through Chicago's nightspots, but this almost certainly followed his initial period at the Sunset. He spent the two months between his debut as a "tenor robusto" and his arrival at the Sunset as a named soloist alongside Adelaide Hall with Sammy Stewart at the Metropolitan Theater. Meanwhile Blanche—with whom he was lodging—crossed town to work with Erskine Tate's band at a rival theater, the Vendome.[3]

The time that Cab and Blanche had spent together on the road with *Plantation Days* had given him an opportunity to learn many aspects of stagecraft and presentation from her firsthand, given that he had barely any close contact with her in the early 1920s. While she was developing into a seasoned trouper, he remained in Baltimore. She was, according to Cab's grandson Christopher Calloway Brooks, who knew her in old age, "a truly electrifying performer."[4] Her wild dancing and uninhibited singing were undoubtedly a prototype for much of Cab's own act. She made a conscious break with the tradition established by the classic blues singers such as Bessie Smith or Ma Rainey who stood forward on-stage and sang over the footlights directly at the audience, irrespective of whether they were being supported by a pianist or a full pit orchestra. Instead, Blanche developed numbers in which she interacted directly with members of her supporting band. Cab was later to do this by encouraging his instrumentalists—and thereby his audience—to shout back verbal responses in answer to his lyrics. The most famous example was to be "Minnie the Moocher" but he also created routines in which he alternated musical phrases with his sidemen such as "The Scat Song." The immediate precedent for this was to be found in Blanche's act. In the surviving early movies of Cab at work, we can no doubt see plenty of nuances directly derived from her vocal and terpsichorean performances.

Blanche's experience with the Smarter Set, with *Buzzin' Around*, and with *Shuffle Along* had brought her into the heart of a milieu of African American entertainers who were taking forward performance traditions that can be traced back to African origins. As the blues expert Paul Oliver says in considering survivals of musical forms that found their way to the New World, "West African collective song is antiphonal, following what has frequently been termed the 'leader and chorus' pattern. In this the vocal line of the leader is often improvised and changes with every verse sung, while the responses of the chorus vary very little."[5]

Oliver's words accurately describe a technique Blanche used regularly, but they also define Cab's eventual "hi-de-ho" routines, which can be seen as a direct linear development from African antiphony. Blanche's vaudeville experience also linked her with a line of African American entertainment that had emerged from minstrelsy in the late nineteenth century, and spawned a genuinely new form of musical theater. The revues in which Blanche appeared were the continuation of a genre that emerged in the 1890s, and which, in the words of Thomas L. Riis, "make a collective statement about the diversity of the black community's musical and dramatic skills."[6]

The brightest female star of those turn-of-the-century revues was Aida Overton Walker, and in the 1902 musical *In Dahomey*, in character as Rosetta Lightfoot, she delivered a song by James Weldon Johnson and Will Marion Cook called "Leader of the Colored Aristocracy." This was built around a call-and-response pattern, in which she is "yearning" and "learning" to "make a proper show." She also sang a Harry von Tilzer song of social aspiration, "Vassar Girl," in which a "dark belle" enters the elite (and at the time all-white) ladies' college. In order to do so, Walker was dressed in the finest contemporary fashion.[7]

In her choice of material, her manner of delivery, and her stage presentation, Blanche Calloway can be seen as the heir to Aida Overton Walker. And owing initially to his sister's influence, Cab was also drawn into the show-business lineage of Walker's husband, George Walker, and his stage partner, Bert Williams. This partnership lasted from 1895 until around 1908, and some of the highlights of Williams's routines survive on cylinder and early disc recordings. Their importance to Cab's generation of entertainers can hardly be overstated. Cab's erstwhile guitarist Danny Barker owned a pair of Bert Williams's stage shoes, which he lovingly preserved into the 1990s as a physical reminder of the greatness of this double act, accurately characterized by Thomas L. Riis as "a masked tatterdemalion actor and a fancy dresser."[8] Whereas Williams usually appeared in blackface and presented a racial caricature designed to identify with the hardships of his African American audience, Walker was the exact opposite, an aspirational figure, representing the height of sartorial, verbal, and physical sophistication. Both of them redefined how songs, comedic monologues, and dance routines could be delivered, with a mastery of timing and nuance that was related to the everyday speech patterns of the African American audience, but which had seldom previously made its way onstage, and never with such comprehensive assurance. Cab was to combine elements of both men's art into his own stage persona, taking his dress code and elegant presentation from Walker and his mastery of diction and movement from Williams.

Accounts of *In Dahomey* (in which Williams and Walker appeared alongside Aida Overton Walker) tell of Williams's dance routines, notably a song called "Jig" that is built on a series of two-bar phrases and call-and-response patterns. This prefigures Cab's dazzling assimilation of comparable singing and dancing into his stage persona. Furthermore, Williams's signature tune, "I'm a Jonah Man," contains the minor key verse and major key chorus alternation that was to become a cornerstone of Cab's genre of Minnie the Moocher songs, as well as containing opportunities for the audience to shout back responses. Williams was also known for interpolating spoken comments into his songs, phrases such as "Poor child," or "I'm gonna dance now," much as Cab was to do in later life.[9] Another common element with Cab's vocal storytelling about Minnie was that both Williams and Walker delivered songs in their shows (from *Clorindy* in 1898 to *In Bandanna Land* in 1908) which contained coded linguistic messages that bypassed a white audience, but were picked up immediately by their African American audiences. "As long as black entertainers kept smiling," wrote Riis, "kept up the mask of humor and lightness, submerged and implicitly serious messages went unread by most whites."[10] Blanche's early stage career, which began shortly before Bert Williams's final appearances, gave her plenty to pass on to her brother that she had garnered from the previous generation of African American show people.

Earl Hines, who was to accompany both Blanche and Cab at the Sunset Café, confirmed that, to begin with, Cab owed most of his act to her. He recalled, "To me, she had a better voice than Cab, and although Cab may not say this himself, I think all of his style was hers."[11] The clarinetist Roger Boyd, who worked with her shortly after the Sunset period, remembered her doing a turn that prefigured Cab's swapping of phrases with such solo musicians as the reed player Hilton Jefferson or the trumpeter Jonah Jones. He said, "As time went by I had a little act on stage with Blanche, it was called 'How am I doing? Hey! Hey!' Blanche would sing eight bars then I followed her with a clarinet solo for eight bars, then I repeated what she had sung. It was very popular."[12]

Brother and sister were briefly reunited during late June 1927 in Stewart's extravagant revue to mark the nineteenth anniversary of the Metropolitan

Theater. This featured a twenty-four-strong cast that also included the young Adelaide Hall. Then on July 15 came the landmark moment when Cab joined the lineup of Percy Venables's new revue at the Sunset called *Sunset Glories*. Louis Armstrong was also featured in the show.[13]

By this stage in his career, Armstrong, who was six years older than Cab, had already established himself as one of the biggest names among Chicago's African American entertainers. Recordings with King Oliver, Clarence Williams, and Fletcher Henderson had started him on his way in 1923–25, but his own discs with his Hot Five and Hot Seven, made after his return to Chicago after a spell with Henderson in New York, had confirmed that he was a major musical talent. His record of "Heebie Jeebies" had done much to introduce the art of singing wordless improvisations, known as "scat" singing, to the public. Scat was one major aspect of his art that Cab closely observed and absorbed, as Armstrong performed similar songs in the Sunset revue.

From late April 1926, Armstrong had been the principal jazz artist to be featured with Carroll Dickerson's house band at the Sunset. After Dickerson was fired as musical director, Armstrong himself had been the titular leader of the group for several months preceding Calloway's arrival. Armstrong was already a seasoned performer on the cornet, but during his period at the Sunset he switched to the more incisive-sounding trumpet, and perfected the parts of his act in which he sang and mugged for the crowd.

In this multitalented New Orleans trumpeter and singer, Cab found a lifelong friend, but he also recognized a larger-than-life stage personality from whom he could learn a vast amount more about his chosen craft. He recalled:

> Of course, Louis was singing and playing way before I was, and he influenced me quite a bit. He was the only male singer around at that time, excluding the country boys, who was doing anything other than straight singing, and we became competitors later on. But I don't say that I've ever copied anything from him. Each of Louis' phrases was a thing of beauty on its own. You listened to Louis—you didn't listen to the band.[14]

Because Cab was not an instrumentalist at heart, it was Armstrong's singing that most captivated him, as well as the trumpeter's stagecraft. If he could apply to his own performances much of what he observed in Armstrong, he would be able to dominate the stage in a similar way. Although there are direct musical parallels between the two men in some of Cab's first recordings—a long-held vocal high note in "St. Louis Blues," for example, is directly modeled on the trumpeter's astounding instrumental technique—it is a safe assumption that Armstrong's friendship and influence brought more intangible artistic qualities to Cab's performances than mere imitation.

According to Earl Hines it was Blanche who came to him and Armstrong at the Sunset and begged them to take on her brother. "If you can do anything for Cab," she said, "I'd sure appreciate it because I can't keep him in school." According to family legend, Blanche Calloway was briefly involved romantically with Armstrong at the time, despite her relationship with Waddy, and so the trumpeter was happy to do whatever he could to help her.[15] When Cab joined the show at the Sunset, Blanche, who was also frequently featured in the cast there, was earning quite substantial amounts of money by the standards of the day. Cab recalled that Joe Glaser, who ran the cabaret and later became Armstrong's manager, paid Blanche two hundred dollars a week, which is equivalent to about twenty-five hundred dollars today. By contrast, for his work as a singer, dancer, and even occasional drummer with the house band, Cab himself started at a lowly thirty-five dollars.[16] Yet this was still substantially better than most skilled manual workers in Chicago, and it was to give Cab a priceless opportunity and experience.

Although Louis Armstrong often doubled between the Sunset and other venues around town including the Metropolitan Theater, which meant that he often only appeared for the later sets at the club, Cab enjoyed at least a couple of weeks of being able to watch him every night at close quarters. There were also other regular performers at the Sunset—the singers Adelaide Hall, Edith Wilson, and Jazz Lips Richardson, as well as the dancer Mae Alix—from whom he could learn. The Sunset closed for a while at the end of July 1927,[17] but when it reopened, Cab—whose recollections of playing at the Dreamland almost certainly date from August 1927 when the Sunset was out of action— was again a member of the cast. But by then, Armstrong had rejoined his former leader Carroll Dickerson at the Savoy Ballroom and did not return. Nevertheless, the show business community in Chicago was a close one, and even if Armstrong and Cab did not continue to work alongside one another for the "six months" Cab claims in his autobiography, there were plenty of opportunities for Cab to continue to witness Armstrong in action, and for them to become friends. Cab described Armstrong as "a person you could talk to," and his grandson remembers seeing the two men many years later backstage at the

National Theatre in Washington, D.C., behaving "just like brothers." Their friendship was close, and lasted until Armstrong's death in 1971.[18]

Although he rejoined the Sunset revue in late 1927 as part of the general cast, Cab's chance to shine came one night when Adelaide Hall was indisposed. He volunteered to substitute for her and consequently sang her feature number "Song of the Wanderer" more than passably. From this moment on, as well as continuing his walk-on parts in the comedy revue and his close-harmony singing duties, Cab understudied the entire cast, at one time or another taking over every role in the show to cover for illness, lateness, or other absenteeism. This undoubtedly helped him to develop his prodigious musical memory.[19] Gradually, other musicians who played at or visited the Sunset began to notice Cab, particularly as he rapidly progressed from bit-part player and singer to becoming the club's master of ceremonies, replacing the dancer Ralph Cooper at a salary of sixty-five dollars a week.[20] This meant that as the weekly casts of the revues changed, he enjoyed a degree of permanence, introducing new acts, but also developing his own repertoire of songs and dances. The trombonist and singer Clyde Bernhardt recalled:

> I saw him in 1927 but he was just a cabaret singer then . . . we went into Chicago at night to the Sunset, me and a few of the boys, and we saw the floor show. His sister, Blanche Calloway, she was a headliner entertainer at the Sunset. Blanche . . . was a headliner and Cab, he just had, you know, a part. I think he just got in there 'cause Blanche she had a lot of prestige . . . so I was told. He was singing, he was good . . . but I didn't pay him no mind. But soon he was VERY big.[21]

Bernhardt had an extraordinary memory for details of events and people he met on his travels, not least because he was a lifelong diarist and an energetic correspondent by letter. Because he worked his way around the African American entertainment circuit in the 1920s and 1930s, he knew many of the musicians Cab was later to recruit into his bands, and he remained an enthusiastic fan of Cab's work. Other musicians, particularly those who had already made a reputation for themselves as instrumentalists in the 1920s, but who were then overlooked as tastes and fashions changed to favor singing, dancing, and general entertainment, were more dismissive. The bandleader and banjoist Elmer Snowden, for instance, who also hailed from Baltimore, and had helped give Duke Ellington his start, was bitterly unenthusiastic: "Cab was a dancer, you know he tried to play drums and he tried to play saxophone, he tried to play everything, but he was strictly a dancer."[22]

The way Cab was reported in the press indicates the extent to which he put in the hours to become a thoroughly professional performer. For almost a year he remained just another name amid the lengthy cast lists of those who played at the Sunset, but as 1928 wore on, he began to be singled out for praise in his own right:

> Cab Calloway, master of ceremonies at the Sunset Club, Chicago, gets over his wares an' how. Back in the days (several years ago), when Cab used to warble out "You Gotta Know How to Love" at "Tent Arabia" in his old home town Baltimore, he was hot then. But like new wine, he grows better with age.[23]

As a result of his hard work, Cab was able to send money both to Zelma and home to his mother, who had split up with John Fortune by this time and was ultimately to move to Chicago to bring her younger children to live with Blanche and Henry Waddy. However, hand in hand with such family responsibilities, he increasingly began to enjoy the fast-lane lifestyle of a successful entertainer. He and Waddy pursued their mutual love of horse racing, and along with Blanche they also made the rounds of the city's copious supply of after-hours clubs and gambling dens.

Any thought of maintaining serious study of the law was soon abandoned when Cab met the woman who was to become his first wife, Wenonah Conacher, known as Betty. On the fringes of show business when they first met, she was hustling up more money each week than Cab. Together they became a high-earning, fast-spending couple. They grew inseparable, and not long after Cab became MC at the Sunset, he and Betty moved in together. Despite opposition from both Eulalia and Blanche, within a few months they were married in July 1928. Their main marital home for much of their remaining time in Chicago was a room in a South Side brothel run by a madam named Mae Singleton. No doubt to the irritation of the women who worked there, and the bemusement of their customers, Cab bought himself an alto saxophone. He practiced it for some months, while he took lessons from one of the Brown Brothers, a well-known saxophone quartet.[24]

Well established as the front man of one of Chicago's best nightclubs, with an income that had risen by late 1928 to around $125 a week, and with Betty's money supplying the couple with fine clothes, good food, and the wherewithal for gambling, Cab was settled and happy. The storm clouds of the 1929 stock market crash had not yet gathered and Chicago was still the epicenter of African American entertainment.

Nevertheless, some entertainers were beginning to realize that New York offered even more potential for African American musicians and dancers than the Windy City. The mob rule of the Capone era was far from over, and its stranglehold on Chicago's nightlife left little opportunity for new venues to be created or for more jobs to open up. The turf war between gangland club owners led to several venues being forcibly closed by firebombing or other violent means. Furthermore, the white local of the musicians' union, headed by the up-and-coming James C. Petrillo, was beginning to operate a color bar against black performers being allowed to work in the most lucrative venues. At the same time, the beleaguered city authorities were attempting to clamp down on liquor consumption and racially integrated audiences. By contrast, the entertainment world of New York was still expanding rapidly. In particular Harlem was becoming a focal point for black theaters and cabarets. The Alhambra, the Lincoln, and the Lafayette theaters were all moving into full stride, and the Cotton Club, Smalls' Paradise, and Connie's Inn all offered similar packages to the Sunset in Chicago. A host of smaller clubs and speakeasies employed everything from solo stride pianists to little bands of four or five pieces, often combined with singing waiters and dancing girls. In addition there was the famed Savoy Ballroom in Harlem, whereas in downtown Manhattan there was the Roseland Ballroom, where Fletcher Henderson was resident, and the Kentucky Club, where Duke Ellington had played.

In 1929 Louis Armstrong, along with several of Chicago's other brightest talents, made the move to New York, beginning an exodus that would radically alter the face of Chicagoan entertainment over the next couple of years. At first, the change was barely noticed. Until that point, fashions were cyclical, and entertainers such as Blanche Calloway and Armstrong himself had always returned to the Windy City after periods in New York.

When Armstrong had first left the Sunset Café for the Savoy in 1927, the management assumed he would come back in due course. His departure for New York seemed at the time to be no different, and simply put off the day when he might return. As it turned out, he had gone for good. To take his place, after the club's reopening in late 1927, the Sunset brought in various bands, eventually deciding to hire one that had been working at the Plantation Café, a ten-piece group called the Alabamians. Their "peppy playing" was directed by the alto saxophonist Marion Hardy, and fronted for nightclub work by the singer and violinist Lawrence Harrison.[25] There were two trumpeters, Edward Mallory and Elisha Herbert; two additional saxophonists, Artie Starks and Warner Seals; with Henry Clark on trombone; Ralph Anderson, piano; Lesley Corley, banjo; and Jimmy McHendricks, drums; plus the avuncular figure of Charlie "Fat Man" Turner on tuba. He went on to become Fats Waller's bassist and ultimately a well-known Harlem restaurateur, vividly commemorated in Sy Oliver's song "At the Fat Man's."[26]

Harrison was well connected in African American show business, his father being an established actor, but he was not an outstanding bandleader. Somewhat overstepping the mark in terms of his duties as MC, Cab decided to rehearse the group himself to back some of his own solo numbers, and immediately discovered he had a talent for directing a band. Quickly memorizing the arrangements, he would gesture to the reeds or the brass to accentuate their parts, or signal dynamics to the drums and banjo, and the music came alive. Although Marion Hardy was titular head of the band, it was run as a cooperative and its members soon decided to fire the staid Harrison, and take on the loose-limbed all-singing, all-dancing Cab Calloway in his place.

Fronting this band every night at the Sunset during much of the first half of 1929, Cab consolidated many of the traits that would define his approach to bandleading and singing. In particular, he worked on the idea that he had picked up from Blanche of interacting with the musicians in the band, recalling: "we developed a style of novelty arrangement in which the band members all had megaphones, and I would sing a line and they would hold up their megaphones and respond."[27] Apparently Cab's other role model for this kind of singing, call and response, and energetic interaction was the white novelty bandleader Benny Meroff, who had a legendary reputation for working his audiences into a fever pitch of excitement. As well as dancing around, singing, and conducting, Meroff had a special baritone saxophone constructed in a straight format—somewhat like a cross between a giant soprano sax and an alphorn—on which he grunted gruff solos that were a triumph of comedy entertainment over musical content.

The arranging for the numbers that Cab sang with the Alabamians, and for most of the rest of the group's repertoire, was done by Marion Hardy, not one of the best-known leaders in jazz history, but nevertheless a saxophonist and musical director much liked by his sidemen. He had the reputation for treating them well and paying high salaries of a level normally associated with better known groups. One reason for this was that outside the Sunset he assiduously courted better paying jobs. Clyde Bernhardt, who later worked with Hardy, observed that his was "an entertaining band [that] used to do a lot of glee club singing and they played most of all white jobs. They played a lot of college jobs, college dances, and they were very popular."[28]

Cab's singing, jumping, and jiving in front of the band helped its appeal, fitting in well with the group's existing penchant for mixing entertainment with jazz, and together they played slick arrangements of most of the current songs of the day for college and Sunset audiences alike. However, in 1929 the management of the cabaret passed from Joe Glaser's family to Harry Voiler, who decided that, despite the popularity of Cab and the Alabamians, he needed to refresh the floor show and change the resident group. He naturally assumed that Cab, as the Sunset's MC, would simply transfer his allegiance to Boyd Atkins and his Vagabonds who came in to replace Hardy's band. But Cab now felt that the Alabamians was his band as much as Hardy's, and so to Voiler's surprise he elected to stay with his fellow musicians and leave the club.[29]

With considerable chutzpah, considering he had yet to make a record or acquire much of a reputation beyond Chicago, Marion Hardy capitalized on the band's popularity at the Sunset and persuaded MCA (the Music Corporation of America), one of the country's biggest booking agencies, to take them on. Consequently, from May until October 1929, the Alabamians toured in the Midwest, prior to taking up a spot at the Savoy Ballroom in New York City. The band started its new career in Chicago itself, first at the Cinderella Ballroom, and then at the larger Merry Garden, before setting off on a road tour that took them via Mendota, Springfield, and Peoria, Illinois, to Kansas City, Missouri.[30] The MCA bookers did not hold back in their billings for the band, which was described as "one of the greatest colored attractions in the country today," although interestingly the press notices made more of the fact that the band had been "borrowed" a year or two earlier for a season in Ontario by Jelly Roll Morton than that it was being fronted on this tour by Cab.[31]

Traveling in a fleet of automobiles, as many bands of the day did, and accompanied by Betty and the other band wives, the Alabamians experienced the tour as a novel adventure and great fun. The Kansas City engagement, at the city's popular El Torreon Ballroom, at Thirty-first and Gillham, lasted for two months. Although the comedy routines went down well, and the band played adequately for the dancing patrons, Cab began to get gnawing doubts, worrying that the Alabamians might not be slick and sophisticated enough for New York City.

His instincts told him the band's rhythm section needed a stronger grounding in jazz than its pianist Ralph Anderson was able to provide, and so he set about courting the outstanding twenty-five-year-old player with the city's Bennie Moten Orchestra who had recently made waves on a short tour to Chicago. This young man was none other than Count Basie, who recalled:

> Cab was fronting that band and he wanted me in there. We used to sit on the corner talking about things. . . . I think he almost lost his friendship with some of the fellows in that band because they saw that he was trying to bring me in. But Cab didn't care a damn. It didn't work out, but Cab really was for me.[32]

Even at this early stage in his career, Cab was displaying a trait that he was to follow throughout his many years as a bandleader. As the English critic Albert McCarthy succinctly put it:

> Cab was very much personally concerned with the hiring of personnel and was perspicacious in his selection. If he had wished, it would have been easy to select a line-up of capable but rather anonymous musicians to provide a backdrop for his singing. It is a tribute to him that he never did so.[33]

His doubts about the Alabamians were to prove entirely justified once the band arrived in New York, and he no doubt wished that his blandishments had successfully wooed the young Bill Basie away from Kansas City some eight years before John Hammond finally managed to do so.

So, just how capable were the Alabamians? As it turns out, the Marion Hardy band's one recording session was made soon after it arrived in New York, on October 29. From this, we get the impression of a competent group, but one that is rather lumbering and stodgy compared to the remarkable standards of easy, fluent swing being achieved at the time by Fletcher Henderson, Duke Ellington, and Luis Russell (who was directing Louis Armstrong's principal backing band). By 1929, all these latter orchestras had largely shed the tuba in favor of the more flexible sounding double bass, and their drummers were developing a technique that went beyond the off-beat cymbal crashes and clippety clops produced by Jimmy McHendricks in the Alabamians. In Hardy's group, the banjo and piano are practically inaudible, whereas Ellington and Russell were working out ways to feature them as key elements in their bands' overall sounds. As Cab had foreseen, fashions were moving so fast in jazz at the time that the Alabamians, who had been a great success in Chicago and provided good value entertainment in Kansas City, were already sounding anachronistic by the time the musicians reached New York.

It is intriguing to think that Cab, having fronted the band and sung with it throughout the 1929 midwestern tour, might have made his first records as a vocalist with Hardy (whose name was misspelled as "Marlow" Hardy on the labels) and thereby changed the band's fortunes. But there is no evidence of his distinctive tones in the close-harmony warbling of the "Alabama Magpie Trio" who sing on both the sides that the band recorded, "Georgia Pines" and "Song of the Bayou." Jazz critics have tended to deride the clichéd broken chords, vo-de-o-do breaks, and wailing minor key moans of this close-harmony trio, but what the records confirm is that this was a band whose performances were modeled on white society orchestras every bit as much as contemporary African American jazz bands.

Yet even if it is not possible to discern the rounded tenor voice and perfect diction of Cab Calloway among the Alabama Magpie singers, there is nevertheless a more than even chance that the records do contain his first appearance on record in these otherwise undistinguished performances. According to Cab himself, in a conversation with the English writer Steve Voce, he put his lessons on the alto saxophone to good use, and joined in the reed section, playing second alto on the session. In the same interview, he went on to relate the story of the band's disastrous debut:

> I brought the Alabamians from Chicago to New York . . . and we went to work in the Savoy Ballroom. We were a big flop there because we were playing Chicago jazz, and they didn't like it too much in New York. They were playing the Eastern style, and it had a more solid and cumbersome beat to it. The kids couldn't dance too good to our music, and they really didn't like it. But while they didn't like the band, they went for my vocals.[34]

Already dressed in his trademark white tail suit and using a baton to direct the instrumental interludes between his vocals, Cab was undoubtedly a star turn.

As he described it, the band looked the part as well, in smart black coats and with shoes so shiny they could see their reflections in the toe caps. But the group simply failed to compete when they played opposite the zesty rival attraction at the Savoy, Cecil Scott's band. The Alabamians got their two weeks' notice on their first night.

The band worked around New York for a short period after being fired from the Savoy, and then returned to the Midwest, playing once more back in Kansas City, and going on to revisit the scene of its earlier success in Peoria, Illinois. Cab, on the other hand, decided to stay put in Manhattan, and immediately put in a transfer request to move from the Chicago branch of the American Federation of Musicians (AFM) to which he had belonged, local 208, to the New York local 802.[35]

Normally a musician had to wait six months before being allowed to work regularly with a band in the city of his or her new local. Cab sidestepped the system by not working as a bandleader or jazz vocalist, but returning to cabaret as a dancer and singer, hence nominally becoming an actor. In November 1929, almost as soon as the Alabamians left the Savoy, Louis Armstrong put in a good word for him, and he joined the cast of a revue that had been running successfully since May that year at Connie's Inn in Harlem, *Hot Chocolates*, written by Fats Waller and Andy Razaf. Replacing the juvenile lead, Paul Bass, Cab found himself singing a sequence of hit songs: "Sweet Savannah Sue," "Goddess of Rain," "Rhythm Man," and "Ain't Misbehavin'."[36]

He opened in this show during the strangely calm period of shocked reaction to the Wall Street stock market crash of the previous month. Fortunes had been wiped out, investors watched their remaining stocks rally weakly before falling further back, and banks were forced to close, taking with them the nest eggs of many, many savers. Yet in a spirit of forced gaiety, New York's nightlife continued almost unabated, as audiences sought the escapism and feel-good factor of pacy, dazzlingly produced song-and-dance shows. No longer the front man for a touring band, Cab landed himself a secure place in a long-running revue at a hundred dollars a week in the very center of the Harlem show business world that he was to dominate during the following decade.

In common with anyone arriving in New York at the time, Cab and Betty had been awed by the sheer scale of the city. In those days the George Washington Bridge had yet to be finished, and so their initial approach from the New Jersey side of the Hudson River was by the slow-moving passenger ferry, allowing them to see the full impressive sweep of the Manhattan shore-line and the thrusting skyscrapers of what was already becoming one of the world's tallest cities. In addition to the dramatic impression made on them by the city itself, they were immediately drawn into the vibrant African American community in Harlem, not least because they found lodgings in the three-story brownstone belonging to bandleader Fletcher Henderson. Whereas their former billet in a Chicago whorehouse had certainly put them at the heart of that city's seamy nightlife, they were now ensconced in a buzzing, lively community of musicians, as the Hendersons let several rooms to other Harlem entertainers. Within a few weeks, Cab had met, heard, sung for, and hung out with a broad cross section of the show community.

Hot Chocolates was the second revue that Fats Waller and his lyricist Andy Razaf had composed for the Immerman brothers, George and Connie, at their nightclub, Connie's Inn, after Fats was released from prison in early 1929, hav-ing failed to keep up his alimony payments. The brothers, who also owned a deli for which Fats had once been a teenage delivery boy, had a soft spot for the rotund pianist, and he responded to their invitation to write for them by pro-ducing some of his (and Razaf's) most memorable songs. The first show, *Load of Coal*, had contained the immortal "Honeysuckle Rose," and *Hot Chocolates* included several more of their best efforts, of which the two most famous were "Ain't Misbehavin'" and "Black and Blue."

Connie's Inn was at the very center of Harlem's clubs and theaters, at 2221 Seventh Avenue and 131st Street. A basement club, it had a chorus line with a mixture of dancing girls and drag artists so convincing that they could barely be told apart from the female hoofers. "For half a dozen years," said one review, "Connie's has housed the colored show par excellence. In those years, Connie's has gathered together Negro artists of the first water."[37] Among those artists on the opening night of *Hot Chocolates* was James Baskette, who later became famous as Uncle Remus in Disney's *Song of the South*.

Within days of the premiere, the Immermans realized that their new show had the potential to transfer to a Broadway theater, and by way of tryouts at the Windsor in the Bronx, it arrived at the Hudson Theater downtown on June 20, where it was to run for 219 performances. Louis Armstrong was drafted to star in the stage version, and he stopped the show nightly with his renditions of "Black and Blue" and "Ain't Misbehavin'." Before long, *Hot Chocolates* was run-ning in parallel as a nightclub revue at Connie's Inn in Harlem and as a full stage show downtown, with the principals, including Armstrong, Edith Wilson, and Jazz Lips Richardson, dashing back uptown to appear in the late-night Harlem version after the curtain fell at the Hudson.

When Cab first arrived in New York and renewed his friendship with Armstrong, the trumpeter recommended him to take Paul Bass's place in the version of the show running at Connie's Inn. There, backed by Carroll Dickerson's band and with Armstrong and Richardson also appearing, Cab was surrounded by the musicians who had been such a formative influence on him at the Sunset. He felt he had something to prove to them, by performing the songs better than Bass, using all the techniques he had perfected on the road with the Alabamians. When the Immermans sent a touring company on the road in late 1929, because Cab was still waiting for his union transfer to take effect in New York, he went with it, first to Philadelphia and then to the Tremont in Boston. Playing piano with the touring production was Bennie Payne, who became a firm friend of Cab's, and would eventually be the pianist in his band for many years.

Back in New York after the road tour of *Hot Chocolates*, Cab went on to appear in another show which had strong associations for him. *The New York Age* reported:

> Clarence Robinson . . . will present at the Lafayette Theatre his *Second Plantation Revue* next week. The cast of the *Second Plantation Revue* is indeed a notable one. It includes Eddie Rector, one of the greatest dancers on the American stage, Celeste Cole, undoubtedly the greatest colored woman singer in America, Cab Callaway [sic], a new comer to Harlem and one of the ablest orchestra leaders and Masters of Ceremonies.[38]

By the time this show finished, Cab's AFM transfer was almost complete, and this happened to coincide with the reappearance in New York of Marion Hardy's Alabamians. In his memoirs, and in dozens of interviews, Cab always maintained that the band lost out in a battle of music during its initial two weeks in New York, and that this precipitated his future career. In fact the decisive battle was to take place once the band returned to Manhattan, on May 14, 1930.

Billed as "a war to the finish" and a "Million Dollar Affair in Musical Talent," the contest was held at the Savoy Ballroom, and was, up to that point, the largest band battle ever held. It involved no fewer than six orchestras, of which the principal ones were led by Duke Ellington, Fletcher Henderson, and Chick

Webb. Making up the balance of the contest were the Missourians under Lockwood Lewis, Cab Calloway with the Alabamians, and Cecil Scott. On the night, Henderson ran away with the contest,[39] but there was to be a very fortunate outcome for Cab, as a result of his one-night reunion with his former colleagues:

> The Missourians had a leader and vocalist called Lockwood Lewis, and during the battle I outdid Lockwood Lewis, but the Alabamians were outplayed by the Missourians. So the manager decided to put the Missourians and me together. Most of us stayed put together for the next seventeen or eighteen years![40]

Charlie Buchanan, the manager of the Savoy, through the simple expedient of putting Cab in front of a well-established and more experienced band, had laid the foundation for a landmark recording session just ten weeks later, when the Missourians would be formally transformed into Cab Calloway and His Orchestra.

Chapter 3

Cotton Club Stomp
1930–1931

C ab came from winning his band battle at the Savoy to headlining at Harlem's most celebrated venue, the Cotton Club, in less than a year. Yet he worked rather harder than he suggests in his autobiography to ensure that he and the band were ready to take this opportunity when it arose. Furthermore, almost by chance, the band that he had ended up fronting was better equipped than almost any other for the job of playing at this prestigious club, because in an earlier incarnation it had already worked there for some time.

The Missourians—as the name implies—came directly from the midwestern territory band circuit. In the very early years of the 1920s, when jazz was becoming America's main style of popular music, dozens of similar bands crisscrossed the South, Southwest, and Midwest, bringing this new exciting sound to theaters, dance halls, and even hastily converted tobacco warehouses in small towns and cities spread over a vast geographical area. The territories were a mixture of arable farming land, cattle country, or untamed expanses of plains, forests, and mountains, but wherever river routes, railroads, or highways converged, there would be trading settlements, and even the most isolated of these were, as the territory bandleader Jesse Stone put it, "hungry for entertainment."[1]

Although Cab says in his autobiography that "the personnel of the Missourians was constantly changing," the nucleus of the band he inherited in May 1930 had been together since it was formed by the violinist Wilson Robinson as "Robinson's Bostonians" in St. Louis, Missouri, in the spring of 1923. Trumpeter R. Q. Dickerson, trombonist DePriest Wheeler, saxophonist Andy Brown, bassist Jimmy Smith, and pianist Earres Prince had all been founder members of that group, and were still in the lineup when Cab took over the band. The drummer Leroy Maxey—also to be a Calloway stalwart—had joined the group in mid-1923, within a few months of its formation. Several of these musicians had started out in Kansas City itself, but they all formed their style in the blues-tinged musical environment of the Midwest and Southwest.

Whereas the Alabamians came together as a Chicago cabaret band not long before Cab encountered them in 1928, the Missourians had clocked up several years of experience by that time. After spending the first part of 1923 based in St. Louis, they moved to Chicago as "Robinson's Syncopators," and then for the rest of that and the following year toured widely. Accounts suggest that they ventured as far north as Duluth, Minnesota, and according to the drummer Harry Dial, who later worked with Robinson, "the band played the Pantages vaudeville circuit on the West Coast for a season and then the Orpheum circuit in the East for a season." Not long after their return to Chicago in late 1924, they were hired to come to New York as the house band at the Cotton Club. Robinson's services were dispensed with en route, and the violinist Andy Preer became the group's front man. By December 1924 the group was broadcasting twice a week over the WHN network as "The Cotton Club Dance Orchestra."[2]

This club was to become crucially important in the fortunes of both the band and of Cab Calloway, but at the end of 1924 it had yet to reach the position of dominance in New York's nightlife that it was to enjoy from the late 1920s until it moved downtown in February 1936. Located up a flight of stairs from its modest but distinctive marquee at 644 Lenox Avenue at West 142nd Street, it had started life in 1920 as the Club Deluxe, and the former heavyweight boxing champion Jack Johnson was its proprietor. A couple of years later, from his cell in Sing Sing, the Yorkshire-born New York gangster Owney Madden put out feelers about buying the lease. At the time, Madden was some nine years into a twenty-year sentence for his part in murdering another hoodlum, Little Patsy Doyle. Nevertheless, the club was acquired on his behalf by some gangland associates to coincide with his release on parole in 1923.

Prohibition offered Madden the chance to set up several fresh rackets once he had left prison, and the newly renamed Cotton Club was one of a number of nightclubs in which he took an interest. He swiftly established a sizable business bootlegging liquor in partnership with a former rival, Big Bill Dwyer, and along with the other entertainment venues in his empire, the seven-hundred-seat club offered an excellent opportunity to pass on illicit alcohol to customers in the know. Madden and his partners, Dwyer, Frenchy DeMange, Bill Duffy, Mike Best, and Harry Block, were notorious gangsters for whom murder, extortion, gun and booze smuggling, fight fixing, protection rackets, money laundering, and thinly veiled fraud were all in a day's work.

As outwardly respectable club owners, however, they lured big spenders from the white community in downtown Manhattan to Harlem, where they presented the best in African American entertainment. Although the club's printed menu offered only soft drinks, champagne could be acquired from a knowing waiter at around thirty dollars a bottle, and a fifth of Scotch was just over half that price. These hefty costs did not discourage the spendthrifts from downtown, but they effectively kept the local African American population out, something which was Madden's underlying aim. "The Cotton Club, located at the heart of Harlem at 142nd Street and Lenox Avenue, does not cater to colored patrons and will not admit them when they come in mixed parties," reported the *New York Age*.[3] The only African Americans allowed in the audience were established stars or nationally famous sporting personalities.

The racial overtones of the Cotton Club—both in appearance and attitude—would make a study in themselves. The street-front aspect of the club suggested something of a romantic "Uncle Tom's Cabin" image of the old South, with a log-paneled fascia and a shingled "roof" attached to the front wall, but the pièce de resistance was the setting of the bandstand and tables inside. Cab later described it as "a replica of a southern mansion, with large white columns and a backdrop painted with weeping willows and slave quarters."[4] The tables were covered with red and white gingham, and the African American waiters wore red tailcoats, in the manner of old retainers moving discreetly between their white paying customers. The Cotton Club put on at least two new revues every year, in some seasons refreshing the all-star black cast and the program even more frequently. Generally it presented songs, comedy sketches, dances, and band music rolled together into a vaudeville variety show by such experienced producers as Walter Brooks, Dan Healy, and Lew Leslie.

This was the atmosphere into which the former Robinson's Syncopators arrived in late 1924. Their first records, made just a few weeks later on January 6, 1925, are unremarkable—two stodgy, unswinging blues. But their front man Andy Preer was a shrewd political bandleader as well as a hit with the public, and he managed to keep on the right side both of the mob and of his audiences, to the extent that the band became a permanent feature at the club. As a consequence of such regular high-profile work, in each of its successive recording sessions there is a dramatic improvement. By the end of 1925, DePriest Wheeler's muted trombone and R. Q. Dickerson's trumpet were wailing confidently over a swinging ensemble with punchy brass figures and neat reed riffs on "Everybody Stomp." By February 1927 when the group made its final recordings under Preer's direction, we can hear from its bright, self-assured version of "I Found a New Baby" why it acquired a reputation as one of New York's best bands.

In May 1927, Preer unexpectedly died. Madden and his associates were not sure that the leaderless band would continue to be a sufficient draw for the club without its charismatic violinist and front man, and they set about recruiting a replacement. However, this took time, and it was not until December that their eventual choice, Duke Ellington, arrived. In the meantime the Cotton Club Orchestra supplied the music for the choreographer and producer Dan Healy's new revue *Breezy Moments in Harlem* billed as "the hottest show around at the coolest place in town," which opened in July, and the musicians stayed on for its early fall successor *Blushing Browns*. However, the band was unceremoniously made homeless with Ellington's arrival on December 4, and as soon as the new year arrived, it set forth on the road, touring first with Ethel Waters and then as an attraction in its own right, spending almost all of 1928 in the Midwest, with brief visits to Chicago, Pittsburgh, and New York.[5]

The band started out on this tour under its familiar Cotton Club name, but as the year went on, this began to create confusion with Ellington's band, so it was at this point that the title "Missourians" was adopted. The reed player George Scott (who had joined some time before the band's February 1927 recordings) took over musical direction, while the one-time Dixieland Jug Blower and singer Lockwood Lewis replaced Preer as front man.

While the Missourians were out on the road, Bennie Moten brought his Kansas City band to New York in September 1928, playing in an updated version of the midwestern style at the Roseland Ballroom, the Lafayette Theater, and the Savoy Ballroom. He then returned to Kansas City. Meanwhile, the Missourians' extensive travels seem to have come to an end in April 1929, and when the band reentered the recording studios in June in New York, its months of working together on tour were readily apparent. The tightness of the ensemble coupled with a brash, breezy confidence outdid even Moten's discs, which he had recorded at Camden, New Jersey, during his stay in New York. The enforced return to the Midwest had revitalized the Missourians' sound, and it is easy to discern why Cab heard in its playing the same excitement and swing that had made him want to recruit Count Basie on his visit to Kansas City. The first disc the band made at the June session, "Market Street Stomp," starts with some accomplished and deftly played brass section work, followed by precisely articulated reed riffs, and Wheeler's swaggering trombone. Thornton Blue's clarinet weaves fluently over the ensemble, and even if Andy Brown's tenor already sounds slightly dated for 1929, it is played with great control and certainty. By the time of the band's last recording under its own name in February 1930, although it still overdid the use of the chord sequence from the final strain of "Tiger Rag" as the building block for most of its original pieces, it was showing a real breadth of ability. This ranged from the breakneck display number "Two Hundred Squabble," with showcases for Morris White's banjo,[6] Wheeler's muted trombone, Dickerson's fiery trumpet, and Blue's throaty clarinet, to the plaintive "Prohibition Blues," which captured some of the programmatic flavor of Ellington's writing and arranging. Again Blue and Dickerson were the star soloists.

This was now undoubtedly a band that could tailor its performances for a record, but which clearly also had the skills to put on a live show that more than lived up to its sound on disc. Its only limitation was the vocalizing of Lockwood Lewis, who spoke rather than sang his lyrics with little of the extrovert dynamism that was audible among his fellow band members and that would be a vital part of Cab's act.

There is no more graphic description of Cab's personal vitality than an account by the bassist Gene Ramey who was once on the losing end of a "battle of bands" against him. The band Ramey was playing for had acquitted itself well in its opening set and went into the interval convinced it had done enough to win the contest.

When Calloway came on for the second set he made a remarkably spectacular entry, leaping over chairs, turning somersaults, and indulging in all manner of non-musical showmanship, all the while singing . . . in his most eccentric manner. This so won over the audience that we didn't dare go on again.[7]

The aural equivalent of Calloway's tumbling act on stage can be heard on "St. Louis Blues," one of his two first-ever recordings with the Missourians, cut for Brunswick in May 1930. There can be no more dramatic debut on record by any singer, and his vocal gymnastics are completely unlike anything else in jazz up to that time. R. Q. Dickerson's "talking" trumpet and DePriest Wheeler's muted trombone usher in the piece. Wheeler in particular shows even more brash confidence than on his earlier records, and produces a cross between Tricky Sam Nanton's plunger-muted work for Ellington and the forthright shouting trombone of J. C. Higginbotham in Red Allen's contemporaneous recording band.

As discussed in chapter 2, for his first vocal chorus Cab holds the word "blues" on a high note for eight entire measures, abandoning the normal concept of a lyric and behaving exactly like an improvising instrumentalist. For the two following choruses he delivers something close to the normal words of the song, and then begins an extraordinary babble of scat syllables, mainly built around a "bow-wow-wow" motif that would later turn up in the work of vocalists as varied as Louis Jordan and the New Orleans saxophonist and singer Sammy Lee. The effect is of Cab having not one but two conversations simultaneously, and of creating a vocal language that is already far beyond the normal ideas of scat singing. The full band explodes into action behind him just before the end of the vocal, and he howls like a banshee as the musicians roar past him toward their instrumental choruses.

The arrangement nods in the direction of Louis Armstrong's 1929 recording of the piece, not least in the final vocal chorus where Cab weaves in and out of the band's stabbing chords like a horn player, before the lead trumpeter Lammar Wright punches out the same high-register closing riff as is used on Armstrong's disc. By contrast, "Gotta Darn Good Reason Now," the other track from this session, is nothing like as exceptional, but "St. Louis Blues" was original enough to work its way onto the best-seller lists at the end of 1930 and to put "Cab Calloway and His Orchestra," as the band was billed on the label, firmly on the musical map.[8] The band went on to make further sessions for the Brunswick label in October, November, and December.

These chart the progress of Cab and the band as they found a natural musical language and style together. In due course, he would roll into his singing an astonishing range of allusion, consolidating Armstrong's scatting, timing, and phrasing, but also looking beyond jazz to a wider set of influences that encompassed Jewish cantors, country blues singers, and fast-talking low-life street characters. This stylistic breadth was still largely in the future in late 1930, but clearly the exceptional nature of "St. Louis Blues" gave Cab and his orchestra something to aim at. However, there is no consistency about the output from their next sessions, and this could well be because in the closing months of 1930 the band lacked a regular home, which would have offered it a nightly opportunity to work out what its real strengths were. The best example of band and singer working together is "Happy Feet," where Cab leans way back behind the beat in his vocal, easing out the rhythms of the written melody to something far smoother and more instrumental in concept, and offering an excellent counterpart to Thornton Blue's dramatic clarinet. This scurries all over its range, including some deft phrases in the highest altissimo register. Blue had a rough, vocal edge to his sound in common with such Creole players as Edmond Hall, offering a real stylistic contrast to the most influential style of the decade, the fluency and classical tone of Buster Bailey, who starred in Fletcher Henderson's band.

Almost as good is "Viper's Drag," where Cab's vocal solo is built out of wordless scatting, and includes a sequence in which he sings a phrase in his high tenor range and then answers it as a baritone, becoming a one-man example of call and response.

More interesting are the artistic failures. These include a stilted version of "Jenny Lee" in which the band sounds more like Paul Whiteman's society band than a hard-swinging midwestern jazz orchestra, not least because the trumpet soloist (most likely the newly arrived Wendell Culley) does an accurate recreation of Whiteman's erstwhile star soloist, Bix Beiderbecke. Equally unconvincing is "Yaller," a song that laments the lot of the "high yaller," the light-skinned African American who "ain't even black . . . ain't even white." The potential strength of the racial protest in the lyrics is undermined by Cab's delivery, in which he adopts a tremolo and does a passable impression of Al Jolson at his most saccharine.

Nevertheless, with their recording career under way and playing roughly twice a week at the Savoy Ballroom, this was definitely the period when Cab and the Missourians began to jell as a group. Before he took over as front man, the band's fortunes since returning to Manhattan in 1929 had followed a pattern similar to Cab's own. The musicians had suffered an enforced layoff during the months while Cab had been appearing in *Hot Chocolates* and the *Second Plantation Revue*, because several of the band's members did not belong to the New York local of the musicians' union. Tuba player Jimmy Smith, trumpeter Lammar Wright, and trombonist DePriest Wheeler were all still members of the Kansas City branch, number 627. Like Cab they had to prove six months' residency in New York before being able to make a full transfer to local 802, during which they were restricted in the work they could accept. The period of time that their transfers took to come through was completed at almost exactly the same moment as Cab himself became free to work in New York as a bandleader.[9]

Once his own six months were up, and shortly before the Savoy battle, Cab made a handful of appearances in April 1930 fronting a local New York group led by Earle "Nappy" Howard, who recalled, "Our first gig was with Cab Calloway at Penn University. The night was a big success. Cab gave a big performance, he was at his jiviest and he gave a good report to the Savoy who booked us."[10] Cab and Howard went on to play several times at the Savoy Ballroom and at the Saratoga Club in late April, and this kept his hand in as an orchestra director, but it was never likely to be a permanent arrangement as would become the case with the Missourians. Once they had joined forces, Cab had firm ideas about broadening the band's stylistic palette even further than it had managed to do during its year on the road. He recalled urging his musicians to listen to what was going on around them in New York, and—testament to his interest in rehearsing them—to slow their ballads down further, to work on their dynamics, and to pace themselves carefully in order to produce even more dramatic effects from their up-tempo displays.[11]

According to Cab in his autobiography, there were plans for him and the Missourians to open as the major act at a new Harlem nightspot called the Plantation Club, backed by the Immerman brothers, but this venue was vandalized beyond repair just before its opening night, preventing him from making his debut. However, this raid on "a colored night resort patronized by white fun seekers" in which twenty-five thousand dollars worth of damage was wrought by a gang using "crowbars, picks and axes"[12] took place on January 10, at the time Cab was still on tour in the cast of *Hot Chocolates*. Although there were suspicions aplenty about who was behind this desecration, there was no proof. However, when Harry Block, a shareholder in the Cotton Club and co-owner of the Silver Slipper in midtown, was shot dead at three o'clock in the morning on April 30 by "two pale youths" in the elevator of his apartment building on West Seventy-third Street, the truth began to emerge. According to the newspapers, Block's black notebook containing "the name of practically every racketeer in town . . . suggested so many feuds as a possible background to the killing" that the police had to work through a forest of clues. They soon settled on the theory that this was a revenge murder for the wrecking of the Plantation Club, suggesting that the destruction had taken place at the behest of Owney Madden, who disliked the idea of serious competition on his doorstep. Conveniently for him, Madden was in the hospital being treated for old gunshot wounds when the wrecking and the subsequent killing occurred.[13]

The likelihood is that the Immermans had indeed intended the star of their smash hit revue at Connie's Inn to transfer to become the headline act at their new venture, but not, it would seem, with the band he was to take over the following May.

Once Cab and the Missourians had begun their association that month, for the second half of 1930, when they were not working at the Savoy, they played the Alhambra Theater in Harlem, and alternated between the two Paramount theaters, one in Manhattan, the other in Brooklyn. At the latter, Charlie Davis remembered leading his band the Joy Gang in support of them periodically from September until the year end.[14] Cab also recalled working at a small nightclub on the Lower East Side of Manhattan, bringing home so little money that he and Betty occasionally regretted leaving their lavish lifestyle in Chicago, because she had not resumed working after their arrival in New York.

Ill advisedly, immediately after his victory in the battle of bands, Cab signed a long-term contract with the co-owner of the Savoy, the entrepreneur Moe Gale, in which Gale would become his agent and pay him one hundred dollars per week. Gale, whose real name was Moses Galewski, became known as "the Great White Father of Harlem" as a result of his similar financial involvement with many African American performers, siphoning off a hefty percentage of their earnings should they succeed, and on the back of his most high-profile artists well able to afford his weekly guarantee for those who were less successful. In this case Gale had a shrewd suspicion that before long Cab would be worth many times what he had agreed to pay him over the next ten years. However, in the early fall of 1930 Gale was struggling to find Cab and the band enough work to cover the weekly hundred dollars, until toward the very end of the year he managed to put the band into the Crazy Cat, a club at Forty-eighth and Broadway, which catered to the Times Square after-theater crowd and to a show-business clientele who came in after work.[15] The audience was white, and according to Cab, he reached an even bigger public because there were regular broadcasts from the club.

This residency had an immediate and beneficial effect on both singer and band, as we can tell from their last record session of 1930, made on December 23. All four of the discs they made that day are magnificent, and Cab's version of "St. James Infirmary" was to be his second hit record, following in the wake of "St. Louis Blues." Equally remarkable are "Some of These Days," which gallops along at breakneck speed with Cab's vocal floating eerily over the ensemble, and "Nobody's Sweetheart," which is a good early example of what might best be described as Cab's high tenor wail, again hanging back way behind the beat for maximum dramatic effect. But the record that most firmly points to something new and different in Cab and his band's act was called "Is That Religion?"

Cab assumes the role of a preacher, and his band becomes the congregation. In just the way he had learned from Blanche at the very outset of his career at the Sunset, he interacts with his musicians, drawing their personalities into the performance, and enlisting sounds that would be familiar to anyone who had witnessed the revivalist fervor of an African American gospel meeting. As he intones, a voice comments "Ain't it true? Ain't it true?" and then a chorus of falsetto voices introduce the chorus with "Tell us all about it!"

Such records were not new. There were plenty of genuine sermonizers and preachers whose work appeared in the catalogs of "race records,"[16] starting with Calvin P. Dixon in 1925, and going on to include the Reverend J. C. Burnett, whose "Downfall of Nebuchadnezzar" became a best-seller. But what was genuinely original here was the way Cab and his band were using this genre as a setting for entertainment, and what's more, entertainment in the very kind of nightclub most frowned upon by preachers of the type Cab was emulating. Later artists such as Louis Jordan would take the idea even further in songs such as "Deacon Jones," but Cab's "Is That Religion?" was one of the first not so much to satirize religion, but to use its familiar tropes as a new way to engage an audience. Ironically, it was not an original Calloway idea, but a piece he had picked up the previous spring during his short run of campus and Savoy gigs with Nappy Howard, who recalled, "Cab paid us the supreme compliment. A number we had called 'Ain't That Religion' was played by his band,

and his arrangement was the same as a special arrangement we had made!"[17]
A few months later, when Cab and his new agent Irving Mills started to plan
how to market his band, this kind of song would be a fundamental building
block of their approach.

So how did he move from Moe Gale's hand-to-mouth management to being
handled by the successful agent behind Duke Ellington's meteoric success? In
Cab's autobiography, he recounts how a group of mobsters arrived at the Crazy
Cat and told him to be at the Cotton Club the following afternoon to rehearse
the show, or else. His contract with Gale was to be torn up, and he was to be
employed by the Cotton Club instead.

Dramatic as this sounds, his progress there was slightly less rapid. In late
January he was playing for a week at the Strand Theater in New York, and it
was announced to the press during the course of this show that he would
replace Duke Ellington's band at the Cotton Club during the first week of
February, when Ellington set off on tour.[18] It was a logical choice for the club's
management. They had three years' experience of employing the Missourians,
prior to Ellington's arrival, and in Cab himself the band had a charismatic
leader who was already a vote winner with Harlem audiences, and a far more
versatile front man than Preer had been. Accounts differ as to whether Cab
actually began his run on Sunday, February 1, or Wednesday, February 4, 1931,
but soon he was firmly ensconced at the club, with his band backing the floor
show and also playing for his own high-energy act. The supporting cast included
the Cotton Club regulars Aida Ward and Edith Wilson, who had often sung
there in the Ellington era, plus Louise Cook, Earl Tucker, Dotty Rhodes, Sonny
Boy Dudley, Bessie Dudley, Meers and Meers, Willie Jackson, Three Little
Wards, and the Bon Bon Boys. Such a show was not cheap to put on, even in
the depths of the Depression, but according to the press of the time, the
uptown venues were holding their own against the prevailing tide of financial
disaster: "Clubs in Harlem are the only ones doing good enough business to
hold a good show. White night clubs in greater New York are the real victims
of the depression and feel it to a greater extent than their competitors in the
Harlem district."[19]

Once Cab became the principal headliner at the Cotton Club, his contract
with Gale was also effectively a thing of the past, because by making his move
he had automatically come under the aegis of Irving Mills, who was in cahoots
with Madden and his associates. Under an arrangement begun when the songwriter Jimmy McHugh, a former partner in the family publishing firm Mills

Music, had been appointed musical director and composer-in-residence at the Cotton Club, Mills published all the music performed there. Furthermore, he owned a sizable stake in Duke Ellington's band, which he also managed.

Mills promptly set up Calloway's band along similar lines as a new corporation, in which he, his lawyer, and Duke Ellington owned shares worth 65 percent of the whole, leaving Cab with just a 35 percent interest.[20] Moe Gale was edged out of this deal, but he remained a potent force in the Harlem music world through his joint ownership of the Savoy Ballroom, and he was not above bringing his old "exclusive" contract with Calloway to bear a few months later, when Ellington was working his way back toward New York on the later stages of the tour he had begun in February, just as Cab himself was about to get his first break from the Cotton Club. Dr. Klaus Stratemann, Ellington's chronologer, pieced together the story:

> Ellington's NBC-booked midwestern dates created some tension between NBC's artists bureau and Irving Mills who was apparently infuriated over NBC's alleged mishandling of both the Calloway and Ellington bands. The former had been booked by the chain for a midwestern tour at what Mills considered unfavorable terms, and over his head, in a direct deal with Moe Gale and Herman Stark (manager of the Cotton Club), said to jointly control the majority of Cab Calloway Inc. (Mills held an interest of 40%). Mills retaliated by threatening to pull the Ellington band from NBC's direction and switch to the CBS network at the end of Ellington's NBC-booked engagement at the Lincoln Tavern in Chicago, on August 13. The rift was apparently healed quickly as Ellington continued his tour as scheduled.[21]

The incident gives some insight into Irving Mills and the hard-headed methods he used successfully to manage both Ellington and Cab, whose band was to become every bit as important to his organization as Ellington's as the Depression years wore on. Initially he was able to use Ellington's established drawing power as a means of selling his other bands to theaters and clubs, so that if a club wanted to hire Ellington they would first have to book Cab or Mills's third main aggregation, the Blue Rhythm Band. As Cab's popularity rose to rival, and periodically eclipse, that of Ellington as a result of his residency at the Cotton Club, his band would be similarly exploited by Mills as a reward for booking other less well-known bands in his management empire.

Irving Mills was born in January 1894. He and his elder brother Jack were the sons of Russian Jewish immigrants, and had grown up on the Lower East Side of New York City. Their father died when Irving was eleven, and after working in menial jobs in hotels and theaters, Irving became a song plugger first for Snellenberg's department store in Philadelphia, and then in New York for the publisher Leo Feist, until he and Jack set up their own firm Jack Mills Inc. (later Mills Music) in 1919. Whereas Jack managed the publishing business, Irving took a much wider role in shaping twentieth-century popular music. In the mid-1920s, he had a recording career himself as a vocalist, mainly with medium-sized jazz groups of New York session players, variously including Red Nichols, the Dorsey Brothers, Joe Venuti, and Eddie Lang, under the names of his Music Masters, his Modernists, his Musical Clowns, or his Hotsy Totsy Gang.

In 1926, Mills became the manager for Duke Ellington, and seeing the potential for a different type of promotion from most jazz acts, he applied considerable skill to promoting the artistic side of Duke's work, getting his compositions and recordings assessed on completely different critical criteria from other bands. He combined his continuing work as a publisher with running Mills Artists' Booking Agency, and later also became head of the American Recording Company, which after a period in the hands of Consolidated Film Industries was eventually subsumed into Columbia in 1938.[22]

Mills astutely realized how Cab's larger-than-life personality and unique vocalizing could be used to sell the band, and in due course Mills went to elaborate lengths to package Cab's identity and sell it to the entertainment world. His press kit for "His hi-de-highness of ho-de-ho," produced in 1934, left no detail unplanned as to how Cab and the band would be marketed, from press ads to posters, from band photos to portrait pictures, and from a formal biography to short pithy catch phrases designed for lazy editors to appropriate as previews or reviews.[23]

Mills's influence was immediate. Within a month of Cab's debut at the Cotton Club, he began to sing a high proportion of original material rather than the standard songs by other writers that he had hitherto performed. On March 3, 1931, Cab and the band went into the studio in New York for Brunswick to record "Minnie the Moocher (The Ho De Ho Song)", which according to publicist Ned Washington was because "he and his sponsor [Mills] decided that he should have a special number, suited to his wholly individual style, so they wrote one together."[24] Irving Mills's name appeared on virtually every song he published as either lyricist or additional composer, and "Minnie the Moocher," although it was drafted by Cab, was no exception. Throughout the 1920s, despite a limited formal education, Mills provided lyrics for scores of songs in exchange for a cut of the royalties. Sometimes these were cynical exercises in adding additional verses to extant songs, but he frequently provided all the lyrics himself for completely new tunes, and he also regarded himself as an astute editor of compositions, trimming even Ellington's work down to simpler, more approachable forms that he instinctively knew would succeed with the public. As was so often the case, his instincts for Cab were sound, and the song, with its incorporation of Cab's interactive call and response with the band, and the lyric's creation of a Harlem demimonde of Minnie and the drug culture, became a vital ingredient in creating the persona for Cab that would make him a national phenomenon.

Cab was to record the song many more times in his career, but this original version became the first million-selling disc by an African American artist, and Cab was eventually presented with a gold disc in the fall of 1944. The song had achieved overall sales of close to two and a half million for Cab by 1978, a truly remarkable achievement.[25] It became the template not only for further remakes but also for several other numbers that Cab gradually added to his repertoire as the 1930s went on. Some of these were about Minnie and Smokey Joe, the fictional character who introduced her to opium addiction or "kicking the gong around," whereas others picked up on the "hi-de-ho" catchphrase that the original song introduced. All of these pieces were designed to involve the audience in Cab's musical storytelling, by joining in the "hi-de-ho" responses, and thereby becoming part of the song.

"We did things in the Cotton Club which were fantastic numbers, but related to dope," recalled Calloway.[26] More than any other singer of the time, Cab in his trademark songs— darkly atmospheric minor key "moaners"—dealt almost exclusively with the seamy world of narcotics. This was not necessarily apparent to his white audiences or to record buyers who were not party to the jive language of Harlem, which had its own terms for everything from marijuana to cocaine and opium. "An entire secret language developed," pointed out the musicologist Gunther Schuller, "perpetuated now in the popular song literature of the thirties."[27] It is undoubtedly the case that "Minnie the Moocher" spread that message to those in the know very effectively, and it did so with the same vivid imagery, suggests Schuller, as a dramatically photographed silent movie.

The piece opens with the band playing a simple minor theme over the snare drum press rolls of Leroy Maxey, before a brief cameo by the growling trumpet of R. Q. Dickerson. The mood is Ellingtonian, with Dickerson catching the atmosphere of Bubber Miley's playing on a piece such as "New Orleans Low Down" or Cootie Williams's brilliant moments on "East St. Louis Toodle-o," and making an explicit connection with the sound that the Cotton Club (and Irving Mills) had so successfully marketed as "jungle music." There is also an entirely deliberate attempt by the band's arranger, Walter "Foots" Thomas, to recapture his own setting for Cab of "St. James Infirmary," thereby immediately bringing to listeners the sound of the band's most recent hit record.

The recording balance—maybe at Mills's insistence—puts Calloway far more firmly in the spotlight than on any of his previous records as he enters for his vocal. The band drops way back in volume, and Cab's words can be heard perfectly, including a rather strange mispronunciation of the word "whale." When the band shouts back "Ho-de-ho-de-ho" in the first chorus, Morris White's single string guitar solo sits elegantly behind the massed vocals. The story moves on to introduce Minnie, Smokey Joe, and Minnie's dream of a fortune given to her by the king of Sweden, but for those who were not in the know about the drug-laden imagery of the lyrics, the most memorable aspect of the performance is the constant variation on the "hi-de-ho" call-and-response pattern. This was the aural "hook" by which Cab would become known to his audience, and it gave him an immediately recognizable identity. This was important to him in terms of recordings, but it was even more vital as he built an audience on radio. From very early in his run at the Cotton Club, he was being heard nationally over the NBC "Red" Network, and "Minnie the Moocher" became his calling card for radio audiences everywhere. As the bassist who joined him later in the 1930s, Milt Hinton, observed:

> Cab was not a star that was made by records. He didn't like to make recordings. For Cab Calloway the radio was the thing in those days. There was no television, just radio. At twelve o'clock each night you'd hear Cab Calloway, coast to coast, Hi-de-ho-ing, so people all over the country heard him. And when he went on tour, it was like a rock star of today. People flocked to hear him, in order to see him in person, because they'd heard him on radio. He was exciting to listen to, so they came out to hear the band. So he had a big following from that standpoint.[28]

The year 1931 saw Cab using his base at the Cotton Club to begin his relent-less climb to national and then international stardom. Dressed in his white tie and tails, his long straight hair ruffled into a prototype Beatle mop, and con-ducting with an oversized baton, Cab Calloway crystallized his persona as an entertainer at the club. An accurate impression of how he appeared at the time can be seen in the 1934 movie *Cab Calloway's Hi-De-Ho*, in which his act was filmed on a mock-up of the Cotton Club stage. He holds the viewer's attention with effortless authority. Singing "Zaz Zuh Zaz," his vocal gymnas-tics are matched by exaggerated gestures, and between the vocalizing he moves spectacularly—running the gamut of jazz dance devices from frenetic movement to slow-drag walking. Indeed his movements drew on the entire lexicon of vernacular African American dance, with allusions to nineteenth-century survivals such as buck and wing alongside comparatively recent fads like the black bottom. His gestures and his vocals were designed to bring his band—and thereby his audience—into the act as well, highlighting the differ-ent sections of musicians, and encouraging them to shout or sing a response to his words.

As he throws his head back and projects his voice, displaying his distinctive perfect teeth, his singing is marked by a complete lack of inhibition, and a freedom that matches the finest jazz instrumentalists of the age. At twenty-six years old, when this film was made, he had used his first three years of working regularly at the Cotton Club to consolidate a stage personality that cut through racial and class boundaries. It turned him into an entertainer who connected with all of American society, not just the African American public who bought his discs, or the well-heeled white pleasure seekers who defied the Depression and flocked to Harlem to hear him in person. His daughter Camay witnessed Cab's stage persona in the 1930s firsthand as a child:

> He had this kind of charisma that you just don't see in people today. . . .
> He was a wonderful singer, he was a wonderful dancer, he dressed very
> beautifully, he was charming and that kind of thing. But he also had a
> magnetic something, so that people just gravitated toward him.[29]

In the movie, aside from a frothy plot about a pullman porter's wife who falls for Cab when she hears him on the radio, there are hints that alongside the charm and charisma, Cab was considerably more than a happy-go-lucky, care-free entertainer. He receives a telegram as his train is setting off for New York, saying that a new routine is required at the club. Consequently he rehearses his men during the journey. When the train draws in to its final destination, the porter asks him for advice, and Cab becomes a knowledgeable Harlem businessman, recommending a radio receiver that will accurately reproduce the sound of his band.

There are two nuggets of truth embodied in this fictional presentation. First, since 1930, Cab had increasingly become a perfectionist about rehearsing his band in order to reach and maintain the highest level of performance. Second, although he had made an error of judgment over his first management contract with Gale, he possessed the streetwise guile and innate business acumen to keep himself and his band securely employed by the collection of hardened criminals at the Cotton Club.

In later life Cab's detailed attention to rehearsal was much the same as it had been in the early 1930s. According to his grandson, Christopher Calloway Brooks, this was because his dance movements were an essential ingredient in the way he conducted his musicians:

He would sing the songs, focusing on the cues, and there'd be a lot of places where there were *ritardandos*, and *accelerandos*, and *fermatas*, and he would really have to conduct those. Other times he would have to conduct the verses, because . . . in cabaret with just an accompanist, it's easy to follow the singer taking a *rubato* approach and doing the verse a little differently each time, but if you've got sixteen musicians trying to follow a singer . . . in that circumstance the rehearsal version was going to be identical to what he wound up performing.[30]

The British arranger Alan Cohen experienced this firsthand when he put together a big band to accompany Cab for a BBC broadcast from the Ritz Hotel in London in 1985:

He didn't need a musical director, because it was all built into his act. All the singing and stamping around and scatting, all his hand movements: these were all significant for the band. He was very energetic, he did his special dance . . . and the singing and the hollering, and conducted, and cut off and held long chords, and things like that. It was all built into his act, and so were the tempi.[31]

Playing in that band was the saxophonist Alan Barnes, who recalled that Cab's ebullient smile would disappear from his face as he turned to face the band, gesturing briskly to his musicians what he wanted with a frown, before his grin reappeared as he swiveled back to face the audience.[32]

And in just the same way as Cab's easygoing stage persona hid a lot of this type of behind-the-scenes attention to detail, it also disguised the toughness that had been bred in him as a teenager, hustling up work and running with the gang in Baltimore, and learning his independence at Downingtown. Camay recalls that "he looked classy, but he always had that street streak. It served him well over the years—you did not cross him."[33]

Which was just as well for Cab, because according to the press of the time, the Cotton Club's proprietor Owney Madden and his gangland associates were mixed up in just about every type of urban crime imaginable.[34] Yet just as Preer had done, Cab found favor with Madden and the mob, and with Mills's energetic management behind him, this gave him a significant advantage in the cutthroat world of Depression entertainment. In the months that followed the recording of his theme song, he not only continued to improve his standing with the club's gangland owners but used his innate toughness to set about improving his band, and grooming them into an orchestra of the very highest quality.

Chapter 4

Harlem Fuss
1931–1933

"Cab was making changes," recalled guitarist Danny Barker. "From 1931 he . . . fired one Missourian of the original band at a time. Rumor says he fired them because when he first joined the band they resented him. [It was] a process: to break up a clique in a band. You get a clique in a band, that's trouble."[1]

Barker was later to take over the guitar chair in the Calloway orchestra, but already as a freelance player in New York during 1931 he was a shrewd observer of developments in jazz. The changes that Cab made would have been much talked about at the Rhythm Club, where the city's big band community met socially, and where Barker was a frequent visitor after his arrival from New Orleans in 1930. In some ways Cab's decision to pick off the weaker members of his band one at a time seems paradoxical. The Missourians' great strength until he took over was their tightness as an ensemble, and their collective skill far outweighed the solo talents of individual members, with the possible exception of the clarinetist Thornton Blue, who was the first to leave when the band arrived at the Cotton Club. But it became clear over time that Cab wanted the best of both worlds, to maintain the distinctive swing and midwestern bluesiness of his band, but simultaneously to improve the underlying musicality of his ranks and add to the group's solo strength.

Arville Harris who replaced Blue in February 1931 was not as distinctive a soloist, but he was perfectly competent, and a more versatile section player.

Four months later, in May, the Missourians' long-term pianist Earres Prince was ejected, and Cab's accomplished friend from the touring production of *Hot Chocolates*, Bennie Payne, took his place. The fiery trumpeter R. Q. Dickerson, a key ingredient in the original Missourians' sound, was next to go, being replaced in July by the experienced territory band player Edwin Swayze (whose name, on account of its pronunciation, is often misspelled Swayzee). There was a further adjustment to the trumpet section soon afterward when Wendell Culley was ousted in favor of Reuben Reeves, a brilliant soloist and high-note specialist who had made his name in Chicago as a challenger to Louis Armstrong. By the end of 1931 Cab had replaced one-third of his backing band, in every case with a more skilled big band player, and with the possible exception of Harris, a more promising soloist as well.

Before Barker joined Cab in 1939, he was to experience a similar sequential firing routine in Lucky Millinder's group. In 1934 Millinder was brought in as director of the Mills Blue Rhythm Band, and he immediately adopted an identical policy to Cab's 1931 clear-out of the sections. This suggests the guidance of Irving Mills himself behind both Millinder's and Cab's changes in personnel, urging each of his new stars to take direct control, and to break up any power base that lingered from the band's previous career. It was well known that some 1930s swing bands had influential inner cliques that dictated their entire repertoire and policy, including decisions on who the featured soloists would be, and who was to be marked out for promotion. The Arkansas-born trombonist Snub Mosley, for example, always complained that when he joined the mid-1930s Luis Russell band, it was run by a "New Orleans clique."[2] Crescent City members such as Henry "Red" Allen, Albert Nicholas, Pops Foster, Paul Barbarin, and (although he was born in Panama, and moved to New Orleans as a teenager) Russell himself decided who was in and who was out, often over plates of red beans and rice in the leader's dressing room. Mosley—however skilled a trombonist and singer—was never to be accepted by that inner circle. There is some evidence that the Missourians were a band similarly manipulated by a clique of long-serving members who went back to the early days in St. Louis of "Robinson's Bostonians."

Although Cab valued the experience his men had gained in the Midwest, he did not want to be ruled by it. His judicious substitutions sent out the clear message that he was leader of the band in more than name, and for those who enthusiastically embraced his direction, there were soon noticeable benefits. During the course of his first year at the Cotton Club, Cab's financial position improved dramatically, as he and the band were paid upward of five thousand dollars a week, which is equivalent to over seventy-one thousand dollars in 2010.[3] This brought Cab himself back to a similar level of earnings to that of his final months at the Sunset, and as well as fueling his passions for fine clothes and betting at the racetrack, it also brought an end to what had threatened to be a cause of friction between him and Betty.

In addition to the band's nightly appearances at the club, followed toward the year's end by a short midwestern tour while Ellington temporarily returned to Harlem, there were regular recording sessions, producing two or more new titles virtually every month in 1931. These were also a boost to the earnings of Cab and his musicians. According to Cab's own estimate, by the end of 1931 he was earning twenty-six thousand dollars a year in salary from the corporation that Mills had established to manage the band, plus roughly the same figure again in the form of a profit share.[4]

Given Mills and Ellington's financial stake in the band, however, it was not surprising that the recorded repertoire consisted almost entirely of pieces published by Mills (several being cowritten by him as well). To maximize his profits, Mills had a fondness for issuing as many different recordings of his songs as possible. So it was predictable that Cab would swiftly make cover versions of Ellington's "Mood Indigo" and "Creole Love Call."

The first of these pieces is just an instrumental, with the newly arrived Arville Harris taking the familiar clarinet solo, and Wendell Culley supplying the muted trumpet. The second is almost entirely a band feature as well, with Dickerson's growling trumpet added to the tonal palette, although rather than emulating Adelaide Hall's wordless adornments to the original Ducal recording, Cab restricts himself to a low-key ramble through a single verse of Mills's "official" lyrics at the end of the piece. The atmosphere and the style of the performances are undeniably Ellingtonian, giving the impression that Foots Thomas had probably transcribed the bones of the arrangements from Ellington's records. In defense of this, Cab observed:

> Ellington had at that time the greatest array of sidemen jazz has ever known. Artie Whetsel, Bubber, Tricky Sam, Bigard, Carney, Hodges and Wellman Braud. Braud was just about the finest bass-player around in those days. He was just about the first bassist to pick the bass, and he really started the style. All the guys patterned themselves after Duke's soloists because they had no one else to pattern themselves after.[5]

Fortunately, away from the Ducal repertoire, Cab's band still retained its individual brand of midwestern swing. The underlying Kansas City influence was to remain the basis of the group's development in the early 1930s, setting it apart not only from Ellington but also from Fletcher Henderson's New York–based orchestra. A romping version of "Farewell Blues" with a manic vocal from Cab, made at the same time as "Mood Indigo," confirms that the band's fundamental identity was intact, and in mid-1931 it still employed Jimmy Smith's tuba as its bass instrument, not yet following Braud's new fashion for the string bass.

In the summer of 1931, the Pennsylvania and New York State local press began carrying advertisements for Cab's "Cotton Club Orchestra" making its "First Appearance on Tour."[6] In fact this was another moneymaking ruse for Cab, in a practice well established by bandleaders of the time, namely to take over somebody else's lineup for a small number of out-of-town engagements, leaving his own band in place at the Cotton Club. For this, Cab selected his former occasional backing group, led by Nappy Howard, who recalled, "On July 3rd we hit the road to back up Cab Calloway for two nights in Schmokin [sic], Pennsylvania. . . . The gig was a big deal for him, something like a couple of thousand bucks, which back in those times, was big."[7] Many of the provincial appearances by Cab and his "Cotton Club Orchestra" that were billed within striking distance of New York later in 1931 similarly used Howard's men, who performed an identical function for other well-known leaders, including Don Redman and Noble Sissle—all of them, like Cab, grateful for the extra cash.

Meanwhile Cab was maintaining a high profile with his own band in New York City. A couple of months into Cab's Cotton Club residency, Mills took out full-page advertisements in *Variety* to publicize the band's appearances downtown at the Paramount Theater with dancer Bill "Bojangles" Robinson. Then a German radio broadcaster, "Hectic Helmut," took his microphone into the Cotton Club to record his impressions of Cab and the band, possibly confusing his audience at home with his highly contrasting portrait of New York nightlife, because the other group he recorded was Vincent Lopez's society band at the St. Regis Hotel in Manhattan. Around the same time Cab began to be featured in the gossip columns, not least the one penned by the man who set the style for such writing in 1930s New York, Walter Winchell. He observed:

> Far be it from us to proofread so usually flawless a directory as Donnelley's
> *Red Book*, for its spring-summer edition. But Cab Calloway is a sepia

orchestra director, singer extraordinary, and all-round entertainer. Cab
Calloway is not, as Column 2, page 819 of Donnelley's lists him—a taxi-
cab![8]

As 1931 progressed, New York nightlife itself changed. Two years or so into the
Depression, there was a shift in Midtown from sizable venues with a hefty
cover charge toward smaller speakeasies, whose entry fees included a couple
of drinks for what the larger places would have asked just for admission. Food
prices remained high, but as speakeasies vied for trade, they offered more and
more in the way of entertainment. To compete, Harlem's floor shows offered
even more splendid presentations of numerous artists with singing, dancing,
and comedy. "After all these years," ran one report, "Connie's Inn and the Cotton Club [have] survived. Cab Calloway, the band maestro, serves music hot at
the Cotton Club."[9]

As if to prove its superiority in competing with midtown speakeasies, when
Cab returned from his two-month tour of the Midwest in December 1931, the
Cotton Club launched one of its most lavish revues to date, called *Rhythmania*.
Cab and Aida Ward were the star performers, but the show's real importance
was that it employed a new songwriting team, Ted Koehler and Harold Arlen.
They would rival the huge success that Jimmy McHugh and Dorothy Fields
had brought to Ellington's first shows there from December 1927 onward.
Although Ellington's most enduring recordings from the period are now recog-
nized to be his own compositions, or the pieces he wrote collaboratively with
his sidemen, many of the most popular discs he made in the late 1920s were
drawn directly from the Cotton Club shows and written by Fields and McHugh.
Such songs as "Freeze and Melt," "Harlem River Quiver," "Bandanna Babes,"
"Hot Feet," "Arabian Lover," and perhaps most notably "I Must Have That
Man" and "I Can't Give You Anything but Love" (with Baby Cox and Irving
Mills himself sharing the vocal duties) were recorded by Ellington's band
within weeks of their first performances at the club.

However in 1930, Fields and McHugh accepted a lucrative offer to go to
Hollywood and write movie musicals for MGM. The film company tied them
into a new publishing deal with Robbins Music, and so they ceased to provide
either Mills or the Cotton Club with fresh material. As a parting gesture,
McHugh dusted off a number of older songs he had written in the 1920s with
Al Dubin as the basis for Walter Brooks's *Brown Skin Vamps*, the show that ran
at the club for the three months immediately before Cab's arrival.[10]

Arlen and Koehler had supplied some pieces for the first of the revues in which Cab appeared, *Brown Sugar*. They then set to work to become part of the fabric of the Cotton Club and its entertainment in a way that Fields and McHugh never had. Whereas McHugh mostly worked away from the club's premises as a publisher and song plugger for Mills Music, and Fields wrote most of her New York shows at her family's Upper West Side apartment, Koehler (whose hobby was woodworking) helped design and build Cotton Club sets for choreographer Dan Healy. Meanwhile Arlen struck up friendships with the dancers in the revue, learning the latest steps and rhythms, before going back to his penthouse digs at the Croydon Hotel and crafting what he had heard into new melodies. Apparently Arlen himself was not a fan of the bawdier numbers they were required to write for such risqué singers and comediennes as Cora La Redd and Leitha Hill, but he nonetheless came up with suitable compositions, on the stipulation his name was absent from the published sheet music.[11]

Ironically, in the light of the composer's distaste, Cab himself reserved his highest praise for Koehler and Arlen's "double entendre nasty songs . . . the hurly burly bump and grind mixed with high class swinging jazz," which in his view were more in tune with the genre of African American revue than Dorothy Fields's less "funky" lyrics. He believed the new team produced the ideal "combination of vaudeville, burlesque, and great music and dancing."[12]

In December 1931 Koehler and Arlen wrote virtually the entire *Rhythmania* show, and immediately struck a vein of successful hits. Indeed so confident was Mills of these songs that he had Cab record them just before his tour, a few weeks ahead of the pieces being premiered at the club. "Between the Devil and the Deep Blue Sea" became a jazz standard after Cab's October 21, 1931, recording, but at the same session he made two discs of Koehler/Arlen material that were to be vital ingredients in the Calloway canon: "Trickeration" and "Kicking the Gong Around."

"Trickeration" is one of those fashionable songs of the period about Harlem and its nightlife that helped to cement in the public mind an image of the district as the entertainment capital of the United States. Not only did its lyrics prefigure Ellington's "It Don't Mean a Thing If It Ain't Got That Swing" but it also became a template for Koehler's later Harlem song "Truckin'" (written with Rube Bloom). Arlen's catchy melody and Foots Thomas's sparkling arrangement, with some jaunty clarinet playing from Harris, provide a perfect setting for Cab to deliver not only the lyric but also some of his most virtuoso scat singing to date. By contrast, "Kicking the Gong Around" sets a somber mood, containing far more explicit drug references than in "Minnie the Moocher." In keeping with that earlier song, there is a shout-back chorus for the band, no doubt designed to reinforce Cab's "Hi-de-ho man" image with the radio-listening and record-buying public. For these three pieces, Jimmy Smith forsook his tuba for a double bass, and the band's already hard-swinging beat became lighter and more flexible. Not surprisingly, all these tunes entered the best-selling lists toward the end of 1931, and created a welcome reception for them in the December revue.[13]

Cab was featured in all three songs at the Cotton Club, but also in the program for *Rhythmania* was "Without Rhythm," which—although it was not one of their specialties from the live show—Cab and the band recorded on November 18. This piece shows that his reorganization of the trumpet section had been a great success, starting with Swayze's growling horn, and with a sparkling high-note solo from Reeves in his best Armstrong manner. The entire section leads the final key change and closing chorus, showing some of the band's most disciplined and effective brass playing so far, recorded over its traditional bouncing midwestern rhythm. In his vocal refrain Cab takes the opportunity to lead a couple of choruses of shout-back scat singing with his men.

Thus the pattern was set for the next couple of years. Koehler and Arlen would write a batch of songs for each new revue at the Cotton Club, and Cab would record his own feature numbers at the time, soon followed by other songs from the same team that had been conceived for other members of the cast. Occasionally Cab made versions of material they had supplied to other shows, but for which Mills followed his usual policy of recording the songs as widely as possible. Hence Cab was among the first to record several numbers by the pair that were to become jazz standards, notably "I've Got the World on a String" (which was Cab's ballad feature from *The Cotton Club Parade* in October 1932), and "I Gotta Right to Sing the Blues" (from the *Earl Carroll Vanities*). These were both recorded in November 1932. Meanwhile, a string of Koehler/Arlen pieces more appropriate to Cab's "hi-de-ho" persona were featured both in Cotton Club shows and on record, including "Minnie the Moocher's Wedding Day," "Harlem Holiday," and "That's What I Hate about Love."[14] As well as pieces by other writers in the Mills stable, and a growing quantity by his trombonist Harry White, Cab himself continued to furnish material for the band during this period. It is easy to discern his hand in the scat-orientated lyrics to songs such as "The Lady with the Fan," "Zaz Zuh Zaz," "Jitterbug," and—above all—"The Scat Song" itself.

Such high-quality songs, coupled with Cab's hard work on improving his band, and Mills's astute management were greatly to raise Cab's profile with the general public. His press billings from the time give a sense both of his growing fame and just how successful he had been in creating an instantly recognizable public persona. He offered

> something new in red hot rhythm—something different in hotcha harmony. He is the originator of "Minnie the Moocher," the song that is at present sweeping the country. He also originated the "ho-de-ho-de-ho" jazz cry and when Cab sings it it is one dynamic blast of blues. His voice rings to high heaven with the hottest, happiest, craziest melody you ever heard. Cab Calloway does not only sing, but he is all over the stage, strutting, shuffling and shaking—his dances are never the same in any show.[15]

By the end of his first year at the Cotton Club, 1931, Cab was still broadcasting regularly on NBC's "Red" network.[16] In December he also recorded the sound track for a Betty Boop "talkartoon" of his best-known song, "Minnie the Moocher," for release early in 1932.[17] In the picture—which combines live studio shots of Cab and the band with an animated cartoon—Cab dances a brilliantly effective slow drag in front of his band over the opening titles. His supple movement and slow-motion running on the spot is a prototype of Michael Jackson's "moon walk." The plot, such as it is, is simple. As the teenage flapper Betty Boop and her canine friend Bimbo run away from home, they hide in a tree stump as a cartoon walrus, several skeletons, a trio of convicts, a cat, and four kittens (plus a few additional phantasms) perform a fantasy animation to Cab's singing. The effect prefigures Disney's bad dream sequences, such as the "Pink Elephants on Parade" from *Dumbo* or the "Heffalumps and Woozles" from *Winnie the Pooh*. Then the band roars into "Tiger Rag" and Betty and Bimbo run frantically for home pursued by a shrieking ghostly horde. The brief title section was Cab's first film appearance, but it is obvious that he already had the charisma to be a skilled performer for the camera.

Max Fleischer, the producer of the film, who was the creator of Betty Boop and later of Popeye the Sailor Man, was among the first moviemakers to realize that certain African American performers had achieved considerable crossover popularity with white audiences. *Minnie the Moocher* with Betty Boop was the first of three Calloway shorts he was to make that integrated Cab's singing and dancing into the cartoon world of Betty and her friends. In preparation for the movie, Max's brother Lou Fleischer made special visits to the Cotton Club to study Cab's dance steps and his scat singing, with the idea that the third brother, Dave Fleischer, who directed the animation, could more accurately depict Cab's highly personal style in the cartoon ghosts and animals by creating characters who could replicate his supple steps, starting with the walrus. In the finished films, the reason the principal cartoon characters so closely resemble Cab's dancing is that the Fleischer brothers used Max's invention, the Rotoscope, for the drawings. In this technique, actual footage of Cab dancing the cartoon roles was projected onto a transparent easel, where the animators traced his movements frame by frame, adding the features of the character over Cab's outline.[18]

Cab's larger-than-life personality made the transition to cartoon more readily than did that of the firm's other major African American star, Louis Armstrong. Fleischer's animators were somewhat vexed as to how to integrate into the action a musician who mainly played the trumpet and sang, and who lacked Cab's natural movement. In the end, Armstrong was presented as a disembodied head singing at Betty from the top corner of the screen. There were no such problems with Cab, however, and as far as the live-action sections of the films were concerned, there was not any patronizing treatment of him or his African American band. For the first movie they were all dressed immaculately in two-tone suits with matching brogues, and later they appeared all in white, exactly as they would have been for the Cotton Club or New York's most fashionable theaters.

The depiction of Cab in Fleischer's animated cartoon characters is more questionable. As well as singing for the threatening walrus-ghost in *Minnie the Moocher*, Cab also provides the voice and movements for a hermit-like being in the later *Old Man of the Mountain*. This character makes explicit and frightening sexual advances to Betty, tickling her with his beard, removing her dress and fondling her breasts, having already caused a mass exodus from her small town in a thinly veiled metaphor for black encroachment into white housing areas. Fleischer may have realized the drawing power of the best African American performers, and presented them very professionally in live-action shots, but he was not immune from introducing stereotyping the moment his animators got to work. Nevertheless their skill—particularly for the early 1930s—is undeniable, and the hermit's lips catch every nuance of Cab's high-speed syllabic scatting.

Aside from the glimpses of Cab and his band in live action in the opening sequences of these films, Cab was to make his first movie alongside humans, rather than cartoon characters, in *The Big Broadcast of 1932*, which went on release in October,[19] and caught Cab in his outsize white tailcoat delivering a particularly theatrical version of "Kicking the Gong Around." His mimed hand actions include cutting and snorting a line of coke, presumably an image the significance of which bypassed the director, Frank Tuttle, who was otherwise dealing with such uncontroversial performers as Bing Crosby and George Burns.

Records, radio, and now movies as well helped Cab to feature for the first time in the *Pittsburgh Courier*'s annual "Favorite Orchestra Contest." Mills's publicity machine had done its best for him, according to the paper's report, which ran:

> The incomparable Duke Ellington came into his own again Monday when figures . . . indicated that the internationally famous bandleader with the surname [sic] of royalty was back in first place position again. The voting however showed that Fletcher Henderson, Noble Sissle and Cab Calloway, who were second, third, and fourth respectively were in striking distance of the leader. . . . The tabulation indicated that 13,970 votes had been polled for Ellington, 12,711 for Henderson, 12,104 for Sissle, and 11,899 for Calloway. This is one of the closest foursomes among the leaders which has materialized since the beginning of the contest.[20]

A year earlier, few had heard of Cab Calloway. Now he had come within a couple of thousand votes of the best-known African American bandleaders in a national poll. Two months later, in the same paper's year-end "Band of the Year" vote, Cab dropped one place to fifth. To the surprise of most followers of the scene, his sister Blanche unexpectedly came sixth, her thirty-two thousand votes placing her slightly ahead of her old flame Louis Armstrong.[21]

Cab's arrival in New York and his success at the Cotton Club had not gone unnoticed by his elder sister, who had stayed in Chicago when Cab first set off

on the road with the Alabamians. As he featured more and more in the public
eye, she must have been somewhat peeved to see someone whom she had
groomed, and to whom she had imparted much of her craft as both vocalist and
dancer, overtake her in popularity. Furthermore, Cab's record contract with
Brunswick and his connections with the mob at the Cotton Club had accelerated his career even further.

It was not in Blanche's highly competitive character to let her kid brother
climb so far up the show business ladder without a fight-back. In later life she
was just as feisty a businesswoman as she had been a performer, selling
specialized cosmetics to African American women, in what became a million-
dollar business. She was attuned to success and taking second place was not in
her nature.[22]

In 1931 she determined that she must transform herself from cabaret
singer to bandleader in order to compete on level terms with Cab. So she relo-
cated from Chicago to Philadelphia, where she headlined at the Pearl Theatre,
and was taken up by its management, which was well connected in the New
York-to-Washington corridor. Whatever big band came through Philly on the
touring circuit was promptly corralled into becoming "Blanche Calloway and
Her Joy Boys" for its week at the Pearl. Even local bandleaders found that she
had no scruples about muscling in on their patch. The well-established trumpeter Charlie Gaines, who was shortly to give Louis Jordan his start, and who
had already recorded with the likes of Fats Waller and Clarence Williams,
recalled:

> The owner of the Pearl was a man named Sam Stefal [*sic*] who was also
> the manager of Blanche Calloway. Sam was always trying to get Blanche's
> boys on the radio in our place, but [I] don't worry 'cause I got all my
> radio time and Sam didn't bother me after that.[23]

In early March, Andy Kirk and His Clouds of Joy came into town. The Pearl's
proprietor, whose actual name was Sam Steiffel, somehow or another persuaded the Victor Company to offer Blanche some record dates, and for the
first of these, on March 2, he simply borrowed Kirk's band wholesale to play
the session under Blanche's name. Kirk—by then an experienced player on the
territory circuit—knew that there was a chance that his band would be stolen
away by Blanche, but he wisely decided that the majority of his men were likely
to stick with him. Kirk recalled:

All the while his henchmen were manipulating this arrangement, the manager was inviting me to relax in his office. He'd say, "Here sit in this nice, soft chair. Be comfortable. You shouldn't have to stay down in the basement with the rest of the band." But I knew what was happening. The boys in the band reported everything that was going on.

To ensure no underhanded dealing went on when Blanche and the band arrived at the Camden, New Jersey, studio, Kirk took his normal place in the lineup, playing tuba and bass saxophone.[24]

That same month, the touring band led by bassist Jasper "Jap" Allen was stranded when several gigs fell through during a circuit of South Dakota, Iowa, and Nebraska. Consequently, six of his musicians accepted an offer to come to Philadelphia and join a new ensemble which Steiffel was putting together to form a permanent backing band for Blanche, and to fulfill the rest of her recording contract. With a small number of players, including trumpeter Edgar Battle, poached away from Kirk, and Allen's former trumpeter Joe Keyes, trombonist Alton Moore, saxophonist Ben Webster, and pianist Clyde Hart, Blanche had the nucleus of an experienced band of her own, plus a collection of soloists who could rival Cab's.[25] This was to be the basis for the group that—give or take a few changes in personnel over time—recorded her next three sessions for Victor, and which launched her career as one of the hardest-working touring bandleaders of all. Reed player Roger Boyd who joined her lineup a little later, remembered:

> I was with Blanche for three and a half years and during that time we went on the road with Jack Dempsey. Now that was a band where you begged for a lay-off. We played theatres, dance halls and tobacco warehouses. The small dance halls were just not big enough to hold the number of people who wanted to see us. Our box office was pretty close to Cab Calloway's outfit in popularity. So they would put us in those big tobacco warehouses, those floors in there were so smooth and they could hold large crowds of people. While I was with Blanche we played the whole RKO circuit three times.[26]

So, on the evidence of these recordings, how great a threat to Cab's popularity was his sister? The standout track from the three numbers she recorded with Kirk's band is "I Need Lovin'," which for much of its length seems as if she is simply a single-chorus vocalist in an extant band arrangement, which features the nimble clarinet of John Harrington and the raucous, jiving trombone of Stumpy Brady. But then, just as the song appears to be nearing its end, she puts in a tour de force of acting, becoming a shy, sensitive "sweet sixteen and never been kissed" *ingenue*, desperate to experience every possible variety of grown-up lovemaking. She pants, she pleads for souvenirs of her lover, and above all she gives the impression of wanting a thoroughly disreputable time, especially as she finishes the song on throaty growls and roars, giving a glimpse of her pent-up sexuality. The piece is a quantum leap forward from her 1925 recording of "Lonesome Lovesick," although it plays equally strongly on her acting ability. When Steiffel put her on the road as the first African American female singer to front an all-male eleven-piece band, he knew that her potent sexuality was a selling point that could compete head-on with Cab.

Her first session with her new ensemble has none of the feel of the well-rehearsed, slick touring group that Kirk provided. Instead, the main piece she recorded, "Just a Crazy Song," begins with a simple head arrangement, shared between the band's most experienced soloists, Battle and Webster. But this hardly matters, as the song is simply a vehicle for Blanche apparently copying the "hi-de-ho" call-and-response and scat routines recently recorded by Cab on "Minnie the Moocher." Except that it was Blanche, not Cab, who had pioneered this very technique out on the road before *Plantation Days* even reached Chicago. In his autobiography, Cab tells the entirely plausible story that he first started his "hi-de-ho" routine while singing an early draft of "Minnie the Moocher" on a broadcast from the Cotton Club, when he forgot the words. "I just started to scat sing the first thing that came into my mind," he says.[27]

Yet it would not be hard to imagine that the first thing to spring into his mind was a cornerstone of his sister's act, that he had learned by watching her perform during the weeks on the road of his own apprenticeship. Furthermore, it is highly unlikely that Blanche could have heard Cab's recording of "Minnie the Moocher"—the first recorded example of his use of "hi-de-ho"—when she went in to make "Just a Crazy Song" on March 27, 1931, because "Minnie" had been recorded in New York just three weeks earlier. This was well inside the average lead time for record production in the early 1930s, so it is almost certain that Cab's disc had not yet appeared. Instead, what we have in "Just a Crazy Song" is an aural snapshot of the stage routine that Blanche pioneered *before* Cab entered show business. The scatting, the shout-backs from the band, and a shared chorus of double entendre call and response with Battle's growling trumpet all suggest a well-honed act pragmatically mapped onto a simple head arrangement for the musicians, just as Blanche might have hastily sketched out for a pit band in a theater on the touring circuit.

Unfortunately for Blanche, this was really the start and finish of her originality. Compared with Cab's ability to put across a ballad, and in particular the new, well-crafted ballads being created for him by Koehler and Arlen, or his outrageous risk-taking vocals at high tempi, Blanche—on the evidence of her 1931 recordings—was a one-trick wonder. Her attempts at ballads such as Cliff Friend's mid-tempo "It Looks Like Susie" are risible, and swamped by her band. When she strays from her vaudeville double entendres on "Growlin' Dan" to try and put across a verse about Dan meeting Minnie the Moocher, she sounds like a feeble imitation of Cab. On a carefully fashioned song such as Waller and Razaf's "Concentratin' on You," she is at her best, but this reverts to her well-worn techniques of dialogue with her musicians, and confiding in the microphone that she puts "her shoe on her head" so lovelorn has she become.

Nevertheless, her formidable energy, Steiffel's aggressive promotion, and the fact that Blanche's band was regularly booked into the Palace Theatre on Broadway, and later the Lafayette in Harlem, were briefly to give Cab and his management cause for concern. "Speaking of 'Hot Ladies' the newest belle of Harlem is the sepia Blanche Calloway, who like her brother Cab conducts a jazz band with acrobatic fervor," ran one report. "On Lenox Avenue she is reputedly best dressed of the 'bright skins.'"[28] As a result, Irving Mills' press office was quick to put out a counterclaim of its own: "Harlem's reigning sheikh is Cab Calloway, a saddle-colored Negro out of a small town in Missouri. He has been leading an orchestra in cabaret and vaudeville. His dicty clothes in zebra patterns set the style pace for ebony swells along Lenox Avenue."[29]

In early August 1932, Cab broke the house record at the well-known New Jersey ballroom the Meadowbrook Inn, where he "proved a versatile entertainer as well as director, and his antics on the stage were agile and amusing." It would not have pleased him to find his sister smashing his own record just a few days later, not to mention her billing as "Blanche Calloway the Queen of Jazz and Her Famous Victor Recording, Radio and Stage Orchestra."[30]

If Blanche were the only person to be trading on Cab's growing reputation, given his debt to her, it is unlikely he would have been too bothered. But when he finally expressed his reservations to the press, during a 1932 tour to Chicago, she was not alone. The *Baltimore Afro-American* reported:

> Cab Calloway is peeved at members of his family and persons who say they are his relatives, who [are] attempting to cash in on his current rep. There's a girl playing dance halls by the name of Jean Calloway who claims to be the orchestra leader's cousin, and plays up the Calloway name. Then there's Cab's brother Elmer, playing night clubs, who bills himself as "Cab Calloway's brother." There is also Cab's sister Blanche, who last week billed herself at Proctor's Newark as "Cab Calloway's Sister." There is also a band billed as "Calloway and His Orchestra" playing Chicago which is causing Cab another headache.[31]

Elmer was not a lasting threat to Cab, and it seems his nightclub career was a brief flash in the pan. By contrast, Cab's own family had never heard of Jean Calloway, although in widespread press notices from 1932 she was trading not so much on being Cab's "cousin" as his "niece" and also "presenting her orchestra, made up entirely of men, over the National and Columbia broadcasting chains."[32]

So who was this mysterious singer?

It appears she was the former star of the touring company of Lew Leslie's *Blackbirds of 1928*, Harriett Calloway. In the fall of 1930, after the failure of his *International Revue*, Leslie mounted a new edition of *Blackbirds*, starting a lengthy tour at the Lyric Theatre in Boston, and again starring Harriett, whose press cuttings made much of the fact that she was a former Columbus, Ohio, newspaper delivery girl, and no relation to Cab or Blanche.[33] Harriett went on to pursue a solo career after leaving *Blackbirds*, and she followed Blanche's lead in setting up a band of her own. During Cab's rise from relative obscurity to national fame in 1931, it suddenly became unhelpful to Harriett to have previously denied any relationship with him. Consequently, as 1932 began, she reinvented herself as "Jean" Calloway. Her subterfuge is apparent only from the AFM transfer deposits of her accompanying musicians, because everywhere she toured in the country she registered herself as Jean, except in her home state of Ohio, where—trading on her local reputation—she once again became Harriett, although her accompanying musicians remained exactly the same.[34] Her touring career lasted until 1933, during which time she once again reverted to her original name, and produced some very memorable press notices:

The music of low sounding trumpets, softly calling saxophones, the melody of violins and the beat of drums, will raise the curtain . . . for the feature presentation of the season, Harriett Calloway. Known to the East as the star of Lew Leslie's *Blackbirds*, that famous show that ran for two years on Broadway, Harriett Calloway represents the sweetest ace of modern music to be featured in the middle west this season.

And what a record! Harriett Calloway was the hit of an eight week run at the Riviera Theatre in New York. Her success in Chicago grew into a 3-month holdover at the Adelphi Theatre. She conquered sedate old Boston for a 14-week run at the famous Fremont Theatre. Laurels, honors, hits and plenty of them—that's the record. Harriett Calloway and her Brunswick Recording orchestra, of 12 men artists.[35]

Not long after this, however, she gradually faded from the scene. Blanche meanwhile kept a band going for almost the entire decade. She recorded again for the Perfect label in 1934, but after her first flush of success with Victor, failed to keep up the creative stream of recordings that Cab continued to produce. In 1938 her band went bankrupt, although she re-formed and toured again in the 1939–40 season.

Despite his gripes to the press and Blanche's surprise appearance in the *Pittsburgh Courier's* 1931 popularity poll, Cab ultimately had little to fear from his namesake competitors. Their efforts were in effect a form of flattery to his own success. Indeed, as well as honing his own singing and dancing, he continued to work on strengthening his band to make it capable of competing with every one of the other ensembles to feature in the polls. By the end of 1931 Reuben Reeves had left, to be replaced by Doc Cheatham. He had been the lead trumpeter of Sam Wooding's vastly experienced band for the *Chocolate Kiddies* revue, which took African American vaudeville of the type purveyed at the Cotton Club to every corner of Europe in the late 1920s. He had recently been playing for McKinney's Cotton Pickers out of Detroit when Cab hired him. As well as offering a rock-steady lead to the section, which was not Reeves's strongest suit, Doc was capable of sensitive and lyrical solo playing. It is his trumpet that caresses the melody through a long solo on Cab's 1932 recording of "I've Got the World on a String," prefiguring the playing of other trumpeters such as Bill Coleman and Buck Clayton. Doc was to be a mainstay of the band until 1939.

Equally, Cab recognized that Jimmy Smith had not made an entirely effective transition from tuba to double bass, so he, too, had to go, to be replaced by Al Morgan, a scion of a leading New Orleans jazz dynasty, and one of the most propulsive bassists of the era. If Cab could not hire Wellman Braud, whom he so admired, away from Ellington, then Morgan was the next best thing. As noted earlier, big band double bass playing was just beginning in the early 1930s, and the use of the instrument to underpin large ensembles had its roots in New Orleans, where Braud had grown up. Many of the most successful players, such as Pops Foster (with Luis Russell) or John Lindsay (with Louis Armstrong), not to mention Paul Whiteman's star bassist Steve Brown, all hailed from the city. It was a member of another of New Orleans's jazz families, noted for producing string players, Simon Marrero, who taught Morgan. By the time he joined Cab, Morgan's forceful swing was to be heard on some celebrated records by the trumpeter Lee Collins, and his strong arpeggios and percussive slap technique were to fit perfectly in Cab's band with Payne's subtle piano and Maxey's drumming. Morgan's dexterity and prowess as a bassist can be seen in the number "Reefer Man," which the Calloway Orchestra filmed in 1933 as an insert for the W. C. Fields movie *International House*.

The final arrival in what was then to become quite a stable personnel from 1932 to 1934 was not a replacement but an additional musician, saxophonist and arranger Eddie Barefield, who would still be working with Cab on and off from the 1950s to the 1990s. He recalled:

> Cab Calloway came to the Hippodrome Theatre in Baltimore. He heard Roy [Eldridge] and I jamming one night, and asked me to join the band. When I joined Cab Calloway, it increased his saxes from three to four, and I had to write my own parts as there were no fourth parts in the arrangements. From Baltimore we went to the Cotton Club in New York and the personnel at that time was: Ed Swayze, Doc Cheatham, Lammar Wright, trumpets; Harry White, DePriest Wheeler, trombones, Arville Harris, myself, Andy Brown, Walter "Foots" Thomas, saxes, Bennie Payne, piano, Morris White, guitar, Al Morgan bass, Leroy Maxey, drums. While we were at the Cotton Club . . . we also played various theatres around New York.[36]

In 1932, the band's work settled into a stable pattern. It would work at the Cotton Club for several months on end, and then take off for one or two ten-week tours during the course of the year.

During its resident periods at the Cotton Club, the routine was tough. Cheatham recalled arriving at the club around 7:30 p.m., playing for dancing for an hour or so, and then performing anything up to four complete versions of the floor show, depending on the number of patrons, and how much they were spending. It was quite usual for the band to finish at 4 a.m. If there was also a booking in a theater in Manhattan, Brooklyn, or Long Island, this was simply added into the schedule. Cheatham said:

Cab was so famous that he was booked to play most of the large theaters in New York at one time or another. A theater show would start at about 8 am. In some there was no time to sleep, and we'd be playing five or six shows a day. We used to set up army cots down in the basement, rush down there to grab 15 minutes of sleep, then go right back on stage again.[37]

When the band worked a theater and the Cotton Club in the same week, Cheatham found himself playing for an average of ten hours a day. Yet while Blanche's musicians resented how hard they were worked, Cab's band did not. The material rewards were considerable. "The band looked really sharp," recalled Cheatham. "We had beautiful uniforms and we could change uniforms twice a day."[38] The band valets Harold and Rudolph, both of whom went on to work for Cab for years, kept everything freshly laundered, set up the stage, and transported bulky items like drums and basses. Instrument manufacturers gave their finest products to the band in return for advertisements that proclaimed "as used by Cab Calloway." At one point, to outdo the rival Beuscher company, Vincent Bach gave new horns to the entire brass section. Equally, Selmer ensured the reed players sported the latest saxophones and clarinets. There was plenty of money, fast cars, female fans, and good living, and also—when the musicians went on the road—far more bearable conditions than those that most bands of the time experienced.

In late 1931 Cab's band toured to Pittsburgh and Washington, D.C. Its early 1932 tour took it to Boston, Buffalo, and then on into the Midwest with an extended stay in Chicago. For these first road trips, the band traveled by bus, and played very few one-nighters. Instead, it was booked into theaters for entire weeks. Prior to Cab's visit in the spring of 1932, the Indiana papers ran several stories to whet the public appetite:

No one knows just where the Negroid yodels "Tey-de-Hey" and "Ho-de-ho" started, but they have caught Manhattan. Oh-h say can you scat? I mean can you do the new Negroid yodels such as 'hey-de-hey" and "ho de ho," and "hey-de-ho-ho?" That messieurs and madames, is "the scat." To scat as Webster defines the word, is no longer to "be gone"! However it might be interpreted as a "sound to frighten away small animals"— such for instance as radio listeners.

At any rate, Manhattan is in the throes of a "scat" craze. It's trickled down from Harlem. Every jazz band goes for it. Crooners shiver, wondering fearfully if they will ever be able to put the scat songs over.

Historians of such episodic epidemics are scurrying around trying to trace the sources. Others wrangle over just how the "scat" got started and who was first to "scat." At the moment, the chief contenders for such honors are Cab Calloway, band maestro of the Cotton Club, and Louis Armstrong.

Calloway appears to be most closely identified with its spread, whether or not he was the originator. "Minnie the Mooch" [*sic*] was the first of the "scat songs" to gain general notice.[39]

Soon after appearing in Indiana, the band was at the Oriental Theater in Chicago, and such was its success that it was held over for a second week, causing a widely advertised dance in Albany, New York, to be cancelled. "Chicago just can't seem to get enough of his red hot syncopations, his ho-de-ho-de-ho songs and his original dances," ran one report of the Oriental engagement, continuing, "Cab Calloway will present an entirely new program, new songs, new sizzling rhythms, newer and crazier dances and a new cast of Harlem entertainers."[40] When it finally left Chicago, the band wound its way into Minnesota, finishing up by breaking the house record in Minneapolis with takings of twenty thousand dollars. As April began, Cab returned to Harlem to star in Dan Healy's new revue, *Cotton Club Parade*.[41]

The early fall tour in 1933 started close to home in Newark, New Jersey, and then struck south, via Baltimore and Washington, D.C. The trip was organized by a Mrs. Knowles, from Raleigh, North Carolina, who owned a couple of buses, and booked the band to travel in them to play at a few resorts on the Maryland coast, then through Virginia and on into North Carolina, Georgia, and Florida. Although Cab and most of his men had previously toured in the South and Southwest in some combination or another, it was a considerable shock to return there after the high life they had enjoyed in Manhattan. Recalled Cab:

> In the Cotton Club, we were the cream of the crop and we were used to being celebrities. In New York we were the toast of the town with big cars and sharp clothes and broads all over the place. Now, all of a sudden, we were forced into small broken down buses, and kept out of restrooms and restaurants.[42]

Most of the musicians who made that tour had stories of the privations the band endured. Doc Cheatham remembered it as far less punitive than a tour he had made with Marion Hardy and the Alabamians, not long after Cab had left that group. Nevertheless, they lived and slept on the buses, changing their clothes at their seats, eating on the move, and entering and leaving theaters and dance halls by the rear entrances. Oftentimes the audiences—mainly consisting of white clientele—were hostile toward an African American band. One night a flying Coca-Cola bottle cut Leroy Maxey's head open, but, bandaged up, he finished the gig rather than incur the wrath of a paying public who would feel short-changed if the band stopped early.

In these adverse conditions, Cab came into his own as a leader. He coaxed and cajoled his men into playing at their best, even when they did not want to or in what they felt to be threatening circumstances. Moreover, he used his personal charm to persuade unwilling stage hands to set up for the band, or to placate crowds when the buses were late or broke down. When, toward the end of the tour, Mrs. Knowles appeared likely to renege on her contract, he insisted on being paid in cash—mainly small coins—from the box office before the band went on, setting a guard over it during their set. "We had to wrap it all in bed sheets and stuff it into our instrument cases," recalled Cheatham. "We helped Cab by opening all our cases and taking the heads off the drums, just to hide the money in something."[43]

The result was that Cab forged a bond between himself and his men. Whereas some of the old Missourians whom he had fired might have resented him, he now led a band who knew that he would stick up for them, and lead them through thick and thin. They admired his craft, his skills as a performer, and his charisma. And in return, they would do anything for him. In future, when the band traveled far afield anywhere in the United States, Cab ensured that whenever possible Irving Mills booked them onto a private Pullman train.

They could live in some comfort in a dormitory carriage, with plenty of space for bags and clothes; on the move they could read and play cards in their own saloon, alongside which there were private quarters for Cab. The cars were shunted into a siding at each town where they played. After the gig, the band returned to the railroad station, climbed aboard its Pullman, and as the musicians slept, the cars were hitched up to a train and transported to the site of the next gig.

Irving Mills, forced by the southern experience to take a more direct hand in the business of touring, used the additional travel facilities offered by the train to add a few variety turns to the program, so that Cab was not touring with his band alone, but a scaled-down version of the Cotton Club revue. In its press releases, Mills's office explained it thus:

> The ever present rumor mongers began chanting that Calloway was just a "freak" attraction, and would be forgotten before six months had elapsed. Irving Mills' answer to these comments was to book Calloway for a series of personal appearances, one-night stands, and motion picture shorts, after he had added various novelties to the orchestra act to catch the public's fancy. Cab's star was in the ascendancy and Mills was ever-present to give him the added impetus to carry him higher and higher.[44]

The physical difficulties of touring were greatly reduced as a result of that first southern experience, and by the end of 1933 Cab was able to claim that since he started at the Cotton Club, he had appeared in "sixty-one theaters in sixteen states, and covered every section of the country except the Pacific Coast."[45] But the year ahead held an even bigger challenge in Mills's scheme of things: to follow in Duke Ellington's footsteps and find a new audience in Europe.

Chapter 5

Zaz Zuh Zaz
1933–1934

....

U ntil the end of 1932, all of Cab's records had been made for Brunswick, which in 1930–32 was a subsidiary of Consolidated Film Industries, and whose products were sold to the general market. The discs also came out at the time on several dime-store imprints of Irving Mills's American Record Company, such as Banner, Melotone, Oriole, Perfect, and Romeo, although Mills had actually sold the company some years before this to the same CFI conglomerate. Brunswick and ARC were technically separate financial entities, but they were managed as if they were a single record firm, and although Irving Mills no longer had the status of being ARC's owner, he was still extremely influential in their joint policy.

However, in September 1933, between the band's two extended tours away from the Cotton Club, Cab moved to a new record company, Victor. This was the firm for whom the Missourians had recorded, immediately prior to their association with Cab, and it had also been one of Duke Ellington's principal labels during his early years under Mills's management. It had a distinguished jazz history, having been the home for such luminaries as Jelly Roll Morton, King Oliver, and McKinney's Cotton Pickers. In 1933 Victor was unquestionably the leading jazz record company of the day. Cab's arrival on the label was a significant piece of product positioning by Irving Mills, intended to consolidate his credentials as a bona fide jazz musician, and not merely a novelty singer.

Technically, Victor's engineers produced a fuller sound from Cab's orchestra, and every nuance of his vocal delivery was perfectly caught, even when his dramatic increases in volume caused him to move back from the microphone to avoid distortion. This created a slightly anomalous result on record, in which what ought to have been his vocal climaxes were oddly subdued, but it did prevent the cutting stylus from jumping out of its groove!

In terms of repertoire, Cab and the band continued to develop successful songs along related themes (another shrewd marketing ploy encouraged by Mills), so that Brunswick's releases of "Trickeration" and "The Man from Harlem" were followed up by Victor's "Harlem Hospitality" and "Harlem Camp Meeting"; Brunswick's "My Sunday Gal" had a Victor sequel with "Little Town Gal," and generic Calloway material such as songs featuring Minnie the Moocher and lyrics packed with hi-de-ho responses made an early appearance as well.

One by-product of the new record deal was that Cab had the opportunity to rerecord some of his earlier hits. He had, after all, reprised several of them in the Betty Boop movies, thereby reminding listeners of his most famous songs. Ironically, the only one of these remakes to be released by Victor at the time was the least well known, namely "The Scat Song" in a vastly improved version from the Brunswick original. Both "Minnie the Moocher" and "Kicking the Gong Around" received equally effective makeovers, but for reasons that are now obscure, these remained unissued until the LP era. Nevertheless, the Victor contract brought most of Cab's new recorded work to an even greater listening public than before.

Before the new arrangement began, the band was occupied with film sound track recordings for the final Betty Boop picture at Fleischer Studios, and also for Paramount's *International House*. It then had substantial commitments to touring, so nine months elapsed between its final Brunswick recording session in December 1932 and its first work for Victor the following September. Nobody would describe the corpus of 1932 recordings as lacking in confidence, but the Victor discs exude a greater sense of effortless authority on the part of the band, and a gradual move from the earthy Kansas City bounce of the Missourians to a more generic swing style anchored by the double bass. "Harlem Hospitality," from the second session, on September 21, shows Al Morgan asserting a relaxed New Orleans two-beat over the opening ensemble chorus. With subtle supporting drumming from Maxey and spare comping from Payne and White, it seems that in its nine months away from the studios the entire band had taken a stylistic leap forward. This was principally due to the rhythm section abandoning the 1920s ragtime influence, and adopting the more even swing of mid-1930s jazz. "Harlem Hospitality" slips into a clear 4/4 swing behind Cab's vocal, save for breaks for hand claps and a shout-back in the middle eight measures. The following chorus deftly shifts key before ushering in a duet between Eddie Barefield's alto and DePriest Wheeler's trombone.

For the subsequent session, Eddie Barefield arranged "The Lady with the Fan," based on a lyric by Cab dedicated to a Cotton Club fan dancer named Amy Spencer. This chart is even more swing oriented than "Harlem Hospitality," notably in Cab's first vocal chorus. Here the main function of keeping the beat is shared by White's guitar and Morgan's walking bass, with Payne improvising delightful piano arabesques behind Cab. A long sinuous saxophone section melody follows, a technique borrowed by Barefield from the best contemporary arrangers, Don Redman and Benny Carter, and to accompany it, White plays acoustic guitar arpeggios close to the microphone. The track has incisive solos from Ed Swayze's trumpet and Barefield's alto sax alongside plenty of vocal interchange between Cab and his sidemen.

By far the most influential recording Cab made in his first group of pieces for Victor was "Zaz Zuh Zaz," which was cut on November 2, 1933, the same day as "The Lady with the Fan." Cab writes in his autobiography that "Zaz Zuh Zaz" was nothing more than a few scat syllables corralled together into a tune. It seemed at the time that the piece was just another "minor moaner" in the vein of "Minnie the Moocher," written and arranged by the band's second trombonist, Harry White. Given Cab's talent for storytelling in song, the familiar characters Smoky Joe and Minnie both make appearances in the lyric. However, the track is memorable because of the consistent invention with which Cab sings variations on the "zaz zuh zaz" theme, and the way these are repeated and sung back to him by his band. The most complex call and response in the Calloway canon to date, this song includes effects ranging from falsetto phrasing to some inspired high-speed gabbling of nonsense syllables at the end.

Only a few weeks after "Zaz Zuh Zaz" and "The Lady with the Fan" were recorded, both songs were used in the short 1934 movie *Cab Calloway's Hi De Ho*. Within less than a decade, the movie, the record, and—as will be discussed shortly—Cab's featuring of "Zaz Zuh Zaz" on tour in Europe led to the creation of a youth counterculture in France. The trigger for this was Irving

Mills's decision to follow Duke Ellington's 1933 European tour with a similar arrangement for Cab, bringing him into contact with British, Dutch, and— most significantly—French audiences at first hand.

In addition to the national touring mentioned previously, Mills applied to Cab other ideas that had worked for Ellington, including regular network broadcasts four times a week on NBC, nightly broadcasts on the New York station WMCA, and carefully timed guest appearances on radio shows with Walter Winchell and Rudy Vallée. These activities were supported by a torrent of press releases for the African American papers such as the *Baltimore Afro American*, the *Chicago Defender*, and the *Pittsburgh Courier*, and further film appearances to build on the success of the Betty Boop pictures.

The nature of Irving Mills's management of Cab's career up to this point shows why cultural commentators such as Thomas J. Hennessey have argued that Mills was the first person to introduce standardized management practices to jazz, through his stable of African American entertainers. Indeed Hennessey, and Jeffrey Magee in his biography of Fletcher Henderson, both perceive Mills as creating a "model of success" in his treatment of Ellington that was then turned into a "structured career pattern" for Cab Calloway, and later for other leaders such as Lucky Millinder.[1] The loser in all this was Henderson, who had originally been penciled in to be the first to follow Ellington to Europe, but whose increasing personal unreliability encouraged Mills to focus his attention on his young Cotton Club protégé, Cab Calloway, instead.[2]

At the start of 1934, Mills produced a sizable publicity pack for Cab to warm up promoters prior to his European visit. But the seeds had been sown among the press well before that, starting within days of the conclusion of Ellington's visit the previous year. *Melody Maker*, Britain's principal magazine for jazz and hot dance music, put out the following editorial while Ellington's band was still on the Transatlantic liner on its way home:

Ellington has been here and thrilled thousands of us. So has Louis Armstrong. We are told that Cab Calloway and the Mills Blue Rhythm Band are on their way. Our education, woefully neglected, is being attended to. We now have everything to learn. Let us, therefore, seize all the opportunities to hear these visiting artistes and learn what we can. It is madness and musical suicide not to do so.[3]

From this it is clear that some British journalists, at least, recognized that complete American jazz orchestras offered a valuable experience to European listeners, who had hitherto heard jazz mainly secondhand, through recordings or local musicians. But in contrast to such perceptive writers, there had also been some danger signs during Ellington's visit. Spike Hughes, a talented bandleader and arranger himself, who had absorbed many lessons about orchestral color and timbre from Ellington, also reviewed for *Melody Maker* under the pseudonym "Mike."

Prior to the Ducal visit, "Mike" had been hugely enthusiastic, particularly on the subject of Ellington's original compositions, but when he heard the band in London playing little or none of that repertoire, and presenting (as it might have done on an American variety show) routine features for its members on such standards as "Some of These Days" or "In the Shade of the Old Apple Tree," he was mortified.

"Is Duke Ellington losing faith in his own music and turning commercial through lack of appreciation," he asked in his review, "or does he honestly underestimate the English musical public?"[4]

Hughes went on to lament the lack of such Ellingtonian classics as "The Mooche," "Mood Indigo," and "Creole Love Call." It is highly probable that the audiences who gave Ellington a warm and enthusiastic reception throughout his tour were blissfully ignorant of these particular highlights of his recorded work, and thoroughly enjoyed his band's highly individual treatment of well-known songs. Yet the main reason for the hostile critical reaction from Hughes and those other British writers who shared his views was a direct and unintended consequence of Mills's copious publicity. He had put considerable energy into promoting Ellington as an artist as well as a bandleader and pianist. The critics who had been assiduously primed by this material were naturally disappointed when they got a stage show that mostly bypassed the artistic end of Ellington's repertoire. Hughes's description of Ellington's performance as "turning commercial" was an ominous sign of how Calloway's determinedly more entertainment-orientated band would be received by the haughty British press.

Not that their American counterparts had let the distinction between the two Cotton Club bands go unnoticed. In 1933, *Fortune Magazine*'s Wilder Hobson published a profile of Duke Ellington that clearly pointed out the similarities and differences between his and Cab's band immediately after Duke's return from his first European tour:

Subsequently only one other Negro bandmaster has had a comparable success. This is Cab Calloway, also managed by Irving Mills. In many places including New York, Calloway's gate exceeds Ellington's. Draped in such fascinating haberdashery as a snow-white dress suit with extra long tails, Calloway weaves gracefully before his orchestra and in a high spasmodic voice emits hot arias like "Minnie the Moocher" and "Kicking the Gong Around." He usually plays no instrument, and as a composer has boasted only of the lyrics to the chorus of "Minnie." They begin as follows: "Hi-de-hi-de-hi—ho-de-ho-de-ho." Calloway's vocalizing is sensational, his band is not to be compared with Ellington's.[5]

Such observations concerning Cab's work have persisted from that day to this. Because Cab's band was constructed around him and his persona as a singer, dancer, and entertainer, rather than a set of highly individual soloists for whom compositions were specially tailored, it has suffered in critical comparison. It was not until Gunther Schuller's masterly reappraisal of the band in 1989 in his book *The Swing Era* that any critical weight was put behind what Calloway actually achieved, rather than what a succession of influential critics thought he ought to have been aiming at. Schuller traces the music of Cab's accompanying band from the "exciting elemental jazz" of the Missourians to the "clean, balanced and disciplined" sound of the 1933 orchestra and beyond. He also proposes that Cab was "the most unusually and broadly gifted male singer of the 1930s."[6]

More significantly, Schuller points out that from the earliest Brunswick recordings onward, Cab made a point of featuring his soloists and ensemble alongside his own singing. This was in marked contrast to the critics' favorite, Louis Armstrong, who tended to hog the limelight as singer and soloist through almost all his 1930s large band recordings, with only the very occasional nod toward the gifted soloists who packed the ranks of his orchestra. Attention has already been drawn to the contributions of Cheatham, Dickerson, Reeves, and Swayze among the trumpets, Wheeler on trombone, and Barefield, Blue, Brown, and Thomas in the reeds. But it was during this period when Cab moved to Victor that—along with his band's stylistic shift further into swing territory—he started consistently to strike the ideal balance between his own vocals and genuinely creative, if brief, contributions from his sidemen.

A case in point is "Harlem Camp Meeting," from November 22, 1933. It is a clever and unusually well-balanced composition by Harry White that, as Schuller points out, uses bell-like broken chords to unify an arrangement in which music alone recreates a black church revival meeting. This revivalist genre is one that the band had explored earlier to support Cab's storytelling in "Is That Religion?" Yet here, apart from a few spoken comments, Cab's contribution is what he calls a "scat sermon"—an entirely wordless vocal functioning as an instrumental solo between choruses from Arville Harris on clarinet, Ed Swayze on growling muted trumpet, and Bennie Payne on piano. The solo space for his instrumentalists is generous, and there's also a well-crafted ensemble opening chorus for the reeds accompanied by stabbing brass, and later for a Henderson-style clarinet trio. The rhythm section pushes everything along with verve and élan, with Morgan's bass easily outswinging the work of his hometown counterparts Pops Foster with Armstrong and Braud with Ellington. This recording totally refutes what Schuller characterizes as "the prevailing view that Calloway was merely a novelty singer, given to 'hollering' and 'braying' [whose] orchestra is no more than a functional band relegated to second-rank accompanimental status."[7]

At the next session, in January 1934, "Jitterbug" makes an even stronger case for the total integration of band and singer as a completely interdependent musical unit. On a song jointly written by Cab and Ed Swayze, with some additional lyrics from Irving Mills, Cab touts the recipe for "jitterbug sauce," a fiercely alcoholic mixture, before singing with each section in turn, commenting on the musicians (or "bugs") as he sings. Individuals like "Fat Boy" Swayze, "Father" White, and "Foots" Thomas are introduced by name (or nickname) but there's also a vocal exchange with the full reed section—"these four boys playing saxophone." Even more impressive is the rhythm playing where Maxey's unfussy, swinging drumming propels the band forward with a relentless energy achieved by very few drummers of the time, except possibly the greatly underrated Alvin Burroughs with Earl Hines.

It was thanks to this record that the term "jitterbug" entered the English language to describe dancers with no knowledge of formal dance, who improvised their steps. Over the decade that followed, the word came to be associated with swing dancers of any style. Also, Irving Mills, who had conceived the "Hotsy Totsy Club" a decade before as a means of promoting both a jointly written song and his 1920s radio double-act with Jimmy McHugh, now set up a similar marketing ploy, the "Jitter Bug Society." Members received a card signed by Cab Calloway (President) and the password: "Palsaddictinsomnidipsomaniac." This—the sign-off tag from Cab's record of "Jitterbug"—had to be successfully pronounced and defined for a member to be admitted to the society.[8]

The musical masterpiece achieved by the band from the months preceding its European tour was Will Hudson's "Moon Glow." It featured the band alone without Cab, as had been the case on record only twice before, in the early arrangement of Ellington's "Mood Indigo" and Benny Carter's "Hot Toddy" recorded in September 1932. In this respect Calloway was unlike other leaders. One cannot imagine a recording by Louis Armstrong and His Orchestra from 1934 in which neither his voice nor trumpet was heard, in order to feature only his sidemen, with some extravagantly generous solos. Yet this is precisely what Calloway did on "Moon Glow," turning over the final title of the session that produced "Jitterbug" and "Long about Midnight" to his men.

Hudson himself supplied the chart that gives the opening melody to muted trumpets above long-held trombone pedal notes, and he no doubt crafted the reed harmonies that sat behind the solos from Arville Harris (clarinet), Andrew Brown (bass clarinet), and—for it is his inspired playing that makes the record what it is—Eddie Barefield (alto saxophone). Recomposing the melody, inserting dazzling passages of double (or quadruple) time, and masterfully occupying a series of solo breaks, Barefield transforms the piece into one of the most memorable jazz records of the mid-1930s. Yet as Barefield himself recalled, it happened almost accidentally, and it took the band some effort to reincorporate this version of the piece into its repertoire after the recording session:

> Just before we went on a trip to Europe, we had a recording date for Victor, when we recorded "Moon Glow," the first [*sic*] instrumental Cab recorded. When we went into the studio we did three titles and they wanted a fourth. "Moon Glow" hadn't been copyrighted then, and we had been using it as a play-off. One chorus at the end of a set. So Cab decided we would do "Moon Glow" in three choruses, one ensemble, one alto solo by me, and spots for Andy Brown on bass clarinet and Arville Harris on clarinet. We did one take and that was it. Then we went on our European tour to England, France, Belgium and Holland, and soon after our return we were in Texas, playing a dance. Before they opened up, they played some records, including one of "Moon Glow"

and we all wondered who it was. We went over to the guy who was playing the records and asked. He said "Don't you know your own record?"
So we had to listen to our record of "Moon Glow" to learn how to play
it on stage.[9]

Despite the casual nature of the recording of "Moon Glow," the piece came at
a time when on record date after record date Calloway's band was demonstrating that it was in the first rank of swing orchestras. It could match Ellington for
orchestral color (and used a very wide range of writers and arrangers to achieve
its effects), and it consistently offered solo space to a collection of players who
were able to make really effective use of their half chorus or eight measures
whenever the chance came along. Yet the first critical reaction to be published
as soon as the band arrived in Europe took only passing note of the consummate musicianship of the band members, but dwelled instead on their clothes
and on Cab's singing.

The Calloway band that sailed from New York on February 23, 1934, aboard
the S.S. *Majestic* for Southampton consisted of Doc Cheatham, Lammar
Wright, and Edwin Swayze, trumpets; DePriest Wheeler, trombone; Andrew
Brown, Arville Harris, Eddie Barefield, and Foots Thomas, reeds; Bennie
Payne, piano; Morris White, guitar; Al Morgan, bass and Leroy Maxey, drums.
Harry White was forced to take a later boat, through what was reported at the
time as "sickness," but which may actually have been a passport irregularity. He
arrived four days after his fellow musicians, and missed the opening night.[10]

The Calloway orchestra opened at the London Palladium on March 5 for a
three-week run. The public, it seems, adored Cab's extrovert singing and dancing, and the band's slick appearance and playing. Not so the *Melody Maker*
critic:

> The show was much as we expected, and much as we feared it. The
> most impressive thing about this combination is its sartorial elegance,
> not only on the stage, but in everyday life, for this is a band of coloured
> Beau Brummells.
>
> The applause broke out in a frenzy as Cab strode out to the stage
> waving a large baton. We left it until the second show to review the
> performance seriously, but although a slicker show than in the first
> house it did not altogether remove the impression of dissatisfaction on
> the purely musical aspects.

The band of much talent is not allowed to show its paces; at least in the matter of orchestrations there was nothing worthwhile and Cab sings too much. Judged by what this phlegmatic critic heard there are British bands who play better stuff and are just as proficient musically. Comparison between Calloway and Ellington is impossible.[11]

Assuming that the band played its arrangements approximately the same way as it did on record, then this review seems harsh. Indeed, the opening night's program at the Palladium included several pieces that were deliberately intended to show off the talents of the band as well as those of Cab himself, namely "The Man from Harlem," "Minnie the Moocher's Wedding Day," "Moon Glow," "Rhapsody of Taps" (a dance by Alma Turner), "The Scat Song," "St. James Infirmary," "Reefer Man" (including a tap dance by the Three Dukes), "Minnie the Moocher," "Father's Got His Glasses On," and "The Last Round Up." As an encore the band played its first hit, "St. Louis Blues."[12] Although "Moon Glow" was included in the program, on this section of the tour Will Hudson's arrangement featured Foots Thomas as the main saxophonist, because the record with Eddie Barefield's famous solo had yet to appear.[13]

Cab's own recollection of his experience in London and later in Manchester was entirely positive. "You would have thought we were gifts from the gods," he wrote. "People climbed all over the stage and then tried to tear our clothes off as we left the theater every night."[14] And despite the sniffy attitude of the British musical press, we can get a sense of how Cab actually went over with the public from the French magazine *Jazz Tango Dancing*, which reported: "Despite what the *Melody Maker* thinks, the success of Cab Calloway in England was enormous, and even greater than it was for Duke Ellington."[15]

So why the poor reception in *Melody Maker*, and the impression from it and similar reviews that musicians, in contrast to the general public, were not enamored of Cab's band? Some of the reasons have nothing to do with the music itself. At the time there was a growing attitude of protectionism in Britain, that soon afterward led to the Musicians' Union, in collaboration with the Ministry of Labour, managing to impose a ban on visiting American orchestras. This was on the grounds that they were taking work away from British players. Indeed even when Cab came to England and Scotland in 1934, in order to obtain permission for him to play it was necessary to negotiate an exchange under which Bert Ambrose's orchestra was offered work in the United States.

This system of exchanges was to exert a stranglehold over who was able to perform in Britain for many decades to come, until it finally broke down in the 1980s. Not long after Cab's visit, full American orchestras were in effect banned from playing in Britain. Jimmie Lunceford's band passed through the country but was prevented from appearing, and Teddy Hill's group only managed to perform in 1937 because it was part of a theatrical revue. Artists such as Fats Waller, Coleman Hawkins, and Benny Carter appeared as solo performers with local accompanists, and even when Duke Ellington returned to Britain with Ray Nance and Kay Davis in 1948 he was forced to accept a local backing trio.

Given the British Musicians' Union's stance, there was considerable antipathy from local dance band musicians toward the visiting Americans (and the *Melody Maker* phrase "coloured Beau Brummels" suggests racial antagonism as well). Doc Cheatham recalled that after the excellent atmosphere of the transatlantic voyage, where the band had been "treated fantastically" and invited to play two highly successful onboard concerts for the other passengers, the opening at the Palladium was a distinct comedown. "The minute they announced Cab Calloway, all the musicians in the pit band blew loud discords and started making funny sounds on their horns. A welcome like that was embarrassing for Cab and for us. But we did our act." Doc suggested that sedate English audiences did not like Cab, because they believed he was "a screamer and a yeller," and he reported that the pit band in Manchester, where the band played from April 2 for a week, behaved exactly as their London counterparts had done. It was only during the intervening week in Scotland at the Glasgow Empire that Doc felt the band had been "well received."[16]

As all this was going on, just across the English Channel in France *Jazz Tango Dancing* revealed to its readers that the unpleasant behavior of the pit bands was not simply a matter of racial prejudice or protectionist alarm. Rather it was because there was an ongoing spat between Irving Mills and Britain's most powerful popular bandleader and booking agent of the time, Jack Hylton.[17] Mills had tried to book Hylton's band in Europe on unfavorable terms, and Hylton was in the process of taking Mills to court over alleged breach of contract. Hylton—who had collaborated effectively with Mills on the Ellington band's visit in 1933—was not a man to be crossed, and he had considerable sway in the world of theatrical musicians and pit orchestras. According to the French magazine's reporter, Hylton was at the center of a "cabal" of British musicians who actively opposed Cab's visit.

However, as far as the general public and the uncritical journalists of the national morning newspapers were concerned, there was no problem with Cab or his act. The regular Fleet Street scribes had no axe to grind compared to *Melody Maker* or its associated music press and Cab went out of his way to praise those writers who "were highly interested in our music."[18] The band played to full houses, and between its engagements at the Palladium and on the theater circuit, it squeezed in several other events: a concert at the Trocadero Cinema at the Elephant and Castle in London, with Louis Armstrong among the enthusiastic audience, plus dances at Streatham Locarno, the Astoria in Charing Cross, Sherry's on England's South Coast in Brighton, as well as in North Country dance halls in Leeds and Manchester. Cab, accompanied by Betty, kept up a frantic social whirl. He hobnobbed with royalty, including Edward, the Prince of Wales, who attended the Palladium opening, and he did the rounds of London's late-night clubs, including the Monseigneur and the Kit Kat Club. At each of these latter venues, Cab sang a number or two, either with members of his own orchestra or with the resident bands. He was then filmed by Pathé News for a short newsreel showing "The Gathering of the Bands." In it, after a brief appearance by Mantovani, and before a featured performance by Roy Fox, Cab was called upon to present the prize to Stan Herbert and His Band, winners of the 1934 "All Rhythm Dance Band Contest" at Westminster's Horticultural Hall.

During his brief time off, Cab had a chance to connect with his old passion for sports. He was whisked away to watch Arsenal playing Aston Villa at Highbury soccer ground in North London. He found himself fascinated by soccer and the deft footwork of the players, who had none of the sartorial or regulatory restrictions of contemporaneous American football.

Meanwhile, members of his own band sat in with local jazz musicians at the Nest, in Kingly Street, Soho, which was to be the major haunt for all visiting American jazz players in the 1930s, including Benny Carter, Coleman Hawkins, and Fats Waller. As far as genuine British jazz enthusiasts were concerned, there was none of the protectionist attitude of the pit band players. This was a great opportunity for them to get together with some of the finest jazz instrumentalists in the United States, and the chance was not wasted. The West Indian trumpeter Leslie Thompson, who lived in London and got to know many of Cab's band, said:

There was a difference between American jazz and what was played over here. While our jazz had shades of urge about it, it erred more towards melody and counterpoint. But the American jazz had all that and something else that kept you tapping your foot whether you wanted to or not.[19]

This British visit was Cab's first experience of working anywhere other than the United States. He later said that the lack of overt racial prejudice in Britain, allowing him the opportunity to stay at the prestigious Dorchester Hotel, and which gave him and Betty the chance to eat in open view at the best tables in the finest restaurants, made him feel free. In England he felt he was living as a normal human being for the first time in his life. "In America," he wrote, "it was impossible for a Negro to feel like an ordinary person."[20]

There were other benefits as well. In an article penned at the time for a British magazine, Cab marveled at the knowledge of his audiences, who seemed to be well aware of the careers and recordings of many of his sidemen, as well as his own records. For the first time Cab was meeting fans of his music who actually listened closely, who analyzed and discussed his recorded output, and who had perceptive observations to make about his discs. At the Palladium he danced to the front of the stage and invited the audience to join in with his scat, shouting back the responses along with his band. "I had expected no such voluminous bellows from an English audience. When it came, I was like to die, as we say in Harlem."[21]

If Cab had one criticism of his public, it was that English dancers, although energetically hopping about from beginning to end at his appearances, had little or no skill.

In the States now, the dance rage is the Lindy Hop, which I modestly take credit for popularising at the Cotton Club in Harlem, and which is especially suited to the fast *tempos* of our orchestras. It is an intricate dance, with much foot and body weaving, and includes over two dozen different steps. There are variations of this dance. The novice Lindy Hoppers just do the Lindy Hop. Those who know a little more about it indulge in a double Lindy. And those who have mastered both of these and desire something still more intricate in this dance do the Triple Lindy. It really is the most interesting dance to observe and presents the appearance of a stage speciality. I noticed that a few couples on the floor were dancing in a manner that appeared to me like an elemental Lindy Hop. It had all the appearance of a beginners' class.[22]

On April 9, Cab and the band sailed from Harwich to Holland, before settling in at the Carlton Hotel in Amsterdam, where there was another round of press conferences and a concert on April 14. The band then appeared in Antwerp, Brussels, Utrecht, and Rotterdam before returning to Amsterdam. On April 22 there was a formal concert at the Gebouw voor Kunsten en Wetenschappen in The Hague. Afterward, Al Morgan, Bennie Payne, Harry White, Eddie Barefield, Foots Thomas, Doc Cheatham, and Ed Swayze sat in at the Tabaris Club, where the band led by the expatriate American pianist Freddy Johnson was resident.[23] This was a reunion for Doc Cheatham with Johnson because the two men had toured Europe together in the 1920s with Sam Wooding. By all accounts there was even more riotous jamming than there had been at the Nest in London.

For the final leg of the tour, Cab and his musicians set off for Paris, where they were to play two concerts on April 23 and 24. *Jazz Tango Dancing*, which was the forerunner of the leading French magazine *Jazz Hot*, reported:

> The critics are enraptured. And the public rush to watch and re-watch the man who is called the inventor of "scat-singing." It seems that in Holland, Belgium and now in France, the people show their good taste and take in their stride the antics of Cab, which are not exactly "hot jazz," despite his label the "King of Hot Jazz," as a really enjoyable pastime. I think the Parisian public will take great pleasure from hearing Cab. He is actually the biggest attraction on the American scene at the moment, and it is truly a pleasure to witness him sing "Hi-de-ho" of which he is indeed the king.
>
> His orchestra is of great value, and in my opinion, the band possesses a more solid rhythm than any other American orchestra. When they start to play with their irresistible swing, it is impossible to stay unmoved. Cab Calloway has a marvellous rhythm section.[24]

This was the beginning of France's love affair with Cab, and—almost certainly for linguistic reasons—his wordless scat became the most popular aspect of his work.

By 1934, Paris had a long-established tradition of African American entertainers working in its bars, theaters and music halls. The drummer Louis Mitchell, who moved there from London at the end of World War I, had led various bands, beginning an influx of individual instrumentalists. Following the appearance of Josephine Baker in 1926 with *La revue Nègre*, backed by Claude

Hopkins' Orchestra, with music by Spencer Williams and choreography by Louis Douglas, it was not just the public but Parisian intellectuals who had taken jazz—and particularly a brand of jazz that involved singing and dancing—to their hearts. That same year, the ethnomusicologist André Schaeffner and the critic André Coeuroy had published *Le jazz*, which was the first attempt in any language to analyze jazz musicologically, and to discern its musical lineage. Their book coined the phrase "Afro-American music," and although Schaeffner's personal preferred sounds were Paul Whiteman's symphonic jazz, he made a strong and knowledgeable case for paying serious attention to such artists as Bessie Smith and Louis Armstrong.

Parisian bands such as Grégor and His Gregorians purveyed a style that had plenty in common with Cab's, not least in the way that the extrovert leader Grégor Kelekian danced, dressed, and conducted his band. He was also a somewhat eccentric singer, his high Armenian-accented voice scatting through such popular records as "Doin' the Raccoon." His band members were expert at the same kind of hot breaks and short solos as Cab's musicians, notably on Grégor's version of "Tiger Rag," known as "Le rugissement du tigre" and featuring a young Stéphane Grappelli on piano.

Around the time Cab appeared, there was a considerable amount of live jazz going on in Paris played by black Americans. Just a month before his shows at the Salle Pleyel, the newly formed Hot Club of France presented an evening in which the "Symphonic Jazz" of André Ekyan with "Junjo" [*sic*] Reinhardt competed with the "Jazz Noir" (black jazz) of Frank "Big Boy" Goudie, featuring the pianist Garland Wilson.[25] Small groups like Goudie's were one thing, but full-scale American orchestras were more of a rarity. Cab's band, with its strong rhythm section, its sartorial elegance, and his own dazzling stage presence, fitted the image of how Parisians thought a hot jazz orchestra should appear, even more than Ellington's band.

Even the hard-to-please French critic Hugues Panassié (a contributor to *Jazz Tango Dancing*, but probably not the reviewer cited earlier) was impressed by some aspects of Cab's band, in a summary of its achievements published a short while after its visit in his monumental survey *Le Jazz Hot*. Dismissing Cab himself on account of his "curious sort of voice, whose endless yelling is quickly tiring," Panassié continued:

> In 1932 Cab picked up some rather interesting recruits; the trumpeters, Adolphus Cheatham and Edwin Swayzee [*sic*]; the trombone, Harry

White; and the contrabass, Al Morgan. The swing rhythm of Morgan stimulated the orchestra considerably; thanks to him and to Leroy Maxie [*sic*], Cab Calloway has a rhythmic section of exceptional power. At times the brasses play satisfactorily. Adolphus Cheatham is orchestrally probably the best first trumpet in the world; there is no one like him at leading a trumpet section.[26]

Fortunately the French public were more impressed than Panassié by Cab's "endless yelling." Indeed "Zaz Zuh Zaz" was to become an integral part of French counterculture in the years that followed. The lyrics were picked up by the Swiss-French songwriter and *chansonnier* Johnny Hess, who worked with Charles Trenet in the duo Charles and Johnny. Trenet's subsequent career was to remain true to the *chanson* tradition, and he created memorable musical images of the France of his childhood in songs such as "Douce France" and "La mer." In contrast Hess was fascinated by scat singing, and wanted to encapsulate into his own writing the new sounds of jazz and swing that were making their way across the Atlantic. So in 1938 Hess wrote "Je suis swing," which was to become the anthem for bohemian middle-class French youth, notably—by the early 1940s—those young liberals opposed to the wartime Vichy regime. His light, frothy recording of the song, despite its contrast between the minor key of the verse and the major key of the chorus, lacks the vibrant energy of Cab Calloway. It is more in tune with Hess's background as a *chansonnier*, and subsequently other singers such as Georges Brassens were to incorporate the song into their *chanson* repertoires. Nevertheless, in 1938 Hess saw jazz as a music of rebellion, born of an oppressed people, and a means to turn accepted social mores upside down.

Hess's lyrics included the phrase "Je suis swing, je suis swing, za-zou, za-zou, za-zou, za-zouzé," the latter part of which was lifted directly from the Calloway song. He reprised the idea in his subsequent piece "Ils sont zazous." The importance of this phrase was principally sociological rather than musical. The French social historian Corinne Grenouillet points out that people's musical taste often reflects their political sensibility, and Hess's songs not only codified the rebellious otherness of Cab's sound into French popular culture but created an excuse for his visual appearance to be adopted by disaffected youth as well.[27]

The Paris-based American journalist and jazz trombonist Mike Zwerin aptly described the sartorial style adopted by male "zazous" as they called themselves:

Zazou boys wore pegged pants with baggy knees, high rolled English collars covered by their hair, which was carefully combed into a two-wave Pompadour over their foreheads. Long checked jackets several sizes too large, dangling key chains, gloves, stick pins in wide neckties with tiny knots, dark glasses and Django Reinhardt mustaches were the rage.[28]

Substitute the name Cab Calloway for Django Reinhardt in that description (because Cab was indeed sporting a neatly trimmed pencil mustache in 1934) and the entire inspiration for the Zazou movement—aural, visual, behavioral—can be traced directly to Calloway. As the 1930s went on his clothing became more and more extrovert. The white tails gave way to the prototype "zoot suit," consisting of baggy pants and oversized jackets much as described by Zwerin. Cab often also sported a sizable watch chain and often a large floppy hat into the bargain. Six or seven years after "Zaz Zuh Zaz" was recorded, teenagers in war-torn France were looking for a role model to epitomize everything they hated about the collaborative Vichy regime and its restrictions. "Cab Calloway and the Cotton Club Orchestra . . . provided a sense of collective identity and a designation," suggests the social historian Sarah Fishman:

> The *zazous*, young men and women of seventeen or eighteen, engaged in behavior that rejected Vichy's moral order. Their appearance and clothing symbolized their animosity to Vichy. Contrary to the clean cut look favored in Vichy propaganda, the young men grew thin mustaches and wore long jackets and pants with big baggy knees and legs that tapered to white socks, an outfit that flaunted the textile industry stipulation that clothing should use the least fabric possible.[29]

The Zazous were publicly denounced as degenerate by Jacques Doriot, the ultra-right-wing leader of the Legion du Volontaires Français, the French division of the Wehrmacht. Hess, by contrast, produced further songs of celebration, and gently praised the Zazous' "cheveux frisottés," and their pointing fingers "comme ça" in the air.

His position as a revolutionary role model still some years in the future, Cab's own time in Paris was not quite the easy social whirl he had enjoyed in London. There Betty had joined him in swanky night clubs among clientele where they could witness at first hand the Prince of Wales and his circle doing "the contemporary dances we were doing in Harlem just as well as the hot set at the Cotton Club."[30] Ever since Cab had moved to New York there had been tension between him and Betty. Their high-flying Chicago relationship, in which she was an equal contributing financial partner, and where they enjoyed the same things, had taken a knock with Cab's dip in earnings in 1929–30. His arrival at the Cotton Club with all its financial advantages had restored matters to some extent, but Betty harbored social aspirations. She began saving for a house. She courted a middle-class social set of doctors and lawyers and their wives as friends, and she ceased to join Cab on his rounds of Harlem.

Not surprisingly, he began to get a reputation as a ladies' man, especially as there were so many lithe, attractive, and available dancers in Harlem's nightlife. In Europe, Betty wanted Cab to make his way back to the hotel after his concerts. Not surprisingly he refused, having the chance to meet European fans, including a number of attractive women. In Paris, after the first Salle Pleyel concert, there was trouble. Cab met a young French girl in a bar, and as he was attempting to seduce her in the toilets, Betty stormed in and started a monumental fight.[31]

Doc Cheatham assumed Cab was in some way unhappy with his reception by the French public in explaining what happened next:

> At our last big concert in Paris he didn't show up for an hour after the show should have started. We sent the piano player to look for him, and when he found Cab, he was drunk. We brought him backstage to the dressing room, put a tub of black coffee into him and brought him back to some sort of life, but he was still drunk when he went on stage. This was very unusual, because normally Cab was a fanatic about discipline. But I think the tour had got to him, and he carried on terribly, trying to speak French.[32]

After the final concert, Cab and the band left immediately for Le Havre to catch the liner *Ile de France* for the homeward voyage. Cab had created a bond with European audiences that would be reaffirmed after World War II. In each country in which he played, he had convincingly won over the general public, even if for a mixture of high-minded aesthetics and more pragmatic local politics, he did not have comparable success with the critics. The tour exposed, however, irreparable cracks in his marriage, which was to stagger on for some years as the background to the increasing artistic and commercial success that followed his return home.

Chapter 6

On the Road Again
1934–1937

The best indication of how Cab must have appeared for his European audiences can be seen and heard in a short Paramount movie he made soon after his return to New York, called *Jitterbug Party*. The film includes two numbers shot as if during a radio broadcast from the Cotton Club. Both had been recorded for Victor just a day or two before the band left for Europe and they remained in the repertoire, namely "Hotcha Razz Ma Tazz" and "Long about Midnight." These appear to be more or less entirely filmed as live, with only a few different camera angles cut in later. In any event the synchronization is excellent, and so, too, are the dropped in close-ups of the reed section with Barefield, Harris, and Thomas. Also featured is the rhythm team in a sequence that artfully captures White's easy swing on guitar and Al Morgan's highly visual style of bass playing, slapping the instrument vigorously while simultaneously holding his bow in his right hand.

Best of all, however, is Cab's extrovert dancing and singing, including a splendid coda to "Hotcha Razz Ma Tazz," that is accompanied just by the hand claps of the band, but which gives a perfect example of his flawless timing and bluesy intonation, while in a state of constant movement.

The second part of the movie involves a shift from the relative formality of the Cotton Club to a fictional Harlem nightspot, with some atmospheric pictures of the area after dark, showing the Log Cabin club, the Lafayette Theater, kids playing on the street, food vendors, and the band hurrying in silhouette to play at the after-hours party. Not long after arriving, Cab exhorts them to "swing it!" and Ed Swayze steps forward blowing a clarion call on his trumpet as the rhythm section kicks in. The camera homes in on Payne and Morgan, then frames a cleverly grouped shot of all four reed players, before panning back to show Cab singing "Jitterbug" at the center of a merry line of dancers. Although according to the copyright line in the opening titles the movie was released in 1935, it was obviously filmed in mid-1934, during the final stages of Cab's short-lived Victor contract.

Irving Mills, having brought the band back from Europe, was now clearly following his policy of seeking more exposure for Cab and his band in the movies. This led from 1934's *Cab Calloway's Hi-De-Ho* and *Jitterbug Party* to the following year's *All Colored Vaudeville Show*, which was shot at the Warner Brothers' Theater in Brooklyn. Adelaide Hall and two dance teams, the Three Whippets and the Nicholas Brothers, were also filmed.[1] Unfortunately Cab's contribution was omitted from the originally released cut of this short movie. It was not until 1945, when Warner reedited it and restored the Calloway footage, that it appeared in full form, under the title *Dixieland Jamboree*. Also added was a worthy—and utterly patronizing—voiceover that intoned:

> In America, the Negro has given to music a newer, greater significance, attaining a superb perfection, a pulsating inescapable style. Talented with the gift of rhythm and a spontaneity of improvisation, the American Negro has fused the past with the present to create an art that is characteristic of our time, dancing, singing, and playing such music that swings the whole world.[2]

As if to make the racial overtones of this postwar production even more obvious, the opening title sequence featured a caricature of a minstrel-era banjoist, complete with rolling eyes, large lips, and white gloves. It is a shame that Cab's vocal numbers, including "Some of These Days," and the band's roaring "Tiger Rag" were not released in 1935 without such a demeaning contextualization on the part of Warner's Vitaphone subsidiary.

However, after Mills's efforts to keep Cab's movie profile in the public eye, following the band's absence abroad, his next move in 1934 was to terminate the band's Victor recording contract and bring it back under the wing of Brunswick, in a global agreement for his stable of artists. Although his press releases intimated that this was done for artistic reasons, it is a fair assumption that a level of personal profiteering also lay behind the decision:

> Ever alert for any possible opportunities of furthering his clients' careers, Mills signed a contract with the American Record Company, calling for the exclusive services of Ellington, Calloway and the Mills Blue Rhythm orchestras in the making of Brunswick, Vocalion, Columbia and other phonograph records. The original contract was later renewed for a long period, allowing him carte blanche in the recording studios. He developed and is still developing, many individual phonograph personalities.[3]

The first sessions to be recorded under the new contract were made in Chicago in September 1934, by the same lineup that had toured Europe. The band had not been in New York for much more than a few weeks before it was off on an extended tour that took in Boston, Cleveland, Baltimore, Memphis, San Antonio, Indianapolis, and Kansas City as well as Chicago.[4] Nevertheless, before setting out it had stopped off long enough at the Cotton Club in May for a very particular side effect of Cab's time in London to be noticed by listeners to its nightly broadcasts. "Cab Calloway . . . over the ether Thursday night seems to have gone slightly cockney in his accent," reported a syndicated gossip column, which also seemed to have been in touch with the hostile journalists at *Melody Maker*, since it followed up the remarks about Cab's accent with, "Aside secretly: Cab Calloway didn't go too well with the folk across the pond."[5]

Cab and Betty, attempting to patch up marital matters after their epic fight in Paris, used the short period that they were in New York to move into a new apartment of their own at the Dorence Brooks Building on the corner of St. Nicholas Avenue and 138th Street, right in the heart of a very upmarket area of Harlem. But Cab was barely in his new home long enough to settle in, let alone restart his social life, before he was off on tour.

The most unusual of the discs made for Brunswick at the first Chicago session is "Chinese Rhythm." It has a neatly swinging arrangement by Harry White, with a nicely muted obbligato from Doc Cheatham behind the opening verse and brief solos from Arville Harris on clarinet, Foots Thomas on tenor, and Lammar Wright on open horn before Cab launches into a scat chorus of make-believe Chinese. In today's more politically sensitive climate, this could well be regarded as offensive, but in the mid-1930s it was clearly a comedic stock-in-trade in American—and particularly African American—show business.

In 1938 Slim Gaillard was to record a similar mock-Chinese scat in his Vocalion record of "Chinatown, My Chinatown," and as late as the 1970s the New Orleans trombonist Clem Tervalon incorporated a similar lampoon into his record of that same song. In "Chinese Rhythm," Cab, as was so often the case, pioneered the idea. In this, and other innovations, he influenced the singers of the era more than any African American male vocalist apart from Louis Armstrong.

Cab's overall influence was widespread. Many of the devices used by Fats Waller and His Rhythm, who began recording in May 1934, had already been tried by Cab. For example, numerous Galloway records have the type of farewell aside that Fats was to use, such as "Yeah, Man!" at the end of "Harlem Camp Meeting," or "Palsaddictinsomnidipsomaniac" to finish "Jitterbug." In addition "Harlem Camp Meeting" offers the kind of running commentary on events that Waller loved to use, as Cab confides in his listeners, "What's this coming off here? Looks like one of them good old revival days . . ." Equally, Cab's exhortations to his soloists on "Jitterbug" are very similar to the verbal encouragement that Fats would later apply to Herman Autrey, Gene Sedric, and other members of his Rhythm. Fats and Slim Gaillard were not the only singers to adopt vocal mannerisms from Cab. Among the others, the most consummate imitator was a man also celebrated as a female impersonator, Billy Banks. He managed a fair approximation of Cab's entire style on the acclaimed 1932 series of discs he made with Jack Bland's Rhythmakers, but perhaps his most direct borrowing can be heard on a cover version of "The Scat Song" made with the Mills Blue Rhythm Band the same year.

Of the other 1934 Chicago recordings by Cab, "Avalon" is the outstanding piece, although for once not because of his vocal, but because of the inventive arrangement that includes a flute and guitar chase between Foots Thomas and Morris White. Then Doc Cheatham's trumpet takes up the musical conversation, using a little cup mute that had once belonged to King Oliver to produce a delicate contrast with the flute.

These September sessions were the last to be made by the band lineup that had gone to Europe, and which had remained stable since the summer of 1932. Most discographies are confused regarding the changes that subsequently occurred, but union records show that in January 1935 Harry White left the band to join Luis Russell's backing group for Louis Armstrong, although he continued to arrange from time to time for Cab. This gave Cab the opportunity to enlarge his trombone section to three, and alongside the original

Missourian DePriest Wheeler, he now added Claude Jones, a veteran of Chick Webb and Fletcher Henderson's bands, and Keg Johnson, who had also worked for Henderson. Both these musicians were to remain with Cab into the 1940s.

Ed Swayze was still with the trumpets for the band's next record date, made in New York on January 21, 1935, but he died unexpectedly after entering Mount Sinai Hospital for an operation just ten days later. His place was taken by Irving "Mouse" Randolph.[6]

One reason for the extra trombonist was that after the return from London, Irving Mills had decided to tour an entire Cotton Club revue built around Cab, rather than just him and the band. The larger ensemble played the stock arrangements required to back the additional acts. When Cab's fall 1934 tour came to San Antonio, Texas, it seemed to have added the ingredients of a talent contest as well:

> Cab Calloway and his new Cotton Club show players will present a show at the Majestic Theater Saturday at 11.30 pm. Calloway acts as master of ceremonies and in addition to Nicodemus, Harlem's comical laugh-maker; Aida Ward, star of "Blackbirds" and "Harlem Serenade"; Elma Turner, a rhythmic symphony of tap dancing; and the "Five Percolators" there has been arranged a number of amateur acts. In addition to the amateur frolic on the midnight show Calloway and his Cotton Club players will give an entirely different bill from his regular show.[7]

One reason for enlarging the show and taking an entire revue on the road was that things were changing at the Cotton Club itself. Prohibition had been repealed on December 5, 1933, and much of the raison d'être for the original club disappeared with it. If alcohol could be legally obtained in many a midtown Manhattan nightclub, then why would wealthy white patrons still make the trek to Harlem, however good the show? Moreover, racial tension and the ongoing effects of the Depression were not helping the atmosphere in Harlem, and on March 19, 1935, rioting spilled onto the streets after rumors circulated that a black youth was being savagely beaten by a white shop owner at the Kress Department Store on 125th Street. The press reported:

> Riots and a crime wave north of One Hundred and Twenty-fifth Street discouraged the downtown white trade which had made Harlem one of

the richest—and most raucous—night club sectors in the world. Grim tales of petty robberies, an occasional knifing, and the knowledge that evil lurked in the dimly lit sidestreets of Harlem made couples think twice before venturing uptown. Of course there were those hardy sophisticates who looked upon it all as an additional edge to the evening's entertainment. But your average Manhattanite out for a good night is a docile soul. A last-minute spat with a garrulous taxi driver usually suffices for his brush with the underworld.[8]

It was the beginning of the end for the Harlem club, which was finally to close on February 16, 1936. Later that year it reopened downtown, but from the time Cab left for England in February 1934 until the demise of the original Cotton Club two years later, he did not play there. His entourage consistently used the Cotton Club name, and the 1935–36 season saw his traveling revue launch the most arduous touring he had yet undertaken. There were brief returns home to New York City, during which the show played theaters, but the revue was staged in Boston; Baltimore; Kingston, New York; Binghampton, New York; Chicago; Cleveland; Indianapolis; and Pittsburgh, before finally making its way to the Pacific coast for the first time. It wound its way down from Seattle via Oakland and San Jose to play in Los Angeles, so that Cab could make his first proper Hollywood movie appearance opposite Al Jolson in *The Singing Kid*. Even in what were normally exclusively dance venues, such as the McFadden Ballroom in Oakland, the entire revue appeared, with its full cast of twenty-two. On the West Coast, twenty-four-year-old, fast-talking Nicodemus was still the star comedian, but Leitha Hill, another Cotton Club stalwart, had replaced Aida Ward as featured female singer.[9]

During its peregrinations in 1935, the band returned twice to the recording studios. The January session, made during its New Year layover in New York, and which turned out to be Swayze's last recording, yielded a fresh variation on a familiar theme with "Keep That Hi-De-Hi in Your Soul." It was jointly written by Cab and Harry White, with the usual extra lyrics credited to Irving Mills (although since most of the lyrics are simply wordless scat this looks as if Mills "cut in" to the royalties even more blatantly than usual). Poignantly there is a final solo from Swayze who sounds in fine form, and Eddie Barefield contributes a more than usually nimble eight measures of alto solo.

In July, the band was in Chicago on the midwestern leg of its tour long enough to visit the recording studios and cut five further numbers for Brunswick. Four are unexceptional, but the fifth, "Nagasaki," is one of Cab's greatest vocal triumphs, and one of the most remarkable vocal performances in jazz. It is a masterpiece of scat, a perfect mixture of stream of consciousness and hard-swinging jazz. It picks up on all the promise of the multiple vocal layers of his early "St. Louis Blues" and goes several stages further. Unlike out-and-out scat singers, such as the up-and-coming Leo Watson, who had just started working on Fifty-second Street with the Spirits of Rhythm string band, Cab does more than simply improvise nonsense syllables. He uses the written lyric itself for a launching pad, and—incorporating some of the oriental jive talk ideas from "Chinese Rhythm"—begins to build Japanese-sounding scat phrases from the syllables of the song. Hence we hear "Oh de-sag, oh de-wack," before Japanese syllables such as "Fuji" appear. Gone in a blink, we are in a stream of consciousness that mentions "Ol' Satchmo" in passing, with an instant snapshot impression of Armstrong, before we arrive at the kind of running commentary heard on "Harlem Camp Meeting." We're told we "ought to go down Nagasaki!" but warned "Them cats are muggin'!" before a scat chorus at immense speed that includes high-pitched gutteral Japanese sounds, and a final invocation to his men to "Swing it you dogs!" In the context of nightly touring with the Cotton Club revue, this suggests that Cab had raised his game several notches so that despite the other acts he would be the unequivocal star of the entire show.

It is unlikely that Cab would have read Hugues Panassié's observations on his reed section, regarding the Paris concerts. But after Cab's having honed his own act, as well as improving and expanding his brass section for the 1935 tour, there was now a glaring weak link in the band, which the French critic had pinpointed:

> The saxophone section has not a very commendable style; it includes—alongside Eddie Barefield, who plays alto saxophone and baritone saxophone equally well, and Walker Thomas [sic]—two extremely mediocre soloists, one of whom, Arville Harris, often improvises clarinet solos in the most frightful taste.[10]

In September 1935, Cab was offered the opportunity by Irving Mills to bring in a radically more imposing reed soloist to replace Harris, namely the former star of Blanche Calloway's band, and a veteran of Andy Kirk and Fletcher Henderson's orchestras, tenorist Ben Webster. Apparently after working briefly with Willie Bryant, Webster had spent part of August in Duke Ellington's band as a temporary replacement for Barney Bigard. When Bigard returned, Webster left, but made it known to Ellington and Mills that it was his ambition to join Duke on a permanent basis. There being no vacancy at the time, Webster's biographer, Frank Büchmann-Møller, speculates that it was Mills who suggested he team up with Cab in the interim, and help to solve the Calloway band's reed section problems. Webster greatly liked the stylish travel by Pullman and the excellent salary Cab offered. He joined the band, replacing Harris, during a short stop in Toronto en route to the West, and stayed with it for the filming of *The Singing Kid*, remaining in the lineup for another year, until March 1937.

It seems that Al Jolson pictures were not made in a hurry—certainly not at the breakneck speed with which Cab's Vitaphone and Paramount shorts had been filmed in the East. Jolson himself told the press that "I only make one picture a year and I can't take the chance of a flop. That's why I took so much pains with it."[11] To some reviewers all the pains in the world would not be enough to rescue *The Singing Kid*, in which Jolson simply reiterated all his stock performance clichés: "eye-rolling, wide grinning . . . and singing his famous 'mammy' songs with traditional gusto."[12]

Nevertheless Cab's period of shooting on the picture lasted for over two weeks, from January 12, 1936, until the end of the month. There were a few moments away from the set, not least for the band to join Jolson on his weekly radio show, on which Cab performed "Wa Hoo," "I Can't Give You Anything but Love," and "Boots and Saddles."[13] In the movie Cab and Jolson sang a new Harold Arlen song, with lyrics by E. Y. Harburg, "I Love to Sing-a." Cab also performed "Keep That Hi-De-Ho in Your Soul," and "You're the Cure for What Ails Me." Another song by the Arlen/Harburg team, "Save Me Sister," was not only featured in the movie but was to become one of Calloway's finest records in the church-influenced "sermonizing" genre when the band recorded it in Los Angeles for Brunswick on January 27. Harburg's lyrics pick up plenty of church resonances, talking of the "straight and narrow way," "that Devil revelry," and how the singer's "heart needs salvation," but it is Cab's delivery, his orational rise and fall, his imploring to the sisters of the title, that gives it the dramatic ingredients which bring it to life. The song was recorded in January 1936, when Cab was twenty-eight years old, but his assured delivery is borrowed directly from the sounds he had heard in his teens while his mother was playing and his sister singing in the church back in Baltimore. However, that sensational performance is not to be heard on the sound track that accompanies the appearance of Cab and the band in the picture, because white studio musicians recorded the music even though Cab and his men appear on screen. Owing to a mixture of union agreements and standard industry practice, Warner Brothers rerecorded all its sound tracks separately from the shooting stage, and in this instance chose to use the house band to accompany Cab.[14] The same studio players back up "the chorus of black beauties imported from Harlem"[15] who took time out from Cab's touring revue to appear in some of the larger choreographed routines.

In hindsight it seems bizarre to import one of the country's finest jazz orchestras to Hollywood to appear in a movie, and then dub its music out of the sound track. Yet there is a clue to the prevailing Hollywood attitude at the time to African American musicians, because the same studio suggested that Cab and the band appear in "whiteface" for a promotional photo with Jolson in his traditional burnt cork. There was a heated discussion between Cab and the studio bosses, who eventually climbed down over what was reported at the time as "utter disregard for their rating as artists."[16]

Despite what might be perceived as negative signs about their employment prospects, both Eddie Barefield and Al Morgan opted to leave the band in Hollywood, to try and make a living there. Barefield believed he could make a go of organizing his own band to play in the many clubs and bars on Central Avenue in Los Angeles, which was at the time a jazz center to rival Harlem, or New York's burgeoning Fifty-second Street. Morgan, especially in the light of Cab's experience in the studios, elected to stay for more surprising reasons. According to his successor Milt Hinton:

> The movie people just loved this big bass player and when the band were filming, Cab would look around and find the cameras on Al instead of him, which he didn't care for very much. Some director told Al that every time they made a movie that required a band they would give him a job, so Al quit the band right there in California and went into the studios.[17]

Morgan managed to make a reasonable living in Hollywood, although his studio career did not quite materialize as fully as he had hoped. After gigging briefly with Les Hite's orchestra at the New Cotton Club in Culver City, he spent the next couple of years working in Eddie Barefield's new band at the

Club Alabam. He took time out to play and record with Fats Waller when the pianist came to Hollywood to appear in a movie, organizing a sextet to play with Fats for almost three months at the Famous Door.[18]

As Cab's band made its way back east, he recruited replacements for Barefield and Morgan. On reeds, he brought in the very experienced multi-instrumentalist Garvin Bushell, who joined the band at its first stop on the way home, in Indianapolis.[19] And a few days later in Chicago, at the suggestion of Keg Johnson, Cab went along to hear Milt Hinton, a young local bassist, who was making a name for himself with the band led by veteran New Orleans drummer Zutty Singleton. Milt said:

Now the fact I was with Zutty meant a lot as Zutty was a king and if Zutty would hire me, I must be okay. When the band hit Chicago, Cab comes down to the Three Deuces all dressed up in a coonskin coat and a big derby, sits down and has a drink with Zutty. I played my set with Zutty and the finale with Art Tatum, and then Zutty calls me over to his table.

"You're going."

I said, "Going where?"

Zutty said, "With Cab Calloway. Cab asked me to let him have you."

I said, "Nobody asked me if I wanted to go!"

Cab said, "If you want the job, be at South Street Station tomorrow, the train leaves at nine in the morning."

I said, "But I have a contract with Zutty, I can't just walk out!"

Zutty said, "No, you go with Cab. I'll get another bass player. You can't pass this up."

So I telephoned my mother, told her what was happening, that I was leaving Chicago with Cab Calloway's band, and she packed my things in a canvas bag.[20]

The train left on time with Hinton on board, heading the 150 miles or so west to Moline, Illinois, where the band was due to play a dance that night. The young bassist, still only twenty-five years old, had mainly played around Chicago, and his only real touring experience had been with the violinist Eddie South, who had never traveled in style as Cab's band did. Hinton was amazed by the luxury of the Pullman car and the easy sophistication exuded by his fellow bandsmen, who were by the spring of 1936 one of the two best-paid big bands of African American jazz musicians in the United States. Each man earned $100 per week—only Ellington's orchestra took home more, with a wage of $125. With his friend Keg Johnson looking out for him, Hinton took over Morgan's comfortable berth on the lower rank of bunks—a privilege normally reserved for the senior members of the band—and that afternoon he was taken to see Cab in his stateroom at the end of the car. In the morning, Cab and Ben Webster had stumbled late onto the train at Chicago's Sixty-third Street Station, having missed the departure from the terminus after a night on the town, but now Cab looked fresh, sober and businesslike.

The interview was not a particularly auspicious beginning for the bassist who was to become the longest-serving Calloway sideman of all. Cab told him that he would keep Hinton on for the road tour just as far as New York. "We get there and I'm gonna get me a real bass player," he said.[21]

However, when the band picked up Hinton in Chicago soon after leaving Los Angeles at the beginning of February, it was about to make a lengthy sweep through Illinois, Indiana, and Ohio. Apart from a fleeting visit to the Apollo Theatre and the record studios in May, it was not due back in New York City until August, when after a few theater dates, rehearsals were scheduled for the grand opening of the new downtown Cotton Club on September 24. Consequently, Hinton had the best part of six months to prove himself.

As Hinton stepped on stage for the first time in Al Morgan's suit, which was several sizes too big, his debut in Moline seemed to be no more promising than his brief interview with Cab. His sleeves flapped over his hands, making it difficult to pluck the strings easily, and he had also had his hair greased into a pompadour, so that the longer strands at the front were slicked to his scalp and sculptured upward to create what was then the most fashionable look. In the heat of the lights he could feel the grease beginning to melt. There was no time for rehearsal, and Hinton was initially nonplussed by the raw power of Cab's brass and reed sections, as they played directly toward him. Because Morgan had been a featured soloist, the bass player stood slightly to the front of the band, between the piano and Cab. Morgan had not been a great reader, so there was little or no music for the bass. Over the roar of the horns, Hinton had to listen hard to the piano to discern the correct chords, although the more difficult changes were called out to him by Bennie Payne.

Suddenly the spotlight was on him. Cab announced "Reefer Man," which had been Al Morgan's feature. Whereas Morgan was a powerful proponent of the slap bass style, in which the string was released against the fingerboard of the bass to make a percussive slap as the note sounded, Hinton was a more subtle and mobile player, relying less on brute force and more on instrumental agility. Despite the oversize suit flapping round his arms, his hair now either standing completely on end or flopping limply downward, he took his chance and plunged into the opening solo, on the chord of F major. It seems that not even a fragment of Hinton being featured on this tune survives from any of the band's airshots, but an excellent example of his virtuoso pizzicato playing can be heard on "Pluckin' the Bass," from August 1939. From this it is possible to imagine the impact on his fellow musicians and the audience alike of his fast, accurate playing, using slapping as just one of an arsenal of percussive techniques, and displaying impeccable intonation through the entire range of the instrument. Urged on by the band, Hinton played a lengthy solo, before Cab brought everyone in together for the vocal and ensemble sections. At the end, the lights came back on Hinton, and Payne whispered that he was to keep going as long as possible on his own and then fall backward exhausted. Payne slid round from the piano stool to catch him. The crowd went crazy, and more importantly Hinton had earned the respect of his fellow members of Cab's orchestra.

Most significantly, this included Ben Webster.

As a soloist, Webster was really to come into his own at the end of the decade when he finally joined Duke Ellington. Yet even in 1936 he was already highly experienced and was by far the most high-profile instrumentalist the band had included since Cab took over the Missourians. Stocky, pugnacious, and with slightly bulging eyes that inspired his nickname of "Frog," Webster was the epitome of the combative midwestern musician. His section mate, Garvin Bushell, described him thus:

> He was a typical product of Kansas City at that time. Kansas City was a fast town where the people were on top of everything—in the line of music, gambling, hustling, and all that. Some of the sharpest characters in the world came from there, I think Ben was influenced by the hustlers and the pimps—he had their mannerisms.[22]

Partly because of this rough, tough streetwise character, and partly because he had made his reputation independently of both Cab and the Missourians, Webster formed a far closer friendship with Cab than had any of the other musicians in the band. The two of them became drinking buddies, visiting clubs, taverns, and whorehouses together in many a town or city as the band's railroad cars wound their way across the United States. Or they would set off in Cab's green Lincoln automobile, which was carried in the band's baggage car, in search of a more far-flung social life. Occasionally this brought troubles of its own, such as during a visit to Youngstown, Ohio, when thieves targeted the parked car while Cab and Ben were otherwise engaged. The press reported, "Cab Calloway hi-de-doed into police headquarters to sing the blues about the loss of $1500."[23]

When he was not carousing with the boss, Webster was an indefatigable sitter-in with local musicians or other touring bands. The culture of competition was deep rooted in Kansas City's musical life, and Webster wanted to play small group jazz as often as possible to keep his improvisational juices flowing, away from the big band charts that he played night after night with Cab. As guitarist Danny Barker, who joined the band in 1937, said:

> It was a very monotonous deal sitting on a stage playing one and a half hour stage shows four, five, sometimes six times a day, seven days a week, for months and months at a time. Playing the same songs over and over, under the hot stage lighting. When the stage show was over you went to the small crowded dressing room, always near the roof of the theater. You practiced, worked with your hobby and wrote letters. Many musicians could not take the daily routine, blew their tops and quit. Others waited till after the show and went to a restaurant, cabaret or joint.[24]

In Milt Hinton, Webster found the ideal companion for his rounds of after-hours jam sessions, particularly after the bassist had been with the band long enough to buy some sharp clothes, and to have his uniform altered to fit. On the one hand he was a young impressionable musician who would look up to Webster, but on the other a reliable bass player, who knew the right chords, and whose support would make the tenorist sound better. The two of them began practicing together while the band was on the road, Webster imparting the chord changes that he preferred to use on his favorite numbers, but also taking the chance to work out some of his most devastating cutting-contest solos in advance. For Hinton it was a daily lesson from a master improviser.

Webster was also quite cavalier about offering his services to other leaders for record dates. It had become an unwritten law in Cab's band that while a musician was a member of it, he would record only for Cab. Webster took no notice of such a convention, and played on several sessions, often taking Hinton along as well. His appearances included a reunion with Ellington on "In a Jam," and a number of dates with Teddy Wilson, accompanying Billie Holiday. At first Cab was furious, shouting, "I don't want my musicians making everyone else sound good!" But when Webster threatened to quit, Cab quickly changed his tune, purring at him and Hinton, "I'm glad to know I've got musicians everyone else wants."[25]

Webster's independence, and the aloof brand of cool exuded by the other newcomer to the reeds, Garvin Bushell, whose father had taught him to fight intolerance with intelligence, triggered a gradual change in the relationship between Cab and the band. Cab was still an autocrat when it came to rehearsing his routines, just as he had been at the early days in the Cotton Club. The Missourians respected him, having both experienced his effective leadership in the South and witnessed the way his zeal for practice had transformed them from raw midwesterners to a slick and tight-knit New York band. Doc Cheatham revered him as "one of the greatest bandleaders who ever lived."[26] On the other hand, Bushell and Webster had been around the block a few times, and they were quite dismissive about Cab's musicianship. Bushell wrote:

> He was a little rougher than he should have been on musicians. On the stand he was a tyrant. He ran his orchestra with an iron hand, not giving much room for your decisions, your concept. . . . At rehearsals he'd scream and holler at you into submissiveness—he thought by acting that way he could make up for his limited knowledge of music. That was a mistake. Cab couldn't really conduct, but in those days there were a lot of phoney conductors.[27]

It was to be an irony that Cab's desire to improve the band by bringing in a higher quality of musician triggered doubts among his men about his own abilities. To the newcomers his inventive capacities as a dancer, his innovations as a vocalist, his remarkable timing, and his ability to connect with the public were unimportant. Could he sight-read a score? Could he hear tiny harmonic mistakes in the sections or tell if one member of the reeds or brass was fractionally out of tune? Could he beat in a number at precisely the right tempo? These were the measures by which instrumentalists accustomed to playing for so many hours each day sized up the musical abilities of their conductors.

By the end of the decade when players like Dizzy Gillespie arrived in the ranks, they were much freer with their opinions, Dizzy holding forth with the view that "Cab was no musician."[28]

Well before that, experienced players coming into the band noticed its shortcomings, often things that Cab himself had started to overlook through familiarity. Bushell was irked by Leroy Maxey's increasing tendency to drag, by Bennie Payne's unswinging foursquare attempts to compensate by pushing the beat, and by Morris White's lack of volume.[29] Before the end of the decade, the band would acquire a new guitarist and drummer, as Cab finally addressed these issues. However, in early 1936 this was still some distance into the future, but the beginning of the underlying change in attitude dates from the tour that followed the band's return from California.

Yet Cab was not short of ideas about drawing his men together, which would help to bond them as a unit outside music. Just before the trip to Europe in 1934, the press reported, "Cab Calloway has organized a basketball team with the boys in his band and played games with local quintets in Rochester and Syracuse, losing both matches."[30]

By the time of the midwestern tour in 1936, the basketball team had become a band institution, and Cab himself would frequently turn out with it. In the summer months, there was also a baseball team drawn from the ranks, which took advantage of the chance to play during the daytime whenever the band worked in one city for several consecutive nights. For this endeavour, members of the Cotton Club revue, the dancers, and the valets were all pressed into service, but Garvin Bushell, Milt Hinton, Claude Jones, Leroy Maxey, Bennie Payne, and DePriest Wheeler all played regularly for the band team along with Cab.[31]

The band also bonded through having its own private language. First, there were nicknames for the musicians, and second, the men spoke to one another using a brand of jive talk that only the hippest of Harlemites would have understood. Doc Cheatham, Keg Johnson, Mouse Randolph, and Foots Thomas had all had their nicknames for years before joining Cab. But the other members got their names from the band. Lammar Wright was "Slop," DePriest Wheeler was "Mickey," Claude Jones was "Wiggy," Andrew Brown was "Flat," Garvin Bushell was "Bull" or "Butch," and Ben Webster was "Frog." In the rhythm section, Morris White was "Fruit," Leroy Maxey was "Cash," and Hinton started out as "Fump," but later became "the Judge."

There had been jive talkers in the lineup since the days of the Missourians, but Webster, after his many years on the road with various bands, had turned it into a fine art. By using almost impenetrable slang, musicians could pass comment on those around them without being understood. Hence you could let your fellow musicians know in code what you thought of—for example—a girl, a car, or a restaurant. In due course, with the various editions of his *Hepster's Dictionary*, a guide to the "Language of Jive" first published in 1938, Cab himself capitalized on the day-to-day speech of his musicians, but it was Webster who was the catalyst. Milt Hinton recalled:

> After a while it got to be a natural way of speaking for him and a group of other guys including me. A girl was a "soft," a guy was a "lanc." "Pin" meant dig or look or see. A "short" was a car, an ugly girl was a "willow-ford." You could put words together and make sentences like "Pin that soft on your right duke finaling from the short." That meant, "Look at that girl on your right getting out of the car."[32]

Given the amount of time that he spent with Webster, it was inevitable that Cab would become one of the most enthusiastic advocates of jive talk, not least because it chimed with the Harlem slang that had become the bedrock of his repertoire of Minnie the Moocher songs. Not surprisingly, however, in the list of terms defined in his *Hepster's Dictionary*, "the official jive language reference book of the New York Public Library,"[33] there is no reference to any of the drug-related slang applied to Minnie and her friends "kicking the gong around." Equally the lexicon of marijuana terms to do with "reefers," "vipers," and "tea" is excluded. There were some aspects of jive talk that needed to remain private, in order not to discourage innocent fans and record buyers.

When the band finally returned to New York, there was a week's residency at the Apollo Theatre in mid-August, and then a short period of time off before the rehearsals began for the opening show at the new midtown Cotton Club. "Since Broadway won't come up to the sepia belt," shrilled the press, "Harlem is moving down. Already preceded in the downtown trek by a number of lesser late spots, Lenox Avenue's aristocrat The Cotton Club, is forsaking its familiar locale for that of Broadway and Forty-Eighth Street."[34]

The new premises consisted of a huge upstairs room at 200 West Forty-eighth Street. In the early 1930s, it had been known as the Palais Royale, where one of Owney Madden's gangland associates, Ben Marden, had presented African American stars including Ethel Waters in fast-paced revues that also featured a scantily clad dancing chorus of young white society girls.

The singer Phil Harris (later best known for providing the voice of Baloo the Bear in Disney's *Jungle Book*) had also become a big hit there after moving to New York from Hollywood's Cocoanut Grove.[35]

After the last of Marden's successful revues in 1934, the club had changed hands, briefly becoming known as the Harlem Club, and run by the Immerman brothers as a downtown version of Connie's Inn. Immediately prior to being refurbished by Owney Madden and Herman Stark, the room had been called the Ubangi Club, specializing in cross-dressing revues. When the Ubangi moved to a new location a little farther down Broadway, work began on recreating the "southern" atmosphere of the original Cotton Club, while retaining some of the more theatrical features of the old Palais Royale, including boxes and a ceiling with molded cupids and cherubs.[36]

The new show at "one of the brightest shining lights in the glittering array of mid-town Manhattan night clubs"[37] was more lavish than anything that had been presented at the old uptown club. Cab shared top billing with the tap dancer and singer Bill "Bojangles" Robinson, whose specialty was dancing up and down stairs. Having conquered the stage in a lengthy career, he was now— at a reputed salary of five thousand dollars per week—just beginning to make a name for himself in movies. A couple of years before, Robinson and Cab had resorted to fisticuffs when Cab refused to play a benefit concert that Robinson was organizing. Cab's daughter Camay Calloway Murphy recalled the aggressive side of her father's character, and this came to the fore when Robinson, whose popularity had earned him the nickname the "Mayor of Harlem," condescended to Cab, "When I say we're going to do a benefit, we're going to do it." Cab, still considered a young upstart by the Harlem elite, refused, and challenged Robinson, whom he described as "a vulgar tough man" to a fight. After a long tussle, in which neither overcame the other, the two wound up being the best of friends. Cab did the benefit, and their careers often coincided as the 1930s went on.[38]

Most of the names from Cab's touring Cotton Club show were reabsorbed into the cast of the new revue at the club itself, which included Avis Andrews, the Berry Brothers, Dynamite Hooker, Broadway Jones, Anne Lewis, Katharine Perry, White's Maniacs, and the Tramp Band, as well as several teams of dancers. There was new music by the songwriters Ben Davis and J. Fred Coots, whose repertoire for Cab included "Copper Colored Gal" and "The Wedding of Mr. and Mrs. Swing." In characteristic fashion, Irving Mills (who was also Coots's publisher) ensured that Cab recorded the new pieces a week before the club officially opened on September 24, 1936. The first of these songs, "Copper Colored Gal," gives us a good impression of how the band must have sounded in the show. Its confident, rich-toned ensemble plays slickly behind Cab with short but effective solos from Mouse Randolph, Garvin Bushell, and an authoritative Ben Webster.[39] The opening theme of the wedding song bears a striking resemblance to Ted Koehler and Jimmy McHugh's "Spreading Rhythm Around," recorded by Fats Waller and featured by him in the previous year's movie *King of Burlesque*. However, once Deacon Calloway starts intoning the nuptial service with responses from his band, the piece takes a satisfyingly original turn away from the earlier song.

In striking contrast to *The Singing Kid*, the band's return to New York was also marked by another Vitaphone short movie *Hi De Ho*, but this time with an entirely African American cast. Burnet Hershey's flimsy screenplay involves a young Cab whose mother is worried by the hours he spends listening to the radio and conducting a miniature orchestra. This offered a simple opportunity to intercut footage of Cab and his real-life orchestra playing out the fantasy. At the same Brunswick session as "Copper Colored Gal" the band had recorded a novelty song, "Frisco Flo," and another vehicle for Cab's favorite collection of syllables, "The Hi-De-Ho Miracle Man." A day or two later, these new numbers were duly reprised in the film. But the standout track in the movie is a simply dazzling version of "Some of These Days." It is a far cry from Cab's original record of the song from 1930. This version features a sparkling flute solo from Foots Thomas, a brilliant guitar solo from Morris White (who is backed on rhythm guitar by Keg Johnson, who temporarily lays down his trombone to supply some Hot Club style swing), nimble trombone from Claude Jones, and a taste of Buster Bailey–inspired clarinet from Garvin Bushell. Yet the most memorable thing about this brief tune is Cab's vocal expertise and dancing. He seems to be scatting at double speed, with lips, teeth, and tongue working overtime to add percussive consonants, before a wild display of footwork that finishes with him spinning round on the spot like a ballerina. More than any film appearance up to this point, Cab's own performance shows why he was such a charismatic front man for the band, and it certainly explains why the Cotton Club had been so eager to reengage him for its downtown debut.

It was in the week following this recording and movie work, leading up to the actual Cotton Club opening, that an event occurred which proved an interesting test of Cab's leadership qualities and the band loyalty he had attempted to build up. All the band members belonged to the New York local of the AFM, which was designated by the area number 802, with the exception of Milt Hinton, who carried an area 208 card from Chicago. On the road this had made little difference, because in whatever city they visited, all the musicians had to deposit their cards with the local union, which was entitled to a percentage of the band's fee. But just as Cab had to do when he arrived in New York, it was now necessary for Hinton to deposit his card with the local there, and to wait six months before he could play regularly in the city. He had gotten away without doing this while the band was playing for a week at the Apollo and at a few other dance dates around town, but moving into a long-term residency was a different matter. A union official checked everyone's card at the final Cotton Club rehearsal and gave Hinton the bad news. Local 802 took a particularly dim view of out-of-town musicians coming in to play at smart new midtown venues.

Cab's initial reaction—preoccupied as he was with fronting a new show, rehearsing new dances, and mastering fresh lyrics—was consistent with Hinton's first interview in the Pullman. Cab told him he could see the band manager Mr. Wright and collect his fare back to Chicago. Then he set about recruiting Chick Webb's bassist, Elmer James, to play the show.

Yet the camaraderie that had built up on the road worked in Hinton's favor. A day or so after the opening, Ben Webster, Keg Johnson, and the band's "straw boss," Foots Thomas, cornered Cab. They pointed out to him that Hinton knew the book backwards and was the band's ideal bass player. Didn't Cab realize how big a name he had become himself? Who was he to be pushed around by the union? And couldn't some of the mobsters who owned the place, Madden, Stark, and their gangster friends, sort the whole business out quickly by having a quick word with somebody high up in the union?

Appealing to Cab's vanity was certainly a sensible strategy, but the three spokesmen (apparently also accompanied by the senior member of the brass section Lammar Wright) were astutely chosen by their colleagues. Cab was personally close to Ben Webster; he acknowledged that the tough-talking pistol-packing Texan, Keg Johnson, had found Hinton in the first place; and he also relied on Foots Thomas to help with rehearsing the band and to conduct the first and last sets of the evening. Elmer James was good, but he was not in the same league as the young Chicagoan bassist. So Hinton found himself summoned back to Cab, who told him he could stay. Also, because the union rules allowed him a limited number of appearances in New York, he would be required to play the two most high-profile shows a week, the ones that were broadcast nationally at midnight on Monday and Wednesday nights, until he had worked out his six months and could rejoin permanently. He was also able to join the men for recordings and occasional brief forays out of New York, including a one-nighter in White Plains and a short hop to Canada for a few nights.

To further make the point to Cab, on its broadcasts the band contrived to feature Hinton more prominently than usual in some of the arrangements on the nights when he played. Consequently, for his part, Cab pulled some strings to get the transfer through in twelve weeks. "Elmer James played his heart out," Hinton later recalled. "But what was more important to the band was the time we'd spent on the road together. They liked me and thought of me as one of them."[40] Cab came out of the affair seeming more decisive than he actually was. His band came out of it with one of the best bassists in jazz, who would remain in the job for eighteen years. Between its members there was a new sense of solidarity, which had ironically been most forcefully reinforced by the reed section's most assiduous freelancer, Ben Webster.

The opening of the new Cotton Club once again gave Cab and the band a regular New York home, usually for two spells of up to three months a year, with the rest of the time being spent on the road. This way of life continued from the fall of 1936 until the closure of the Cotton Club in June 1940. Although Cab was consequently away from his Harlem apartment for months on end, this did not prevent Betty from persuading him to invest sixty thousand dollars of his considerable earnings into building a new home in the North Bronx at Riverdale. She had selected an all-white neighborhood, which caused considerable problems when they finally moved in during 1937, with signs reading "Nigger Go Home" planted on the front lawn during the night.

The house that Betty had planned in order to help bring her and Cab closer together ended up being one of the reasons they eventually split up. Cab was not prepared to live in an alien neighborhood with no bars and no socializing, so he would not forsake his uptown lifestyle, the friends, the atmosphere, and the after-hours gatherings to which he headed every evening once the show was over in midtown. Among his closest friends was the *Esquire* cartoonist E. Simms Campbell, one of the first African Americans to break into the national press. The two of them often drank until dawn, enjoying the vibrant atmosphere of Harlem by night.

In between his troubled marriage and his Harlem friends, Cab found time to keep in contact with Zelma and Camay. When the band worked its occasional

weeks at the Apollo Theatre on visits back to New York between Cotton Club
shows, Camay was often invited along.

> I would always have to stay backstage. He would say to me that he
> would never let his family take the seat of a paying customer. He would
> put me on the side of the stage, so I saw all of his shows in profile.
> Once, when he was at the Apollo there was a new dance called
> "Truckin'," and at the end of the show they would pull kids up out of the
> audience up to come and "truck" across the stage, and that time he let
> me come out and join in and "truck." I was backstage but I joined in the
> dance, I went in and out between the curtains, when most of the kids
> were out front on the apron. No-one really saw me, but he knew I was
> there.[41]

On these visits, Camay seldom got to spend all that much time with her father.
Even in the dressing room there were always people coming and going, but he
would be sure to talk to her, and she became part of the extended family of the
band. One of the valets, Rudolph, would often look after her, or she might be
put in the care of one of the musicians.

> I had a big crush on Bennie Payne. He'd hug me and lift me up off the
> ground, and then he'd take me up to the dressing room, where the
> showgirls would dress. I'd be able to put on some of the big head-dresses
> that they were wearing, or the little shimmy dresses, so that was always
> very exciting.[42]

It was Rudolph who brought Camay's monthly support check up to the aunt
with whom she lived in New York, and he was also the man trusted to place
Cab's bets on the horses, wherever the band found itself, on days when it was
impossible for Cab to get to a racetrack himself. At this point in the mid-1930s,
the band, with its attendant valets and dancers, was more of a family to Cab
than either his wife or Zelma and Camay. When the orchestra first installed
itself in a new dressing room, Lammar Wright would set up a little stove and
cook for everyone, and despite the protocol of distance between Cab and his
men, and the criticisms of his musicianship from some members, an inevitable social bond grew up between them. Just as had been the case with Milt
Hinton's acceptance into the ranks, this bond grew stronger away from home.

Cab always gave his men a paid week off at Christmas, on the principle that having been born on Christmas Day he was never going to work during the holiday season. The tradition began in January 1937 of reassembling to play a New Year date in Chicago and this was also to be a custom that continued for some years, Cab giving his men a train ticket in addition to their Christmas wages, so that they would be sure to appear and not otherwise spend the travel money. At the end of 1936, before its annual vacation, the band made a brief trip south, starting in Richmond, Virginia.[43] Following the 1933 tour of the South, Cab had ventured below the Mason-Dixon Line as little as possible. There had been a short detour taking in Nashville, Tennessee, and Dallas, Texas, via a number of one-nighters in a couple of southern states during the predominantly midwestern tour in the summer of 1936. This year-end trip was another comparatively rare return to the scene of the band's earlier privations.

In some respects things had changed. Coming home to the Cotton Club and working again for Madden and Stark with apparently no expense spared had reinforced the band's links with the mob. "Irving Mills was the designated agent," recalled Doc Cheatham, "but the mob set up everything. One of them was always around. You didn't hardly know it. If you didn't know him, then you wouldn't know who he was. Of course, Cab made big money then. I never saw so much money in my life."[44]

But not even the mob could alter the sense of fear and foreboding that the musicians felt when they crossed the state line into Alabama, or Florida, or Georgia, or Mississippi. They observed the paradox that southern white audiences desperately wanted to hear them, but simultaneously resented them because they were black. In places where there was no access by train, there was an enforced return to traveling by bus. With that came all the old problems of segregated toilets, a sparse supply of restaurants, and appalling hotels. On an earlier tour, Barefield, an ex-prizefighter, had knocked out three aggressive southern whites who clambered onto the bus looking for a fight. This time, Keg Johnson rescued Ben Webster from an argument by firing his gun into the air to break up what was developing into an ugly fight behind a theater. Bushell stopped an apparently violent angry drunk from coming into Cab's dressing room in Longview, Texas, by sweet-talking him in his best, urbane, New York manner. The fellow proved to be the editor of the local paper, and the following day entertained Cab to cigars and whisky in his office, but that had not prevented him from fisticuffs with Harold, one of Cab's valets, shouting at him to "Take yo' black-ass hands offa me!"[45]

The worst incident was at a black dance in Johnson City, Tennessee, where after a knife was pulled on a white spectator, the police moved in with unparalleled brutality. They stopped the band and told the musicians to leave by a side door. A bus took them to their Pullman cars at the local station. Then the police savagely beat many of the clientele and shot others, with reprisals spilling over into the neighboring houses. Screams and shots could be heard from the train, and rumors reached the band of several otherwise unreported deaths.

After the band returned to the Cotton Club for the spring, its tour in the early summer of 1937 was much less eventful, being restricted to the safer territory of the Midwest and Canada, taking in Minneapolis, Cleveland, and Montreal, as well as cities closer to home in Massachusetts and New Jersey. When it ended in August in Canada, the band prepared to install itself once more at the Cotton Club in early September, where Cab was to introduce a new dance craze called "Peckin'," based on a song the band had recorded in March. Apparently Cab took a live rooster on tour with him to study its steps and imitate them in his own choreography.[46]

At the club, Cab was to star opposite Bill Robinson in a new *Cotton Club Parade* with the aim of repeating the previous year's success. However, Robinson had only recently come back from Hollywood, where he had been choreographing the Ted Koehler/Jimmy McHugh musical movie *Dimples* for Shirley Temple. Just as the Cotton Club show was in midrehearsal he got the call from Twentieth Century-Fox to return to the West to costar with Temple in *Rebecca of Sunnybrook Farm*. Because he had a lucrative contract with the studios, he left New York immediately, and the young Nicholas Brothers got their big break, with the sixteen-year-old brother Harold mastering most of Robinson's routines in a few days. Robinson's eventual return in December introduced a new dance to New York, the "Bill Robinson Walk." He and Cab made a formidable partnership, although as a result of a sequence in the movie *Stormy Weather* in 1943, Cab's name would be permanently linked for posterity with the genius of the Nicholas Brothers.

While all the Cotton Club cast changes were afoot, the two saxophonists who had helped to transform the band's reed section, Garvin Bushell and Ben Webster, both left the band. Bushell believed that Cab engineered his departure, trumping up charges that he was not paying attention or fitting closely enough with the reeds. Cab was never good at firing his men, and it may be that he simply felt it was time for a change. In any event, Bushell and Chick Webb's lead altoist Chauncey Haughton simply swapped jobs.[47]

    Webster, on the other hand, was no nearer joining Duke Ellington. It took him another three years to do that. But he was just bored by not playing enough small group jazz and having insufficient solo space in the Calloway orchestra, so regretfully he handed his notice in to his carousing buddy Cab, telling him it was final and irrevocable. Cab asked Webster to suggest a replacement, and so he proposed the tenor soloist Leon "Chu" Berry, who had already made an impact with Teddy Hill and who was currently working in Chicago with Fletcher Henderson. Berry was also well known around Manhattan as a jam session sparring partner of the combative trumpeter Roy Eldridge. Cab offered Berry the job in late July, and before the summer tour ended he came to join the band in Cleveland, sitting alongside his predecessor to learn the book.[48] On the night Webster finally left, Cab went out and got very, very drunk.

Chapter 7

Chuberry Jam
1937–1939

"Chu Berry made a great turnabout in that band," recalled Milt Hinton.[1]
During Ben Webster's time as the principal tenorist for Cab, he had played
some fine cameo solos, for which the band provided excellent backing. However, even in August 1937 as Webster took his leave, the Calloway orchestra
was generally perceived as a slick, well-oiled machine to support Cab's singing and dancing, rather than primarily being an instrumental jazz group in its
own right. Less than a month after Chu Berry arrived, the band began to
make purely instrumental records that jazz enthusiasts and critics would
take every bit as seriously as those by Ellington, Lunceford, or the recently
arrived Count Basie. The bulky bespectacled tenorist was the catalyst for
change.

For a start Berry agreed to join only on the condition that for as long as
he was in the band, Cab would never pick up his alto sax and try to play it
in public—something he had occasionally done since the band's return to
the Cotton Club. Second, Berry recognized the frustration that the band
members felt by having to play the same show night after night. Unlike
Webster, he believed that the solution was not to rush off and sit in at every
possible jam session as an antidote to his main job—although Berry was
always ready to blow at any time anywhere—but to introduce more jazz
and more solo opportunities to the sets played by the band itself. Hinton
continued:

We didn't have much solo work in Cab's band because it was all featuring him. "You've got all these great musicians in the band," Chu told Cab. "You should really let the guys play sometimes." . . . He carried on: "Next time we make a record, why don't you sing on one side and feature the guys on the other side?"

So when we did get to the studio, Cab said, "OK, why don't you guys do something for the other side!" And that's how we began to get features.[2]

Cab was no less zealous than he had always been about rehearsing his own routines with the orchestra. However, one of Garvin Bushell's criticisms of the band was that although Foots Thomas had taken great pains to improve his alto playing, not least by introducing him to Merle Johnson, New York's most highly regarded teacher, there had been no commensurate effort to sort out the fine details of the group's overall sound in its purely instrumental repertoire. Thomas and Johnson helped Bushell center his tone, improve his articulation, and make his pitching more accurate, yet he was acutely aware that collectively "nobody ever rehearsed us to pick up the loose ends."[3] By his mere presence, his remarkable musicianship, and his enthusiasm, Berry altered that, as Milt Hinton recalled:

> Cab wasn't interested in rehearsing the band. He was an artist. . . . We organized that band ourselves. The trombones would get together and have a trombone rehearsal, the trumpets the same. We did the dynamics of the orchestra ourselves, because this was our chance to do something together. I remember the trumpets discussing whether to use hand vibrato or lip vibrato on a particular arrangement.[4]

The effects of Berry's arrival are immediately obvious. Earlier in 1937, the band had cut one instrumental, "Congo," which has an urgent "jungle" beat, and a rather hesitant Webster solo for less than a chorus, with some slightly scrappy ensemble playing. Even "Manhattan Jam," Webster's last record with the band, is a dated arrangement by Harry White that—apart from a few scatted breaks by Cab—mainly features Garvin Bushell's clarinet over a rhythm section in which Hinton's slapped bass deliberately harks back to the Al Morgan days.

In the first group of eight titles cut after Berry's arrival in August 1937 there are two full-blown instrumentals, "Queen Isabella" and "Savage Rhythm," demonstrating that the tenorist's subtle persuasion had worked on Cab. Apparently a very effective line of argument Berry used was that the band had nothing to play when Cab was off the stage, saying: "We can't hi-de-ho if you ain't there." He urged Cab to add some better instrumental charts to the book, and to improve matters in the short term, Berry swapped arrangements with other leaders such as Chick Webb and wrote head arrangements of his own.[5] The first of these new pieces to be recorded, "Queen Isabella" (written by Foots Thomas and Chu Berry, with words added much later by the Cotton Club's new lyric writer, Benny Davis), shows greater section discipline than six months before. The medium swing tempo is ideally suited to Maxey's ability to drive the band, but it also has a strikingly good solo by Doc Cheatham, prefiguring the Armstrong-influenced style of his later career, and disproving his often-expressed view that he was typecast as a lead trumpeter with no solo space. It is possible that Berry recognized Cheatham's hidden solo potential and lured him into the open, but in any event his playing is a fine curtain-raiser for Berry's own full chorus of tenor saxophone solo.

Hinton maintains that Berry tuned his instrument slightly sharp, to cut through the ensemble better, and aided by a key change in the first note of his solo he positively leaps into the limelight with a dramatic flourish worthy of Cab himself. Whereas most of Webster's best solos for Calloway insinuated their way into a song, holding hidden menace, but often just failing to arrive at a convincing destination before they were over, Berry judges his thirty-two measures to perfection. He borrows some ideas from Coleman Hawkins, notably a kind of broad tremolo on rising phrases, and running simply up a chord before then moving the arpeggio upward by a step or half step. However, the tone, at once bleating and fluffy, and the compositional logic, are all his own. The band had never before played host to an instrumentalist whose musical personality was as strong as Cab's yet who also offered a complete aural contrast to the leader's extrovert persona. At a stroke, Berry had lifted the band's game musically, and provided it with a means of commanding the stage when Cab was in his dressing room.

The follow-up track, "Savage Rhythm," originally the flip side of the same 78 rpm disc as "Queen Isabella," is an equally accomplished example of Berry's influence. The section playing is exemplary as are the dynamics. Mouse Randolph kicks off the solos, and after a minor interlude, Berry starts with another dramatic break and then lets his ideas flow, again dominating the proceedings, and pointing toward a splendid final ensemble chorus, with strong riffing and a memorable minor key coda.

In one respect, Cab's instrumental records were following a national trend among big band leaders, because the fall of 1937 saw many of them who routinely included plenty of vocals focus on purely instrumental jazz. In particular, according to the show business columnist Charles G. Sampas, there was "a tendency on the part of the maestri to pair off their ace instrumentalists into clambake crews." Sampas, whose work appeared in papers in New England, noted that the Benny Goodman Quartet, the Bob Crosby Bobcats, the Tommy Dorsey Clambake Seven, and Ben Pollack's Pick-a-Rib Boys were all recording as "bands within a band" during that same season. With the encouragement of Irving Mills, who had recently been named managing director of the "Master" and "Variety" divisions of the American Record Company, Cab followed this small group trend, too. He allowed a septet from his band to make some discs under the name of Chu Berry's Stompy Stevedores. Sampas continued:

> It was hardly thought that the colored combos, while they dote on swing and reserve all their symphonies for jiving would become engulfed in the chamber tide. Yet that is exactly what is happening. . . . Where nothing mattered but his own hi-de-hoisms, Cab Calloway now steps aside for a swing fiesta inspired by Chu Berry and a half dozen stompy stevedores culled from his clan.[6]

With Mouse Randolph, Keg Johnson, and the Calloway rhythm section, Berry's small band cut four titles for Columbia and Variety (both part of Mills's empire) in September 1937. The standout track is Berry's own "Maelstrom" in which Randolph excels with some forceful playing in the Henry Allen mould, and the saxophonist's solo is a similarly strong statement to those on his debut discs with Cab. These records obviously impressed both Mills and Cab, because before long a comparable small group called the "Cab Jivers" would be added to the program on the full band's live appearances.

The two instrumental tracks cut by the Calloway big band in August also set a precedent, so that at the next session by the full orchestra in December, Cab again turned over two numbers to his men with exceptional results. However, by this time there had been another personnel change, with New Orleans–born Danny Barker (who had guested on Berry's small group sides) replacing Morris White on guitar. On "A Minor Breakdown" and "Bugle Blues," the latter including two brief choruses of wordless scat from Cab amid the sequence of instrumental solos, the rhythm section has a lighter feel than previously, with what Barker called his "big fat chords" cutting through the ensemble. His unhurried sense of time connected perfectly with Hinton's bass to give the rhythm section a lift it had never before attained. Chauncey Haughton's mobile clarinet lines also suggest that he was an able replacement for Bushell. Because Haughton had worked for Cab's brother Elmer during his brief foray into band-leading, and then for Blanche Calloway's touring group, he was almost family.

Elsewhere on this December 1937 record session, Cab's vocal performances were as excellently performed and highly personal as ever. Within five months of his arrival, Chu Berry had brought a whole new dimension to the band, even though he occasionally fell asleep on the stand after jamming all night. Cab himself was quick to recognize this achievement. "I didn't know if he would leave Fletcher to come with me," he reflected, "and I felt a little guilty about trying to steal him from a friend, but, well, business is business."[7]

The same sentiments had no doubt been behind the decision to fire Morris White, another of the surviving Missourians. In his time, White had been a fine replacement for his Missourian predecessor Charlie Stamps, and he had managed the transition from the banjo two-beat of the 1920s to the smoother four-four of the swing-era guitar very competently. His soloing was usually brisk and precise, and as he demonstrated in the film of "Some of These Days," he had a formidable single-string technique. Yet in the large theaters where the band played, or even in the new Cotton Club, the complaint from his fellow musicians was that he was inaudible. As Freddie Green was to prove in his fifty years with Count Basie, this was not a matter of amplification. Green's acoustic guitar cut through the roaring brass and reeds of Basie's band in the largest of venues. His subtle placement of chords and precise beat were felt as much as heard, but their absence was immediately noticeable. White had no comparable strategy for being audible and did not develop his volume. After scuffling to find work for a while, he went on to play briefly with Lionel Hampton and then gently disappeared from the music business.

Barker came from a different school of guitar playing from either Green or White. Like White he was an ex-banjo player, an instrument he was to take up again in the late 1940s vogue for traditional jazz, but as the 1920s ended he had been among the first wave of banjoists to transfer to the guitar. Since 1930 he had played around New York in New Orleans–style rhythm sections organized by his uncle, the drummer Paul Barbarin, in particular making several excellent records as a freelance with the trumpeter Henry "Red" Allen. The ebb and flow of the New Orleans street beat was in Barker's soul.

Until a few months before he joined Cab, Barker had served his time as a guitarist in the Mills Blue Rhythm Band, fronted by Lucky Millinder, where he had formed part of a memorable rhythm section with the pianist Billy Kyle, bassist John Williams, and drummer Lester Nichols. This band was so good, and its rhythm team so impressive, that in the summer of 1937 it famously beat the Basie orchestra in a battle of the bands in Baltimore. With Millinder, Barker modeled his playing after John Trueheart, an unsung hero of Chick Webb's band, with densely voiced chords that cut through the overall sound to create a cushion for the soloists. He seldom took solos himself, preferring to specialize in the business of rhythm playing. It is highly likely that Chu Berry—who already knew Barker's work—had a hand in his arrival with Cab, because as Barker said, "his bag was a rhythm section. He liked four men chomping a chord pattern."[8] Barker had also worked with Harry White, who was still supplying arrangements to Cab, and no doubt he put in a good word as well.

Nevertheless Barker's actual recruitment to the Calloway band was prompted by the reorganization of the fall 1937 Cotton Club show to accommodate Bill Robinson, when he reappeared from Hollywood. This involved ousting the young Nicholas Brothers, who as noted had covered for him in his absence. Several parts of the show were rejigged around Robinson's stair- and tap-dancing act, and consequently the producers decided to look for a blues singer to provide a contrast. Yank Porter, a much-in-demand drummer for African American shows who had his ear to the ground in New York, suggested to Barker that his wife, the singer Blue Lu Barker, might fit the bill.

Blue Lu always coyly denied that her nickname had anything to do with the salty songs and double entendres in which she specialized. Her corpus of discs, made for Decca from August 1938 onward, suggests otherwise, with titles like "I Got Ways Like the Devil," "I Feel Like Lying in Some Other Woman's Husband's Arms," "Handy Andy," and above all "Don't You Make Me High." This last song is better known by everyone who has heard it as "Don't You Feel My Leg," and apparently it was this piece that Lu chose to sing at her Cotton Club audition, some nine months or so before she first recorded it.

Cab and Betty were sitting alongside Bill Robinson and his wife in one of the boxes looking down on the stage as Blue Lu, accompanied by her husband, began to sing. The Cotton Club rehearsal pianist Hughie Walk joined in, and with all the skill for which he was renowned, found the right chords immediately to fit with Barker's guitar. The chorus girls and show dancers took up the song as well, snapping their fingers and singing along with the chorus, "Don't you feel my legs. . . ." With the whole place swaying in time, Barker was sure they would get the gig, especially when the cast gave them a spontaneous round of applause at the end. As the noise died down, Cab's valet motioned for Barker to follow him backstage.

When he reached the dressing rooms, Barker found Cab arguing with Bill Robinson, who was incandescent with anger that anyone would dare to sing a risqué song in front of his wife, at the same time somewhat undermining his point about gentlemanliness by producing a torrent of four-letter words. Cab tried to calm him down, and then turned to Barker:

> "What you doin? Where you working?"
> I said, "I ain't working."
> He said, "Want a job?"
> I said, "That's why we came here, to get a job."
> He said, "I'm not talking about 'we.' I said, do *you* want a job?"
> I said, "Yeah, what kind of job?"
> He said, "In my band."
> I said, "That's a surprise to me. Sure I'll take a job, play guitar in your band."[9]

Barker was directed to find Rudolph and sort out a start date the following week, and to get measured for his uniforms. As he left he got an evil look from Robinson, but he had landed the guitar chair in the band, which he was to keep right through the height of the swing era for eight years, until the end of 1945.

He was more fortunate than another young man who auditioned a few weeks later, according to the syndicated New York gossip column by George Ross:

> A pathetic looking darky approached Cab Calloway at the Cotton Club rehearsal last week and gave him a letter of recommendation from vaudevillian Frank Burt.
> "This says you dance, sing, mimic, juggle, and play six instruments," remarked Calloway. "Tell me son, what don't you do?"
> "Eat," was the laconic rejoinder.[10]

Right through the fall of 1937 and again from early in 1938, the band continued to work at the Cotton Club, staying until shortly before the end of March, when Duke Ellington returned to the venue for a new edition of *Cotton Club Parade*, and Cab went out on the road.[11] The lengthy period in New York allowed Barker to settle into the rhythm section, and during the first three months of 1938 there were two productive record sessions that turned out ten titles in all. At the January recording date the band once again made two instrumentals, but although these were new arrangements commissioned at Chu Berry's suggestion from the prolific Ralph Yaw, they are relatively bland. The first of them, "Rustle of Swing," has a fine Mouse Randolph solo and some characteristically strong soloing from Berry, and "Three Swings and Out" features the same soloists with some neatly played section backing. Nevertheless, apart from these solos, the overall sense is that these discs could have been recorded by almost any swing era big band.

The group's own personality, with precise section work, and a rhythm section that could challenge the Count Basie Orchestra for swing, comes out best on this particular session when it is fulfilling its main function and backing Cab. The song "I Like Music (Played with a Swing Like That)" gives him an opportunity to sing a plum-pudding mixture of conventional lyrics, scat, and running commentary, accompanied by cameo appearances by members of each section. These include a slapped bass solo from Milt Hinton and some dramatic drumming from Maxey.

By contrast the output from the March 1938 date is more consistent, building on the band's distinctive sound from previous years, while modernizing the rhythm somewhat and adding new orchestral effects. "Skrontch"— an Ellington composition—moves at a brisk pace and Cab negotiates the difficult lyric with great precision over the angular melody. Barker noted, "He was a great performer and he knew what he wanted. His showmanship was carefully arranged. He learned his arrangements and the band played them to perfection. And he was a helluva singer. Cab Calloway had good lungs."[12]

Two other songs from the same session demonstrate this perfectionist approach to tricky vocals equally well. First, "Peck-a-Doodle-Doo" is a jaunty nursery song, but Cab swings it strongly, setting the stage for a hard-edged solo from Chu Berry and some fine trumpet work from Randolph. The arrangement is unusual for the band in that it features a trombone "choir," but overall the group retains its driving sense of swing from the time of Berry's arrival. Second, "Hoy Hoy" is a medium-paced, relaxed swinger, by Con Conrad, that gave Cab a new strain of vocalese to incorporate into his act.

In the final instrumental to be recorded before the band went out on the road, "At the Clambake Carnival," there are some new sounds in the tonal palette. The trombone choir reappears, this time effectively backing both Chu Berry's and Chauncey Haughton's solos, Keg Johnson takes a high-note solo trombone chorus, and Bennie Payne slips over to the vibes, Danny Barker's rock-steady guitar keeping a pounding rhythm going behind him. The work that the band had put in to improve and finesse its sound is obvious.

This was just as well, because the first months of 1938 saw the consolidation of a relatively recent phenomenon in New York City, the mass adulation of Benny Goodman by a youth audience. Goodman's season in 1937 at the Paramount had led to extraordinary scenes with jitterbugging in the aisles, but the acme of his rise to fame was his band's concert at Carnegie Hall on January 16, 1938. The significance of this event was adroitly picked up by the journalist and short-story writer Damon Runyon in his new syndicated column, "The Brighter Side." Clearly he was not greatly enamored of jazz or swing, beginning his piece,

> We do not care for swing any more than we do for the sounds emanating from a machine shop, but we do not underestimate it. We are well aware that swing at this time holds the most tremendous vogue of any style, form or system of noise-making in the history of the U.S.A. The youth of the land are practically lunatics on swing music. The old folks too are pretty much swing minded. It is one of those national obsessions that spring up at intervals and last until they wear out.[13]

Going on to relate the extraordinary scenes of Goodman's success in the city, Runyon spelled out the threat to Cab:

> It is difficult to say why one swing band is accounted swingier than another, since they all go in for the same type of musical disorder, but that is the fact. For a long time, a sepia colored young fellow from Harlem named Cab Calloway was the kingpin of the swingers, with his shrieking voice and his wild and woolly method of band leadership. Indeed he rather typed the swingband leaders. Then along came this Benny Goodman, a young chap more prosaic looking than Calloway and less articulate and spectacular, to knock the swing addicts right out of their chairs.[14]

The "swing era"—as it was to become known—had well and truly arrived in Manhattan. Now white bands such as Goodman's, and those of both Dorsey brothers and Artie Shaw, would mount a more serious challenge than ever before for the disposable income of swing enthusiasts. As Lewis A. Erenberg put it, "Goodman became a hero not only to a mass white audience, but also to black swing fans who acknowledged his racial innovations and to the Left which believed him an ally of the popular front."[15]

Yet Cab was well placed to resist this assault on what Runyon perceived as his hitherto preeminent position. Through his recordings, broadcasts, and constant personal appearances, his core popularity straddled the African American audience and the white public. However, although he had taken his share of the youth market, which Goodman adroitly targeted, this was not his primary fan base. Cab's real strength was that Mills had worked hard to secure his position as an all-round entertainer as well as a swing bandleader, using several strategies. First, the Cotton Club gave all his activities a strong foundation and lent his traveling revue an excellent brand identity. Second, he had been a regular broadcaster on the radio for years, and when he was in New York his Cotton Club shows still went out three nights a week across the country. Third, his constant touring in between Manhattan residencies had built up a huge following, black and white, throughout the entire nation. And finally Irving Mills's continuing marketing campaign was to give him some additional ways of grabbing public attention in the early months of 1938.

Most important, in terms of national fame, the strategy of making regular movie appearances meant that Cab was now to be seen in full-length features as well as short subjects. In the late summer of 1937 he and the band had shot a version of his recording of "Mama, I Wanna Make Rhythm," for an all-star picture called *Manhattan Merry-Go-Round*. This had a fully interracial cast, and Cab's band appeared alongside those of Ted Lewis, Louis Prima, and Kay Thompson. As well as the stars Leo Carrillo, Ann Dvorak, James Gleason, and Phil Regan, the baseball legend Joe DiMaggio had a walk-on part, as did the singing cowboy Gene Autry. The movie came out in the early spring of 1938, continuing to show throughout the year, and Cab's contribution was, as one press report put it, "a specialty number delivered in the 'scat' manner made famous in the dusky maestro's 'Minnie The Moocher.' "[16] In other press reports the hand of Irving Mills may be detected in the exorbitant claims made for this relatively modest movie:

If a thousand years from now some enterprising archaeologist should wish to learn all about entertainment in the year 1937, complete in all its phases and furbelows, that historian should excavate "Manhattan Merry Go-Round" the Republic Production . . . Cab Calloway and his Band . . . furnish the piece with several new hit tunes which will be whistled the length and breadth of America within a few short weeks.[17]

As well as the movie, which gained plenty of column inches across the country, Mills chose the first three months of 1938 to launch the first edition of Cab's *Hepster's Dictionary*. Dubbed *Cab Calloway's Cat-alogue*, this slender volume gave show business hacks the chance to ruminate on the decline in standards of English that swing had brought about. "The King's English is taking a terrific beating," ran one typical piece. "Name almost any article and . . . the sepian sharpies (dudes) of the dusky belt have another name for it."[18]

Jive talk had been present in the world of jazz and blues since the dawn of the twentieth century. Among musicians, and show business communities such as Harlem, it was subliminally integrated into everyday speech. Since the Ben Webster days, out on the road, jive had increasingly been used privately by the Calloway band, and throughout Cab's entire recorded history jive terms were slipped casually into his lyrics. Now there was a concerted attempt to make it the main plank of a marketing campaign, by which Mills would emphasize Cab's hepness, and thereby make Goodman and other competitors seem even more "prosaic" than Runyon had described them.

There was a clear role model for Mills's marketing methods. In the 1920s, when Jimmy McHugh had worked as the commercial manager for Irving Mills and his brother Jack's publishing firm, McHugh had managed to place stories in the press about almost every aspect of the company's output. A fire in a neighboring hotel prompted McHugh to teach the pajama-clad guests his latest songs, a seashore expedition was an excuse for a photo call with an outsize drumfish to promote a ditty about fishing, and if all else failed McHugh simply wrote about himself, extolling his marketing talents to the world. In his very early days, plugging songs for Irving Berlin, McHugh had noted that the high-brow press would work itself into paroxysms of outrage if lyricists such as Berlin took liberties with the English language. During a decade of publishing and song plugging together, Irving Mills absorbed plenty of lessons about niche publicity from McHugh, and he recognized that Cab's image—what Runyon had called "kingpin of the swingers"—would be greatly reinforced by promoting the language of Cab's songs as a mysterious secret argot. All he needed to do was to collate the band's own everyday slang, and turn it into a pamphlet for distribution first to the press and second to fans. The premise was that those in the know would understand the nuances of hi-de-ho-ing, while journalists could profess horror at the mangled English involved. A typical story, largely based on Mills's press releases, but dressed up a little by its author, ran:

> They talk a picturesque lingo up in the Black Belt, a "jive" so odd only your true Harlemese understands it. "Jive" for instance means lingo or speech. It is an instinctive speech, almost an unknown tongue, and peculiar only to the New York Negro.
>
> Say, for example, you are walking along Lenox Avenue and you hear someone say, "The Chic's schmaltz but she's a V-8." This means "The girl is sweet and sentimental but she's unapproachable."
>
> Well Cab Calloway decided to do something about it. Cab is a "hep cat." And a hep cat is one who is in the know, a thoroughly wise guy, and Cab reasoned: "Maybe I ought to spread the gospel of our jive . . . Maybe I ought to wise up everybody so they can understand what we are talking about . . . But how'll I do it? You can't just pick it up in a day or a week . . . You can't just tell it . . . So I think I'll edit me a dictionary . . . A hepster's dictionary."
>
> Shortly thereafter a neat little brochure entitled "Cab Calloway's Catologue" was deposited on your correspondent's desk. And it's quite a cat.[19]

To counter Benny Goodman's success with the youth market, Cab gave his fans their own means of communicating. Even if they were "beat to their socks" (flat broke), they could still remain "mellow" (fine) if their "main queen" (sweetheart) "had her boots on" (knew what it was all about). At the end of the day they "nixed out their garments" (undressed) and "copped a nod" (went to sleep). Like all slang, from the moment much of it was published, it was out of date ("capped"), but the little book provoked hours of harmless fun with readers who had seldom if ever heard Harlem street slang spoken in real life, and with journalists who protested that this was "English as she never should be spoken."[20]

In his radio broadcasts, following the example of the white bandleader Kay Kyser, who presented a spoof "Kollege of Musical Knowledge" based on university campus slang, Cab introduced a brief series of sketches in which "Professor Calloway" elucidated various aspects of hepster slang to "pupils" drawn from the ranks of his Cotton Club Orchestra. His "Cab Calloway Quizzicale" was still being featured on his radio shows in the mid-1940s.[21]

Once on the road for a tour of Canada, the Midwest, Southwest, and South that lasted until the end of August, the musicians themselves refreshed their private vocabulary with new expressions, keeping the idiom alive and flourishing. Such was its grip on their everyday speech that many musicians from Cab's band were to continue to use the jive talk of the mid-1930s for the rest of their lives. Doc Cheatham, in his nineties, would ask his drummer or bassist if he'd managed to park his "short" near to the Sweet Basil Club in Greenwich Village where Cheatham's quartet played each Sunday, to be assured everything was "ready" or "solid." In the 1980s, Danny Barker would still refer to his guitar as his "box," as would his contemporary with Fats Waller's band, Al Casey.

The language also spread way beyond the narrow orbit of the band and its members. In 1938, slang expressions from Cab's book were picked up by other musicians wanting to sound equally hep. Nobody would have described Tommy Dorsey, the urbane, bespectacled "sentimental gentleman of swing," as a natural jive talker, but when he took over Walter Winchell's syndicated gossip column for a couple of issues that summer, he—or his ghost writer—managed to pen the entire piece in jive talk, complete with the following pithy observation on what made particular musicians effective jazz soloists: "I think it was Coo [sic] Berry the sax player with Cab Calloway who said 'some folks when they blow in all that comes out is spit.' It's not a nice way to say it but it's the difference between a real gate and a fake gate."[22]

On 23 March, Cab's touring entourage set off for its long peregrination through Ontario, Minnesota, Illinois, Wisconsin, Missouri, Alabama, Texas, and Tennessee with a slightly different lineup from the previous year, including the comedians Stump and Stumpy, the Six Cotton Club Boys (a precision dancing team), and once again the blues singer Avis Andrews. For promoting the tour, Irving Mills's office left nothing to chance. Virtually identical panel advertisements were placed in all the local papers on the itinerary, and many an editorial began in a similar vein to this: "If you see the walls of the Majestic Theater rocking and swaying for a week after Saturday, it won't be an earthquake. It will merely be the fact that Cab Calloway and His Orchestra have taken over the theater with their big new stage show."[23]

There were some changes afoot in the band during this tour. First, Doc Cheatham's childhood friend altoist Jerry Blake (the adopted son of Alice Blake, a Nashville widow, but later known by his baptismal name Jacinto

Chabania) came into the lineup from Fletcher Henderson's group. Blake joined Cab as an additional member of the saxophone section, but also became musical director for the band, taking over this responsibility from Foots Thomas. Two Calloway insiders recommended Blake to Cab, Chu Berry, who had worked alongside Blake with Henderson, and Cheatham, who had first-hand experience of Blake's arranging skills with Sam Wooding, watching him use a portable organ that he set up in the dressing room to work out instant charts of the latest hits.[24]

The other change took longer to effect, but Cab was beginning to share his band's apprehensions over Leroy Maxey. On a medium tempo swing chart, Maxey was one of the finest swing players, able to boot the band along and create momentum. But at slower tempi he could drag, and there were similar problems with some of Cab's fast flagwavers. According to Hinton he "never listened enough to keep up."[25] By this he also meant that Maxey never bothered to keep an ear cocked to what was going on in the wider world of jazz and popular music. He did what he did, just as he had done since the 1920s, when he was an innovator on the tom-toms and in using the bass drum pedal. Although since then his kit had expanded to look like the one that Sonny Greer used with Ellington, his playing range as a drummer remained relatively limited and he seldom used the tympani, chimes, temple gongs, and other paraphernalia that adorned the stand. More to the point he was not a natural soloist and even his best-played breaks on record held the possibility of imminent collapse at any moment.

Particularly following the January 1938 Carnegie Hall concert by Benny Goodman, which had featured Gene Krupa's flamboyant playing on "Sing Sing Sing," Cab felt he needed a drummer who could play a comparable role with his band. In later life, Maxey was to claim that he left Cab through ill health, but Milt Hinton told Gene Lees:

> When Gene Krupa started playing all those drum solos, Cab wanted drum solos. Maxey was a great show drummer, but he didn't know how to take drum solos. Cab got him to take a solo one night, and he got so hung up on it, he stood up and sang the rest of it. Cab fired him and got Cozy Cole, who was with Stuff Smith and a hot drummer around New York.[26]

Cole was a veteran of one of Blanche Calloway's many touring ensembles, but since 1936 he had been playing with Smith at the Onyx Club on Fifty-second

Street. The violinist had a raw, exciting style of playing and knew exactly how to build up excitement over chorus after chorus. Cole's snare-drum-based style—"digging coal," as other drummers called it—pounded out an urgent four to the bar that perfectly supported Smith's riffing violin. From his after-hours visits to the club, Cab liked what he heard, and was keen to hire both Cole and the band's star trumpeter, Jonah Jones. It took him a while longer to poach Jones away, but once his band was back at the Cotton Club in the late fall of 1938 he managed to persuade Cole to join him. As it happened, the time was right, because Cole, always a perfectionist and a fanatic for practice to the very end of his life, was getting tired of the life of excess which playing with Stuff Smith involved. Jonah Jones recalled:

> I was drinking 100% proof and smoking marijuana because Stuff wanted you high every night. One time, before Cozy went to Cab, me and Cozy decided to stop drinking. We got to work and Stuff kicked off "Stomping at the Savoy." Then we went into "Mood Indigo." Stuff turned round: "Something's wrong. Cozy? You high? Jonah? You high?" We told him we were taking it easy. Stuff said, "If everyone's not high by the time we come off the break, there'll be a $10 fine for anyone who isn't high." And he brandished the little flask he kept in his pocket for emergencies. We went out the back and got loaded just to avoid that $10 fine and Stuff was happy.[27]

For Cozy, quitting obligatory booze and drugs, focusing on playing drums for one of the finest of all big band rhythm sections with Payne, Barker, and Hinton, and having solo features written for him by the band's growing posse of professional arrangers was a huge step up toward international fame. He was also a man of ideas when it came to the role of a big band drummer, saying to the other instrumentalists in Cab's band, "I'm not going to play solo drums behind your solo, but I'm going to feed you a certain foundation that will make you feel good while you are playing." He believed he had to know the style of every individual in the band to create the right drum backdrop for each of them.[28]

Before Cole arrived in the ranks, there were three record dates to be made, which were to be Maxey's farewell sessions with the band. Of these Cab's nod to another recent craze, "Boogie Woogie," is rather pedestrian, with Haughton producing a clarinet chorus that is clearly modeled on Benny Goodman's style.

For once Chu Berry sounds slightly overwhelmed by the piece, although the final choruses are good examples of band riffing. There's a similar clarinet cameo on the otherwise riotous "Miss Hallelujah Brown"—a joyous celebration of a former church sister who discovers jazz. Cab's somber preacher mode gives way to jaunty swing, and the track shows Maxey at his best, providing excellent support for a fine Chu Berry solo, and laying down a firm off-beat for Cab's last eight measures. By contrast, one of the band's first forays into Latin territory, "The Congo Conga," has fine additional shakers and claves, some excellent lead trumpet from Cheatham (who was later to spend time with Perez Prado and other Latin leaders), but in this less familiar genre Maxey's drumming lacks the driving precision that Cole would later supply to perfection.

On "Shout, Shout, Shout," an instrumental, the band runs through a stack of big band arrangers' clichés, from trombone choirs to clarinet trios, but the only moment of real drama is a stratospherically high trumpet solo from Lammar Wright, who according to Doc Cheatham often played his regular parts an octave above the written pitch just to make them more interesting. Maxey's farewell as a "show drummer" can be heard on Cab's features from these fall 1938 sessions—executing the breaks and fills on the latest addition to the "Minnie" saga, "Mister Paganini, Swing for Minnie,"[29] then subtly supporting Cab's theatrically enunciated "Jive (Page One of the Hepster's Dictionary)," and adding off-beat cymbal work and snare fills to the year's popular hit song "F.D.R. Jones."

The contrast between these sides and Cozy Cole's first feature for the band, Edgar Battle's composition "Ratamacue," made in February 1939, could not be more startling. The rhythm section comes alive as a jazz unit, excising any flavor of a theatrical big band. Cole dictates everything from the drums. His soloing is deftly precise and driving, his backing to the ensemble is a mixture of flamboyant snare and tom-tom work with powerful hi-hat off-beats, punctuated by flams, fills and rimshots. Behind Cab's singing, Cole delivers the same confidence, for example on "Ad-De-Day (Song of the Cuban Money Divers)" where a long snare-drum roll takes us from Cab's first vocal to a storming ensemble chorus. His sense of dynamics shades the whole performance, and it is immediately obvious that he is playing for the entire band in a way that Maxey never managed. As a result of Cole's arrival and an ongoing sequence of changes in personnel, 1939 was to be a year in which Cab's band transformed itself into an even more competitive jazz big band. It now offered serious rivalry to all the established swing orchestras of the time, as well as being fronted by an entertainer who by dint of his movie appearances and hepster slang had managed to remain ahead of the changes in fashion and style. Yet throughout all these subtle shifts, he never abandoned his public's love of Minnie the Moocher.

Cab himself publicly welcomed the changes to his band. In a 1939 newspaper interview he announced that future performances would contain less scat and more ballads from him, and that he would be making constant improvements to the band. He retrospectively welcomed Blake to the lineup, saying his arrival was part of a series of long-planned moves for "increasing the saxophone section to five men for a better balance, emphasizing melody in our arrangements, and acquiring such star instrumentalists as Chu Berry and Cozy Cole."[30] Cole's arrival coincided with one of the longest sustained periods the band had spent in New York since it originally opened at the Harlem Cotton Club in 1931. From September 1938 it was to remain in the city for the best part of a year.

For the 1938 fall season the downtown club was given a compete makeover, with new murals by the designer Julian Harrison and a revamped entrance lobby and bar. The show that opened on September 28 was a glamorous and star-studded edition of a *Cotton Club Parade* revue, although the club's racial undertones were still readily apparent in the stage set, which was labeled "Col. Cosgrove's Plantation." Fortunately, the revue itself contained no "plantation" sketches, and was a zesty sequence of fast-paced items built mainly around Cab, his band, and the Nicholas Brothers. The singer June Richmond was also on the bill and consequently guested on a couple of the band's late 1938 recordings. Some of the songs that Cab had recorded for Irving Mills shortly before the show opened were allocated to other singers in the company. Among them, Sister Rosetta Tharpe, one of the more secular of gospel singers, took over "Miss Hallelujah Brown," no doubt using the same band arrangement as Cab had done, and Mae Johnson sang "Congo Conga." Meanwhile Cab himself offered his audiences lessons in jive from his *Hepster's Dictionary*.[31]

Just before the refurbished club opened, Cab had made a nostalgic visit back to Harlem. Gossip columnist George Ross reported,

Up Harlem way, sentiment hung so heavy the other night it fairly dripped. The Plantation Club which stands on the site of the old and famous Cotton Club decided to bring together the three most famous celebrities who had ever appeared there. They called Ethel Waters, Cab

Blanche Calloway (courtesy
Christopher Calloway Brooks)

The first Cab Calloway Orchestra, 1930: (l to r) Earres Prince, piano; Walter Foots Thomas, alto saxophone; Cab Calloway; Andrew Brown, tenor saoxphone; Morris White, banjo; Thornton Blue, alto saxophone; Leroy Maxey, drums; R. Q. Dickerson, trumpet; Lammar Wright, trumpet; Jimmy Smith, tuba; DePriest Wheeler, trombone. (courtesy Frank Driggs)

Cab Calloway Orchestra, 1931: (l to r) Bennie Payne, piano; Lammar Wright, R. Q. Dickerson, Reuben Reeves, trumpets; DePriest Wheeler, trombone; Cab; Leroy Maxey, drums; Morris White, banjo; Arville Harris, Andrew Brown, Walter Foots Thomas, reeds; Jimmy Smith, bass. (courtesy Frank Driggs)

At the Cotton Club: Doc Cheatham, trumpet; Harry White, trombone; Al Morgan, bass; Foots Thomas, tenor saxophone; Andrew Brown, alto saxophone; Cab. (courtesy Frank Driggs)

Hi-de-ho at the Cotton Club, 1935: (l to r) Lammar Wright, DePriest Wheeler, Edwin Swayze, Keg Johnson, Doc Cheatham, Claude Jones, Bennie Payne, Leroy Maxey, Cab, Eddie Barefield, Morris White, Arville Harris, Al Morgan, Andrew Brown, Foots Thomas. (courtesy Frank Driggs)

En route to London: New York percussion shop owner Bill Mather (center) with (l to r) Lammar Wright, Al Morgan, Andrew Brown, and Foots Thomas. (courtesy Robert Gore)

The band visiting Doc Cheatham's parents in Nashville. Doc (center) surrounded by his parents, with Cab to the right of Doc's father. (courtesy Doc Cheatham)

Calloway baseball team, 1936. (rear, l to r) Bennie Payne, Claude Jones, Cab, unknown, Garvin Bushell, unknown, DePriest Wheeler. Front: unknown, Milt Hinton, Leroy Maxey, unknown. (courtesy Frank Driggs)

Never far from the Pullman: Danny Barker in the Chicago railroad yards, 1940. (courtesy Frank Driggs)

Bill Robinson, Lena Horne, and Cab during filming of *Stormy Weather*, 1943. (courtesy Christopher Calloway Brooks)

Cab in *Stormy Weather*.
(courtesy Frank Driggs)

The Cab Jivers: (l to r) Milt Hinton, bass; Danny Barker, guitar; Al Gibson, clarinet; Buford Oliver, drums; Tyree Glenn, vibes; Jonah Jones, trumpet; and Ike Quebec, tenor saxophone. (courtesy Danny Barker)

The Cab Calloway
Orchestra, mid-1940s:
new faces include
Dave Rivera, piano;
J. C. Heard, drums;
Paul Webster and Shad
Collins, trumpets.
(courtesy Danny Barker)

The band in 1946,
seen from the
rhythm section.
(courtesy Danny
Barker)

Cab and Ike Quebec
working the crowd
into a frenzy, Toronto,
1945. (courtesy Frank
Driggs)

Cab and his daughter
Chris, early 1950s.
(courtesy Frank Driggs)

Solo artist on the road:
Cab on his way to
entertain the troops,
Florida, 1952. (courtesy
Frank Driggs)

Members of the family at Lido Beach for Cab's eldest daughter's wedding: (l to r) Camay Calloway Brooks, Dora Hughes (aunt), Booker Brooks, Zelma Martin (née Proctor), William Martin, Nuffie, Camilla Coverdale, Cab. (courtesy Christopher Calloway Brooks)

In concert in the 1980s: Cab and Christopher Calloway Brooks (guitar). (courtesy Christopher Calloway Brooks)

Cab as Curtis in a scene from *The Blues Brothers* (1980). (courtesy Frank Driggs)

Calloway, and Duke Ellington, and the reminiscences—and tears—
flowed in an unceasing stream. Ethel did her classic rendition of one of
the great torch songs of our time, "Stormy Weather," the song that cata-
pulted her to fame. Cab went into "Minnie the Moocher" . . . and
Ellington played his "Black and Tan Fantasy".[32]

Such public uptown reunions were rare, and Cab seldom played in Harlem any
longer, although much of his social life was still based there. Normally, after his
traditional New Year trip to Chicago, he would have returned briefly to the
Cotton Club downtown for the spring of 1939 before heading off on the road.
This year was different. The fall revue continued to play at the Cotton Club
from January through early March. There was a two-week break, and then on
March 28, the club launched a glittering new revue to coincide with the imminent New York World's Fair. For the first time ever the venue was to remain
open right through the summer, and Cab, Bill Robinson, and "100 Sepian
Stars" played to packed houses who experienced "by all odds its most successful cavalcade of dynamic singers, rippling feet and flashing limbs."[33]

Such a long residency allowed Cab to continue to tinker with his lineup,
some changes being forced on him and others being a matter of choice. The
first sequence of changes was not planned. Early in 1939 Doc Cheatham was
taken ill on the bandstand at the Cotton Club, and although his devotion to
Cab was deeply entrenched, he was forced by his health to leave the band. "I
was worn out, through traveling and not eating right," he recalled.[34] Several
discographical sources suggest that Shad Collins, who was drafted to replace
Cheatham when he went home for six months to his parents in Nashville to
recuperate, actually joined the band as early as 1937, but Collins spent that
year in Teddy Hill's orchestra, with whom he traveled to Paris (where he
recorded with Dicky Wells). He was still with Hill, touring to Baltimore, among
other places, in 1938. When Cheatham became ill, Collins had just returned
to New York, and being temporarily unemployed, he was quickly drafted as a
short-term replacement, before taking up a job with Count Basie.[35] He was to
join the band on a full-time basis in 1941, but meanwhile Cheatham's departure left Cab with a problem.

Since 1933, Cheatham had been the band's lead trumpeter, leaving Wright
free to solo occasionally, and allowing Randolph to save his lip for the most
demanding solo role. If necessary, Wright could take over the lead duties, but
this altered the balance of the section. Without Cheatham this left the soloing

to Collins and Randolph, who sounded relatively similar to each other. Cab's first thought was to return to his original plan and hire Jonah Jones away from Stuff Smith. However Jones was not keen to join at a time when the band was immersed in a huge revue, with little or no opportunity to play jazz:

> I figured Cab's band wasn't the place for solos because his show was so big. He had eleven boy singers and tap dancers, Bill Bailey (Pearl Bailey's brother), The Miller Brothers and Lois, it was wonderful! What a show. But there were no chances for trumpet solos, whereas with Stuff I had all the solos I wanted. I'd be there blowing and Stuff would be playing riffs on his violin, muttering into my ear, "One more, Jonah! One more!"[36]

Consequently Jones turned him down, but recommended to Cab that he hire Dizzy Gillespie, a young firebrand soloist from South Carolina who was making a splash with Teddy Hill's band, both in the Savoy Ballroom's pavilion at the New York World's Fair site in Flushing and on the band's regular visits to the Apollo Theatre.

When Doc Cheatham returned to see his old colleagues on his way to play with a Latin band in Paris—a career move that was stymied by the outbreak of World War II—he sat in on Dizzy's audition with Cab. According to him, "they were undecided about Dizzy, what he was doing. So they decided to get another guy, and they chose Mario Bauzá. He made the job, did a good job on lead."[37] Some time after the end of March, the Cuban trumpeter Bauzá replaced Collins, and Wright returned to his original role. This was a canny move by Cab. Bauzá had been the lead trumpeter for Chick Webb, and had recently spent several months with Don Redman's band. Originally a woodwind player, he had developed into an exciting, flamboyant section leader, with the brash tone and split second precision of the finest Cuban brass players, and the ability to shape the sound of the trumpets more forcibly than Cheatham, who had been a skilled, but gentle perfectionist in the Louis Armstrong mould. Bauzá was also to encourage Cab to continue to add Latin numbers to the repertoire, such as October 1939's "Chili Con Conga."

A few weeks after Bauzá's arrival, Mouse Randolph unexpectedly left to join Ella Fitzgerald's new band, the group that had been Chick Webb's Orchestra, until the diminutive drummer's untimely death from tuberculosis of the spine in June 1939. Consequently in August, having already auditioned and being a protégé of Bauzá, Dizzy was hired as the Calloway band's main soloist. As Dizzy told the story, he clinched the job by taking over Bauzá's chair for a couple of nights.

> One night he sent me down to the Cotton Club in his place and told me
> to let Lammar Wright take all the first parts and then when it came
> time for a solo, blow. Cab didn't know me; I didn't even report to him,
> just put on the uniform and sat down. I could play fly then, from being
> in Teddy's band, so when I took my solos everything would be fine.[38]

The trumpet section would remain constant until March 1941, with Bauzá playing lead, Wright taking occasional solos, and Dizzy being featured as principal soloist.

The trombones were also to undergo a change as DePriest Wheeler, another Missourian, was to leave at the end of 1939. He was replaced by Quentin Jackson, and a few weeks later, Claude Jones was replaced by the multi-instrumentalist Tyree Glenn. In the reeds, Chauncey Haughton, despite his uncanny ability to deliver Benny Goodman–influenced solos, was replaced by one of the finest lead alto saxophonists in the business, Hilton Jefferson, and Jerry Blake moved across to play second alto and clarinet.

The year in New York saw Cab's band slowly but surely reinforce its jazz credentials. Looking back wistfully on his time in the orchestra, something he still dreamed happily about every night until his old age, Doc Cheatham observed perceptively: "He had to change the band, because he knew he wouldn't be able to scream for the rest of his life."[39]

Chapter 8

Dizzy Atmosphere
1939–1941

....

The extended time that Cab and the band spent in New York during the 1939 World's Fair brought about some changes in Cab's own life. In 1937, after moving into the house that he and Betty had built in Riverdale, they decided to try to have a baby. The intention was to bring them closer, but this was in reality again papering over the cracks in their failing marriage. Although Cab was on the road for much of that year, they were together often enough for Betty to recognize that she was unable to conceive. Consequently, as Cab related in his autobiography, they decided to adopt a child. Betty wished to keep this decision secret from her social circle, and in an elaborate pretense she left town to "have the baby." She returned early in 1938 with two-month-old Constance.

From the very beginning of Constance's life, it became clear that all was not quite right with her. Betty and Cab sought advice from various medical specialists, but the unanimous conclusion was that Constance was educationally subnormal, and might never be able to live a fully independent life. Far from bringing Cab and Betty closer together, this was the wedge that finally pushed them apart. Cab recalled Constance as "a sweet, dark-haired little girl, struggling to cope with things."[1] Yet despite a degree of tenderness toward the girl, soon after her arrival Cab moved permanently out of the family home to live in a succession of New York hotel suites.

In effect, he and Betty lived separate lives from the spring of 1939 onward. Nevertheless, just as his older daughter, Camay, received monthly checks and was invited to see him while he was in New York, he felt a similar sense of responsibility for his new daughter. This meant that for the first few years of her troubled life he visited her frequently. But as the separation between him and Betty became ever more acrimonious, the visits got further and further apart, so that by the time Constance reached adulthood they seldom happened, and once she was in her thirties, she and her father lost touch completely.

Until he met his second wife, Nuffie, in 1942, Cab had, as Bennie Payne put it, "so many women you couldn't keep track of them."[2] He was a huge star by 1939 and during the previous twelve months, his had been the highest earning African American band, ahead of Louis Armstrong, Fats Waller, Chick Webb, Duke Ellington, and Jimmie Lunceford, with an average gross of seven thousand dollars per week.[3] Rich, successful, famous, Cab was clearly an attractive catch, and, becoming an ever more passionate womanizer, he took his pick from the best-looking Cotton Club chorus girls and Harlem's most fashionable females. But he met no one who kindled the affection he had felt for Zelma, nor who offered him the kind of fast-lane companionship he had originally enjoyed in Chicago with Betty.

In later life, apart from performing on stage with his third daughter, Chris, Cab was to keep his family life entirely separate from his professional life, and the seeds of this disciplined compartmentalization go back to 1939. From his nightly stage appearances, and the string of attractive companions on his arm, nobody would have guessed that the effervescent front man of the Cotton Club was going through a difficult patch in his personal life. The only clue to those who knew him well was that he used every opportunity to spend his free hours in the daytime at the racetrack. Habits were formed during that long season in New York that would stay with him into old age. For the most part his band members remained tight-lipped about Cab's sequence of girlfriends, but his fondness for going racing was a foible they all remembered. "He was perfect, personable," recalled Danny Barker, "and he had no vices other than, I think, them horses."[4]

From January until April he followed the races at Aqueduct in Queens, which in those days retained its faded Victorian grandeur, still looking very much the same as it had when it opened in 1894. (The track was dramatically remodeled in 1941, with a new clubhouse that became something of a second home to Cab.) From April until July, Cab went a little further afield to Belmont

Park at Elmont, on Long Island. Then, any time off that he could manage in August was spent upstate for the series of summer meetings at Saratoga Springs, before the fall saw him return to the late season at Belmont. It was an interesting year to be going racing in New York State as all the local tracks were progressively introducing the "pari-mutuel" system of betting, in which all bets of a specific type were pooled and the payout based on the size of the pool. There was considerable pressure applied to the owners of the tracks to outlaw illegal betting rackets, with the state threatening to close them down if they did not conform to the new standard. Empire City, Saratoga, Aqueduct and Belmont all brought in apparatus during the 1939 season so that they could start 1940 "fully equipped" to operate the new system. The advantage for Cab was that from now on, even when he was away on the road, he would be able to place "offtrack" bets exactly as if he were there in person.[5]

Given the opportunity, he always greatly preferred to be there in person, although those who met him in the clubhouse or the stands hardly recognized the extrovert character he normally displayed. Instead he studied form silently and intently, keeping to himself. He was not the only bandleader to behave differently when he reached the track, as his former manager Stan Scotland recalls:

> One day I met him at the track, I guess it was either Aqueduct or Belmont, and we were walking under the stands while he was looking at his racing form. Coming towards us is another gentleman, also with a racing form, and we're converging, when I see the other gentleman is Count Basie. Cab and Basie come close to each other, and I'm standing on the side. They don't even look up at each other, they're both looking at their racing forms, and they start to go, "Uh, huh," "Hmm, hmm," "Uh huh." Neither of them uses any language until they finally go, "Uh, huh, yeah." "Hmm, hmm, ok." Then Basie walks away, and they both know exactly what horse they're going to bet on in the next race. Basie goes right to the restroom. I say, "Cab, why's he going to the restroom, when the horses are coming on to the track?" Cab looks at me and he says, "Basie stays in the restroom for every single race, because he believes that's lucky."[6]

Cab did not share the passion for racing with any particular member of his own band, but since Ben Webster's departure, he had begun to socialize from time to time with his musicians, rather then remaining aloof as he had in the pre-Webster years. "You could get drunk with him and bring him home on your back (and I did that many a night)," recalled Bennie Payne, "but the next day when he raised his hand for the downbeat, he didn't want to know nothing about what happened the night before."[7]

Miraculously able to recover from the wildest nights on the town (his grandson Christopher Calloway Brooks recalls Cab sweating out his hangovers in the hottest and steamiest of shower baths), Cab's perfect stage presentation had now become second nature.[8] Cab's musicianship may have still been called into question by one or two of his bandsmen, but there was no doubting that he was extremely serious about discipline in the orchestra. During the long months on the road he mentored his men, helping them to maintain a smart appearance, dealing promptly with alcohol problems, forbidding marijuana (despite the subject matter of his most popular songs), and ensuring that gambling did not get out of control. When Milt Hinton lied to the road manager, Mr. Wright, to obtain an advance that was immediately won away from him in a gambling session with his bandmates, Cab read the riot act to his men, forbade Hinton from gambling, and saw that the money was paid back.[9] He urged his musicians to respect hotels, and not get into trouble, or make waves with local women. If they made a good impression wherever they played, then they would be likely to be asked back, unlike groups who trashed their accommodations and publicly made merry with the local maidenry.

Both on the road and in New York, Cab was a stickler for professional appearances, supplying several changes of band uniform, and insisting that his men wash between sets in order to look fresh and smell clean when they came on stage. According to Milt Hinton it was Cab's dislike of tiny flaws in shirts, undershirts, or socks that led to the band's private myth of an imaginary bat that ate up ragged clothes. It began with Cab sticking his finger in the hole and tearing until the garment was ruined, forcing his man to replace it. Soon the band took matters into their own hands—or at any rate fingers. "You better watch those holes, man, or the bat's gonna get you," was the remark when anyone spotted a flaw in a fellow musician's garments, and if the garment wasn't promptly replaced it was de rigueur for the man who had spotted the hole to insert his finger and pull, just as Cab would have done.[10] The bat was equally hungry when it came to hats that were becoming threadbare or greasy, back in those days when every well-dressed man was obliged to wear a hat, or what in jive talk was known as a "chapoo."

To keep up morale during the long New York season, the band's baseball team played regular matches. Danny Barker recalled them turning out against teams from other theaters, or playing waiters and busboys from neighboring hotels.[11] Cab was nicknamed "the general" by his men, but to his face he was called "Fess" or "Professor," the highest mark of respect by big band musicians for their leader.

One unusual reason for the growing bond between Cab and his men is that he and several of the band had become Freemasons. Apparently it was Doc Cheatham—already a Mason before he joined Cab—who instigated this, making the point that a national fellowship of friends and allies was no bad thing for a band that was constantly on the road. A friendly Masonic conductor on a train or a bus might help to alleviate the worst Jim Crow conditions of travel, and there might be similar privileges regarding accommodation. In the late 1930s, rather like the AFM local branch structure, Masonic lodges were segregated into black and white. For the most part, white grand lodges refused to acknowledge their black counterparts, despite the brotherly rules of the Masonic "craft," preferring to operate within the racially divided social mores of the time.[12] The African American Prince Hall lodges traced their history back to the eighteenth century, when a black Bostonian called Prince Hall and fourteen other free men of color were made master Masons in an Irish Constitution military lodge. In 1784, these men broke away to create the first African lodge, which in due course split from, but observed most of the practices of, Anglo-Irish Freemasonry.

It is estimated that in the decade when Cab and his men joined there were between five and six thousand black lodges in thirty-seven states, with around 750,000 members in all. During the spring of 1937, Cab, Milt Hinton, Ben Webster, and Garvin Bushell joined the Prince Hall Pioneer Lodge no. 1, in St. Paul, Minnesota. Keg Johnson joined soon afterward, and from time to time, further Calloway musicians were recommended and initiated as the band passed through the Minneapolis area. "There were enough of us in the band to have our own meetings on the road," recalled Hinton. "Sometimes backstage between shows we'd have a short meeting and conduct readings."[13]

The arrival of Dizzy Gillespie into the trumpet section in August 1939 brought in a character who did not so readily fit into the framework that Cab had established for himself and his men, either socially or musically. Some months after Dizzy had joined and proven himself as a soloist, he was recommended to join the Freemasons. However, almost certainly tipped off by another member of the band about the young trumpeter's hot temper and unstable character at the time, the lodge officials took against him and refused to accept his nomination. Apparently this was owing to the fact that his marriage certificate lacked an official signature.[14] The rejection symptomized a wider suspicion among the senior musicians of Gillespie, whose most heinous crimes were to play the fool on stage, despite being a naturally gifted musician, and to question many aspects of the band's life and work that had been taken for granted for years.

In particular it was the two most recently arrived high-profile soloists in the band who sought to keep Dizzy in his place—Chu Berry and Cozy Cole. Both of them were featured in the band-within-a-band, the Cab Jivers, playing a "jam interlude" in each show. The *Brooklyn Eagle* reported that the little group "includes bass, guitar, drums and sax, and beats out some nifty hits."[15] Berry's prowess was praised, along with Cole who had "the fastest pair of hands with drumsticks we have ever seen."[16] According to Dizzy, the members of the quartet—even including Hinton and Barker, who often practiced with him after hours—snubbed him, deliberately overlooking the idea of bringing his sparkling trumpet playing into the little group.

> When I came into the band, as far ahead as I was with that kinda shit, jump'n'jive, I would've gone right into the Cab Jivers, but Chu stopped it. There was a thing on his part against me, because I always respected Chu's playing. But he thought I was too young to have that important a job.[17]

In Dizzy's career, the two years he spent with Cab came at a time when he was still forming his own style. His 1937 records with Teddy Hill, notably a rousing version of "King Porter Stomp," show him to have mastered several elements of Roy Eldridge's style, and to be a promising soloist. By the time he arrived in the Calloway band he was starting the quest for a more complex style of his own, although it was not to be until 1943, some time after he left Cab, that his mature bebop style would come together fully. The result was that in live performance and on record with the Calloway band, his output is very uneven. Frequently there are solos that show more than an inkling of the great soloist he would become, but there are as many examples of solos that fail to coalesce, where bright ideas dissolve into nothing. This counted against him joining the Cab Jivers, which needed to rely on dependable quality from all its members to justify the solo space the group was given in Cab's shows.

Nevertheless, twenty-one-year-old Dizzy's entry into the lineup had a dramatic effect on the full band, which can be heard on the instrumental tracks from three successive recording sessions covering the time leading up to his arrival and his own first recording with Cab in August 1939.

Back in March of that same year, "Floogie Walk" sounds similar to the first instrumentals the band made after Chu Berry's arrival, save for the brisk rhythmic control of Cozy Cole. Mouse Randolph takes a typical but unadventurous Armstrong-tinged trumpet chorus, and there is space for Chauncey Haughton to emulate Benny Goodman at some length. The next session from July finds the trumpets without an effective soloist. Randolph has gone, Bauza is playing lead, and neither Collins nor Wright takes the spotlight on Earl Bostic's jaunty arrangement of "Trylon Swing." Again Haughton's clarinet is given plenty of space and there's a fine solo from Chu Berry. Also in July Cozy Cole cut his second major feature with the band, Edgar Battle's "Crescendo in Drums." Here, in between a succession of solo spots for the drums, Berry is prominently on show.

On August 30, the band made "Pluckin' the Bass," featuring Milt Hinton, written by Roy and Joe Eldridge and arranged by Chappie Willett. It is a tour de force of bass playing, with Hinton's percussive slapping accompanying his own ringing statement of an arpeggiated tune, but the other solo that leaps out for attention is Dizzy's. Berry and Haughton both play flawless swing choruses, but whereas these two men had brought something of a breath of fresh air into the band a year before, compared to Dizzy's fiery performance on this tune, they now sound predictable.

The take that was originally issued, with an athletic leap into the instrument's upper register in the second eight bars of Dizzy's solo, clearly suggests that a new and exciting style of trumpet playing had arrived in the band. There follow some repeated notes in which—rather as Lester Young was prone to do by using "false" fingering on the tenor saxophone—Dizzy uses different valve combinations to play the same note, subtly altering the timbre on each repetition. Dizzy powers into his upper register immediately on the second, even more confident take, although possibly because of a less well-formed solo from Berry, this remained unissued at the time. As well as positioning the repeated note and altered valving idea more effectively, this time around Dizzy incorporates some startling phrases borrowed from Eldridge, including a repeated figure that runs up and then down four semitones.

A pair of brief appearances on Cab's vocal numbers "For the Last Time I Cried over You" and "Twee-Twee-Tweet" from that same August date display

Dizzy's ability to make a strong statement when the chance arose. This effective use of limited solo space would not have incurred the ire of Berry and Cole, nor ultimately of Cab himself. But what none of them liked was that Dizzy was constantly pushing at the boundaries of his ability. Instead of "sitting there making that money," as Dizzy put it,[18] he was never content to do again what he had done before, as the two very different takes of "Pluckin' the Bass" demonstrate. "Diz's biggest problem," said Hinton, "was that he'd try playing things he couldn't technically handle. I'd often hear him start a solo he just couldn't finish."[19]

In Danny Barker's view this musical restlessness was because Dizzy found many of the arrangements trivial.[20] During late 1939, Cab was beginning to hire some of the best arrangers in the business, Edgar Battle, Earl Bostic, and Benny Carter among them. But Cab's biggest hits, the charts the band played most frequently, were mainly still the old arrangements by Foots Thomas or Harry White. These held little interest for a trumpeter who had only to look at a part once in order to memorize it. Quite naturally, Dizzy began experimenting. In the case of some big band trumpeters, such experiments came in the form of technical challenges. In the 1950s, Clark Terry became so familiar with the Ellington book that he taught himself to play it left-handed, and then with the trumpet turned upside down. He had a finger support soldered onto the left hand side of his horn so that he could play one-handed, and on some arrangements amused himself by playing alternate four measure sections on his trumpet (held left-handed) and his flugelhorn (held in his right).[21] This is comparable to Lammar Wright's excursions into the higher register in Cab's band, when he transposed his parts up an octave at sight. Yet in neither of these cases was the overall sound of the band compromised. Indeed it was part of the challenge to do something technically audacious and *not* be noticed. Dizzy on the other hand *wanted* to be noticed, as Bennie Payne recalled:

> From time to time during a performance, Dizzy would just take off in double time. Man it was wild. . . . Cab was very meticulous about music and he'd get mad as hell. "What the hell you trying to do with my band?" Cab would holler at Dizzy. Dizzy would just smile and all Cab could say was "Just play it the way it's written."[22]

Cab tried all his bandleader wiles on Dizzy—initially offering him substantial solo space, and then commissioning arrangements from him. But Dizzy's restless spirit was not appeased, and Cab became increasingly vexed as to what to do. Sometimes Dizzy coerced the whole trumpet section to "cut loose" from the written arrangements, adding spontaneous decorations and making simple riffs more complicated, which seldom improved them. In this he believed he was following the example of the altoist Hilton Jefferson, whose impromptu additions to the parts were so perfect that Cab complained when Jefferson's replacement, Rudy Powell, left them out.

Dizzy had a cruel streak in his character. He had left Edgar Hayes to join Cab in a row over money that ended in a scuffle in which the trumpeter deliberately smashed Hayes's spectacles. He carried a vicious-looking knife at all times. He was also the fount of many a practical joke. On the bus, spitballs were flicked, and sheets of cellophane stretched over sleeping musicians and then ignited. On stage Dizzy began to stand up behind Cab's vocals, miming football passes during the torch songs and ballads.[23] It seems his intention was to goad Cab into reacting, but in the end Cab simply concluded that Dizzy was "a pain in the neck," and out of sheer frustration gradually began to reduce his solo opportunities on record and in theater appearances. He also stepped up the frequency of his calls to Jonah Jones to see if he could be persuaded away from Stuff Smith's group to join the band. Cab was still unsuccessful, so despite being less frequently featured than when he first joined, Dizzy remained the band's principal trumpet soloist.

In the meantime, Cab produced some of his own most distinctive and successful records. The session of July 17, 1939, immediately prior to Dizzy's arrival, yielded two outstanding tracks. The first of them, "(Hep Hep!) The Jumping Jive," was another million-selling disc.[24] The tune was written by Cab and the pianist Frankie Froeba, and mixes jive-dictionary-style scat with call and response, except in this case the band responds both instrumentally and vocally. One neat touch is the collectively sung "hep, hep" riff behind Chu Berry's solo.

More extraordinary is the Yiddish-inspired vocal on "Utt-Da-Zay," a Jewish tailor's song, which Cab sings with conviction. African American gospel music and its choral responses were a major influence on "(Hep Hep!) The Jumping Jive." By contrast, "Utt-Da-Zay" has its roots in the argot that peppered the day-to-day speech of Irving Mills. His parents hailed from Odessa, and what the Yiddish scholar Hankus Netsky calls "the language of *meshugas*, *dzhlubs*, and *mamzers*" seasoned his vocabulary. Since 1931, elements of Mills's linguistic heritage had been subconsciously absorbed into Cab's scatting. When Mills teamed up in 1939 with his fellow Jewish songwriter Samuel "Buck" Ram (later an influential figure in doo-wop, working with the Platters), they endeavored to craft a jazz song that drew on the kind of Yiddish folk melodies with which both writers had grown up. Historian Martin S. Jaffee in his 2009 study of postethnic American Judaism discusses the considerable common ground between African American music and cantoral traditions. He suggests that Jewish immigrants arriving in jazz age America found black music to be a constant sound track to their daily life, saying, "Soon they discovered that the mournful minor key of the synagogue's cantoral tradition made sweet harmony with that weeping blue note forged in Southern cotton fields." He then poses the question as to whether music by a Jewish songwriting team such as the Gershwin brothers (or in Cab's case Buck Ram and Irving Mills) "had its birth in a hasidic wedding in Vitebsk, or in some humid Storyville bordello?" It would be hard to better his response that "Cab Calloway had shown the answer is both/and, turning his signature tune 'hi-dee-hi-dee-ho' into an evocative scat of Ashkenazi cantorial virtuosity in his Yiddish number 'Utt-Da-Zay.' "[25]

The scales and a capella melodies of Jewish cantors, as well as occasional Yiddish words, had been one of many elements in Cab's remarkable arsenal of scat devices. Consequently there are distinct parallels with the sounds of the synagogue in some of the improvised lines that he uses in passing during several "minor moaners" associated with Minnie the Moocher and her friends. However, "Utt-Da-Zay" is the first example of Cab picking up and maintaining such a theme throughout an entire recorded performance. Even the instrumental ensemble choruses at the end retain the minor mood, with the strong riffs behind Chu Berry's impassioned solo recalling the Benny Goodman band's interpretation of the Yiddish tradition in "Bei mir bist du schön."

Following the success of this piece, Cab added other similar numbers to his repertoire, "A Bee Gezindt," recorded in November 1939, "Who's Yehoodi?" cut the following spring, and "Nain, Nain," from November 1941. In his daughter Camay's view, this was because such songs appealed to a very distinct element of his listening public:

He had this great Jewish following. A lot of Jewish people came to see him. Nowadays, in the black community, if I say I'm Cab Calloway's daughter it doesn't really mean that much. Among Jewish people, if I say the same thing, they just go crazy. "Oh Cab Calloway, I loved him!" That kind of thing. He had a few Jewish songs, like "Utt-Da-Zay," that he did. And that public was so faithful to him, and would just come wherever he would perform.[26]

As the years went on, Cab worked his cantoral impression into some of his mainstream repertoire, most noticeably in his 1947 signature song, "The Hi-De-Ho Man," which starts with two long melismatic phrases straight out of the synagogue, before settling into a medium swing bounce, and reverting to Harlem jive talk.

Not long after Cab first recorded "Utt-Da-Zay," he made his most successful foray into Cuban territory. With Mario Bauzá leading the brass, and taking over the arranging duties, "Chili Con Conga," from October 1939 is a huge improvement over the previous year's "The Congo Conga." The bongo drums and shakers return in force, but unlike Leroy Maxey, Cozy Cole has no fear of the underlying Latin rhythm, his tom-toms and hi-hat anchoring everything with confidence and verve. For this Bauzá was largely responsible. "I'd stay up with Dizzy and the band's drummer Cozy Cole," he wrote, "teaching them how to feel some of the simpler Cuban rhythms. Dizzy would sing the drum patterns, using nonsense syllables."[27]

Over Cole's percussion introduction, Cab starts with some authentic sounding Hispanic banter with Bauzá before leading into a vocal as effectively tinged with Cuban atmosphere as his Yiddish songs are charged with cantoral melancholy. When the brass sections take over for the last minute of the disc, their stabs, filling phrases, and final riffs sound authentically Cuban. This was no doubt because Bauzá and his eager pupil Dizzy Gillespie were ardent sitters-in with the Cuban band of flautist Alberto Socarras, which played opposite them in the World's Fair edition of the Cotton Club revue.[28] There is a similarly authentic feel to the Calloway band's recording of the bolero "Vuelva."

The same session's "Tarzan from Harlem" is a calculated attempt to fuse Cab's hi-de-ho call and response with the kind of driving drumming that Gene Krupa had used on pieces such as Benny Goodman's "Sing Sing Sing." Cab's upwardly mobile Tarzan cries are answered by the band, and later in the disc he delves into his bag of scat effects, but the central instrumental passage is a hard-swinging tom-tom heavy section that accurately emulates the Krupa-Goodman sound.

This session makes it clear that Cab's efforts to reform the band had paid off. The material recorded as the year in New York drew to a close required his men to be musical chameleons, but everything was played with a degree of polish and sophistication that no previous incarnation of the orchestra had managed on such a consistent level. On Cab's own characteristic scat songs—represented on this session by a novelty called "Jiveformation, Please," which requires him to "shoot the lingo" to his audience—the band is brilliantly well disciplined. This time it is Cab who becomes the chameleon. Assuming the character of Professor Calloway, he draws on another influence in his banter when he "lays down a few phrases" that are directly borrowed from Slim Gaillard. Indeed Cab's quick ear for dialogue actually leads him to imitate Gaillard, which he does brilliantly, including a tiny stumble over "dug this jive" in the penultimate phrase that captures Gaillard's studiously offhand delivery and the cadences of his made-up language, "vout," to perfection.

The long stint at the Cotton Club—which, because the club closed for good the following summer, turned out to be the band's final engagement there—came to an end on September 23, 1939. Even then, the band lingered not far from home, and a week in Hartford, Connecticut, was followed by engagements in theaters in the Bronx, on Broadway, and in Jamaica, Queens. So it was not until late October that the "Jumpin' Jive Man" and his Cotton Club revue, with a sizable cast, set off for Akron, Ohio, and a tour of the Midwest.

In the publicity sent out by Mills, the vocal group the Chocolateers was given name billing, as were Sister Rosetta Tharpe, Chu Berry, Cozy Cole, and the Cab Jivers. Interestingly Tharpe—originally a Pentecostal evangelist but now specializing in a mixture of gospel and blues, billed as "swinging the Southlands"—was featured every night on a most unholy composition. As the Brooklyn press reported during the Bronx engagement, "Sister Tharpe clicks most strongly with a novelty tagged 'Hot Dog, That Made Him Mad.'"[29] This slightly risqué song was written by Cab's guitarist Danny Barker, and he had recorded it the year before with his wife, Blue Lu Barker, and the Fly Cats, featuring Henry "Red" Allen. The lyrics concern a girl who suspects her man of cheating on her, so she goes out with "the best friend he ever had." Audiences hooted with merriment at the pious figure of Sister Tharpe emphasizing every scrap of double entendre in "he'll kiss you and he'll squeeze you and *please* you, and ask you not to do it again."

The band plus its attendant revue was back in New York for a week at the Apollo Theatre before Christmas, but the new year of 1940 found it in Newark, in Boston, and traveling the Pennsylvania industrial belt, before it fetched up in Chicago in early March for a sequence of shows at the Regal Theatre.

There was sufficient time in the Windy City to fit in a record session as well, and on March 8 the band headed for the studios.

At the Regal, as it often did in regional theaters, the band played opposite current movies. In Chicago, the opening features were *Intermezzo*, starring Leslie Howard, and *Everything Happens at Night*, with Sonja Henie.[30] It was no doubt because of the popularity of a well-known film detective opposite whose movies the band was often required to play that it cut "Chop Chop Charlie Chan" at this record session. There were already twenty-three Charlie Chan pictures by the spring of 1940, and during the course of that year the newly hired Sidney Toler, who took over the role of Chan, would add four more to the franchise with *Charlie Chan in Panama, Charlie Chan's Murder Cruise, Charlie Chan at the Wax Museum,* and *Murder over New York.* The film plots were simplistic and improbable. Charlie's huge family of children usually helped their father solve the case. The Calloway song was designed to go over well with moviegoing fans of the detective, although it was a blatant excuse for Cab to indulge in yet another extended vocal in fake Chinese. The idea was to appeal to the best of both worlds—Calloway fans who would roar with laughter at his Chan impression, and fans of the detective who would howl with appreciation at the mere mention of their celluloid hero.

More interesting musically is that this was the session when Dizzy Gillespie's two principal arrangements for the band were recorded. At this point, seven months into Dizzy's tenure with the band, Cab was still relatively enthusiastic about his young recruit. He hoped to flatter the young trumpeter and win his support by recording two instrumental features that he had composed, namely "Pickin' the Cabbage" and "Paradiddle" (the latter designed to feature Cozy Cole). Yet Cab's efforts to rein in Dizzy's clowning and disaffection were in all probability not the only reasons for this timing. In the months leading up to the session another trumpeter had increasingly been getting a very positive press— namely Dizzy's idol Roy Eldridge. Knowing that he had a musician in his ranks who was capable of sounding uncannily like Eldridge, it behooved Cab to feature Dizzy, in the hope of rivaling this new star, or at any rate, capturing some of his reflected glory. In late 1939, when Eldridge was top of the bill at the Apollo, he had received glowing reviews:

> The band is headed by "the all American swing trumpet star," Roy Eldridge. Eldridge has been called one of the greatest trumpeters of all times. . . . The fact that the band is under the same management as

Louis Armstrong prevents me from saying that Eldridge is better than Armstrong, but thousands of people think so.[31]

Dizzy's trumpet solos on the two instrumental scores that he provided display relatively little evidence of his ability to play like Eldridge, yet both are fascinating for reasons that have nothing to do with his trumpet playing. Ironically, Cab was never to make a commercial recording that really did display Dizzy's playing at its best, although unofficial airshot records of the band's live broadcasts show just how effective a solo trumpeter he could be when the band was stretching out on its jazziest arrangements.

"Pickin' the Cabbage" demonstrates the Calloway band's professionalism at sight-reading a new piece of music in a somewhat unfamiliar genre and making something distinctive out of it. Dizzy himself felt that the number "had some effect on Cab's band. . . . A careful listening to 'Pickin' The Cabbage' will show you the musical direction I'd follow for the rest of my career."[32] Like Dizzy's later composition "Night in Tunisia," it is a musical sandwich, consisting of a Latin-tinged outer section over an ostinato bass with a middle eight in swing time. The middle also involves a switch from the prevailing E-flat minor to its relative major. The Latin/swing and major/minor contrasts, coupled with the idea of an implied Latin beat, were indeed areas that Dizzy was to explore in other later pieces, including "Algo Bueno" and "Manteca."

It is absurd to say as Dizzy did in his autobiography that this was "possibly the first use of polyrhythms in our music since the very beginning of jazz." Nevertheless the repeated bass pattern shared by Milt Hinton and Andy Brown's baritone sax is far from straightforward, with Brown's honks and supporting rimshots from Cozy Cole fractionally anticipating the fourth beat of every measure in a way that is almost impossible to notate. Over the ostinato, Jerry Blake's clarinet and Dizzy's muted trumpet play a theme that stresses a slightly anticipated first beat of each bar, so that theme and ostinato together imply a sense of contrary motion. The combination of these two sets of accents placed respectively ahead of the first and last beats creates an effective Latin feel.

In Dizzy's own solo, he attempts something a little more complicated than he is able to complete. The first sixteen measures are dramatic, but a brilliant flourish that ushers in the middle eight is followed up by some rather lame swing phrasing. Even so, the vision revealed by the whole piece is impressive, and the use of four parallel eleventh and thirteenth chords in the opening is more modernistic than the band's everyday fare.

Although "Paradiddle" was principally a vehicle for Cozy Cole, there is some equally adventurous harmonic writing tucked away in that arrangement. In the band's archive, only the second and third trumpet parts of this chart survive. The distinctive vertical hand (with the stems slightly separate from the noteheads) is Dizzy's own, and it bears little resemblance to all the other surviving music in the easily identifiable writing styles of Harry White, Eddie Barefield, Andy Gibson, and so on. Throughout the first and second measures of the main theme, which follows a four-bar introduction, the two trumpet parts descend in parallel intervals of a flatted fifth. This interval, because of its growing fascination for Dizzy and his generation of nascent bebop players, is almost as distinctive a signature as the handwriting itself. It is doubtful whether "Pickin' the Cabbage" was played frequently or even at all on live dates, but judging by the dog-eared state of the parts, "Paradiddle," numbered 102 in the pad, clearly got plenty of use. It was the most effective of all the pieces written to feature Cole, and as one of the two instrumentalists billed by name in Cab's band (Berry being the other), he would have played it often.

There are hints in these two arrangements of the kind of harmonic language that Dizzy would ultimately bring to the development of bebop. In the next year or so, whenever he did get an allocation of solo space on a Calloway disc there are signs that he was moving beyond the influence of Roy Eldridge to lay the foundations for his own improvisational vocabulary. This process was accelerated after he met the alto saxophonist Charlie Parker on a visit to Kansas City with the band in June 1940.

During the band's final weeks at the Cotton Club in 1939 and subsequently backstage at almost every theater they played thereafter, Dizzy took aside Milt Hinton and often Danny Barker as well, to practice with him, and to try out chord substitutions and altered changes. Hinton was sure that it all began right after Dizzy joined in August 1939:

> In the intermissions at the Cotton Club (we did two shows every night, one at eight o'clock and another at eleven thirty) and after the eight o'clock show, the guys would go out drinking and hanging around, but Dizzy and I would sit around and start talking about changes. Dizzy . . . was picking up on all the new changes and substitution chords. We were now beginning to use an A minor instead of a C chord, emphasizing the A in there which is the sixth. . . . So, as it was summer time, we'd go up on the roof of the Cotton Club, up a little stairway from backstage, a

winding fire stairway, and I would take my bass, and we would practise what he was telling me about. He'd show me these new changes. We'd get off at three o'clock and we'd go to Minton's which was up in Harlem, to play there.[33]

Once the band was on the road, the process went on, as Danny Barker recalled:

Dizzy would ask Hinton and sometimes myself to come into one of the empty theater rooms and play experiments. Hinton would always join Dizzy. After a while I would give an excuse, because the more we would jam and discuss music in depth I began to find myself sitting there listening holding my guitar on my lap. . . . Diz was playing extensions, exercises in a whole new dimension. I would figure on playing chords that would be strange to some people, but would be correct with his extensions chord-wise. I'd grip a tonic chord, listen, move up and down the fingerboard. He would say, "That's right what you're doing." But I had never heard it before.[34]

Barker noticed that when he used these substitutions, Bennie Payne, fine musician that he was, did not seem interested or make any attempt to alter the written chords when Dizzy and Hinton momentarily modified the harmony during Dizzy's solos. Equally, Cozy Cole could instantly master the off-center accents in "Pickin' the Cabbage," but otherwise took little notice of the innovations of Dizzy's former colleague in the Teddy Hill band, Kenny Clarke. These new ideas involved moving the core timekeeping function to the cymbals, leaving the snare and bass drum free to drop in accents that fitted the unorthodox contours of a soloist's melodic lines. Cole preferred to focus on his snare technique, constantly assaulting his practice pad offstage to ensure that he played his features and ornamented the band's regular arrangements to perfection. "When Diz was playing his things to come," remembered Barker, "he was machine-gunned with Cole's military diddles."[35]

What does survive, however, in the occasional solos by Dizzy that were included in the band's recordings from late 1939 until early 1941 is an opportunity to chart the early development of this exceptional trumpeter, as he worked out many of the elements that would coalesce into his full-fledged style in the mid-1940s. At the time, Cab referred to Dizzy's more extreme solos as

"Chinese music,"[36] although in later life he acknowledged that the young trumpeter had been an exceptional musician. High points in the records include Dizzy's beautifully sculpted solo in "Topsy Turvy" from May 1940, a masterpiece of high speed dexterity on "Bye Bye Blues" from the following month, a darkly brooding solo in the sinister chromatic and whole-tone landscape of Don Redman's "Cupid's Nightmare" from a July 1940 broadcast, and the prototype of one of his triplet-based bebop runs in "Boo-Wah Boo-Wah" from August the same year.

It seems also that Cab was not sufficiently encouraged by the results of recording Dizzy's first two charts for the band to invite him to do any more. Apparently at Chu Berry's suggestion, he commissioned instead a number of pieces from Benny Carter. In between leading his own bands, Carter was one of New York's most accomplished freelance arrangers. When Cab's band was briefly back in New York in May 1940 it recorded two of his charts, "The Lone Arranger" and "Calling All Bars." The first of these was actually the subject of an abortive session on May 15, 1940, but the version from three days later that was eventually issued shows the band's discipline has tightened up immensely on this complex chart, so much so that it sounds deceptively easy. According to Milt Hinton, Cab originally wished to rehearse the band through the new material himself, but Chu Berry (who is featured on the piece) suggested bringing in Carter instead. It is probable that what has survived from May 15 are Carter's rehearsal takes, and the final recording from May 18th is the end result of his work, directed by Cab. In any event, the sinuous reed melody and brass stabs are characteristic of Carter's best writing from the period, and are played with great precision and drive.[37]

"Calling All Bars" was actually composed by Leonard Feather, the British critic, pianist, and occasional bandleader. Although Feather continued to write for various papers and magazines as an "impartial" critic, he had been signed up earlier in 1940 by Irving Mills to "a long-term songwriting contract."[38] Under it, Feather was to deliver twenty-four titles a year for Mills's Exclusive Publications imprint, and in return, Mills ensured the music would be recorded. Again Carter provided a thoroughly professional chart, intelligently crafted, and a great improvement over Feather's earlier recording of the same piece with his Sextet of the Rhythm Club of London. *DownBeat*'s Dave Dexter praised the "clever Benny Carter arrangement," and concluded that "the band isn't as bad as most musicians make it out to be."[39] Such derisory asides became typical of the 1940s jazz press, which looked down on the commercialism of Cab's singing much as "Mike" of the *Melody Maker* had criticized Ellington's less artistic efforts in the 1920s.

Unfortunately, having commissioned Carter to write these excellent charts, Cab was not impressed by the size of his bill. Instead of the thirty dollars or so Cab usually paid for an arrangement, Carter charged a hundred dollars apiece, plus his rehearsal time. Although the band loved playing this challenging music, Cab was so incensed that he never called the tunes on a live session. It was left to Foots Thomas and Jerry Blake as straw bosses to squeeze them into the occasional first and last sets when the band was playing for dancers before or following Cab's own appearances on stage.[40]

The growing volume of instrumentals in his book seems to have given Cab ideas of what he might be able to achieve as a composer himself. Maybe spurred on by the success of Benny Goodman's Carnegie Hall concert, or perhaps by the subsequent success of John Hammond's "Spirituals to Swing" events, he suddenly announced in the spring of 1940 that he had his own ambitions to create music for the concert hall. The press reported:

> For the past three months, Calloway has spent every available hour work-ing on a symphony, which is tentatively titled "Symphony in Swing Time." Cab hopes to introduce it at Carnegie Hall in New York City. . . . "Paul Whiteman is the inspiration for me wanting to compose a symphony," said Cab, "but unlike Paul's association with George Gershwin's 'Rhap-sody in Blue' which is really not jazz but light classical, my symphony will frankly be jazz. When it is completed I am going to submit it to Leopold Stokowski."[41]

Nothing appears ever to have come of these rather grandiose plans, and the article may well have been based on a fanciful press release from the Irving Mills office of the type that he and Jimmy McHugh used to confect in the 1920s. Nevertheless, a few months later the band did record one piece that comes close to being, if not a minisymphony, then at least a single-movement concerto for bassist Milt Hinton. Andy Gibson wrote "Ebony Silhouette" for Hinton in January 1941. The piece opens with a slowly and dramatically bowed introduction, followed soon afterward by some brisk upwardly moving pizzicato phrases. Thereafter arco and pizzicato sections alternate, and the band sup-ports Hinton's playing just as a classical orchestra would do for a string soloist. As an arco player he has somewhat better intonation than Ellington's more famous bassist Jimmy Blanton, and if his pizzicato phrasing lacks Blanton's urgency, it has an unhurried charm of its own.

In the second half of 1940 and the early part of 1941, the band produced some of Cab's most enduring vocals, including "Are You Hep to the Jive," "A Chicken Ain't Nothin' but a Bird," and "Are You All Reet?" as well as cutting several instrumental discs of a very high order. Fast or slow, these were mainly built around the tenor saxophone of Chu Berry. His most famous solo "(I Don't Stand) a Ghost of a Chance" was made in July 1940, and was rapturously received by the critics. *DownBeat* rightly praised Cab for giving "Chu Berry a whole side to demonstrate his ability on tenor. 'Ghost' is all Chu, and wonderful Chu, but sounding in spots like he has been influenced considerably by Hawkins of late."[42] Yet the same reviewer cannot resist getting in a typical jazz critic's dig at the bandleader, who sings on the other side of the record: "Except for Cab, some nice jazz here." Berry was also extensively featured on "Lonesome Nights" from August 1940, which is another Benny Carter composition. This was almost certainly one of the batch of pieces for which Cab overpaid, that he no doubt recorded (even if they were not featured on live shows) to earn back some of the cost of the arrangement!

After its traditional New Year in Chicago, the band returned to California for the first time since *The Singing Kid* in 1936. It was a demonstration of how successfully Cab had been able to cross over the color line in respect to his audiences that he was booked into Topsy's Roost, an exclusive Hollywood night club. "It will be the first engagement for Cab on the coast in several years," ran one of the reports, "and the first time Topsy's which caters to white patronage, has booked an eastern colored name band for such a long engagement. The Calloway organization is scheduled to remain until well into spring."[43]

As it turned out, the engagement, though successful, lasted just one week, and by March 5, 1941, the band was back in a New York recording studio. The return east was a landmark for Cab, because as soon as the band returned from California, Mario Bauzá left the lineup to join Machito's Cuban band. This was the moment that Jonah Jones, deciding that it was in the interests of his health to seek a change from Stuff Smith's obligatory diet of reefer and whisky, finally acceded to Cab's blandishments. He said:

> Cab had been after me before, but now I told him I would join. Then, contrary to my expectations, I found I liked the band and stayed with Cab eleven years until 1952. When I joined, Cab said: "Jonah, there's

just three things I want: play my music, be on time and wear my uniforms." So I did that and we got on fine.[44]

Although Jones was obviously aware of how long Cab had been urging him to
join, he probably did not stop to consider how Dizzy Gillespie might have felt,
being usurped as the band's principal soloist. Owing to Dizzy's increasingly
irritating behavior, Cab was not in the least sensitive to his feelings, and was
very anxious to make Jonah feel at home. As a result the new man was treated
with a degree of privilege that had never been extended to Dizzy. Not only was
he heavily featured in the stage show, but Cab celebrated his arrival in song.
Jones recalled:

> He had Buster Harding . . . write a chart for me called "Jonah joins the
> Cab." I never thought that would happen. Cab would sing, "Here comes
> Jonah, blowing on his trumpet," and I'd walk round in front of the band
> and I'd do a chorus in F, one in F sharp, one in G, and so on 'til I ended
> up in C. I was the first one ever to do that, to go out in front on my own
> and have Cab announce my name.[45]

In fact Chu Berry and Cozy Cole had both been featured by name in publicity
and on stage for some years by early 1941, but it was certainly true that Jones
was the first member of the trumpet section since Ed Swayze to interact
directly with Cab on stage. The song was recorded on March 5, which suggests
that Cab had made the arrangements for Jones to join him during the period
that the band was away in the West, and having scribbled out some ideas for
the lyrics, he commissioned Harding's chart accordingly.

When Jones came into the section, Dizzy's bebop experiments were still
going on. Jones found Hinton and Dizzy disappearing off into practice rooms
to work on chords, just as they had done at the Cotton Club almost two years
before. "Cab didn't like it," said Jones. "Dizzy'd do something different in his
solos and Cab'd say, 'I don't want that.' Then Dizzy'd do it again, and Cab would
say, 'Give that chorus to Jonah!' "[46] In an attempt to help Jones to understand
what he was doing, Dizzy coerced Jones to join him and Hinton in their practice regimen. He also took Jones to hear Charlie Parker. But as soon as evidence of Jones's new listening habits crept into his soloing, Cab threatened to
fire him, and Jonah reverted to his own habitual style. Dizzy's solos became
fewer and further between on record once Jonah was in the lineup.

As well as starring in Buster Harding's solo vehicle for him, Jones was also featured on a sparkling trumpet chorus on Cab's vocal feature "Geechy Joe," recorded at the same session. As the song went on to become part of Cab's stage repertoire, Jones would finish his nightly solo on a spectacular high E flat, and he usually played his chorus with his eyes closed. Unbeknownst to him, Cab worked up a routine with his baton in which he pointed higher and higher as Jones's trumpet ascended the scale. On one occasion Jones came to work with a hangover, and simply could not face making his usual stratospheric finale. He opened his eyes to witness Cab's clear disapproval, and as soon as they were offstage Cab asked angrily what had happened to the high note. When Jonah explained, Cab told him he *always* expected to hear that note, and whatever he had been up to the night before was no excuse. It was one of the very few moments of friction between the two men for the next eleven years.[47]

The summer of 1941 was spent in New York and Chicago, with long engagements at the Panther Room of the Sherman Hotel in Chicago and the Strand Theater off Times Square in New York. These featured the cast of forty with whom Cab planned to make his autumn tour. Cozy Cole and Chu Berry still received prominent billing, and in the revue were the long-serving "aristocrat of Harlem" Avis Andrews, roller skater Otto Eason, the comedians Moke and Poke, and the "twelve dizzy feet" of "Cab's boys and girls."[48]

As the long hot summer continued, to break the monotony of its theater routine, the band made a number of records, including a remake of Cab's early hit "St. James Infirmary," and "Hey Doc," in which Cab's vocal partner was his recently recruited trombonist Tyree Glenn. On both of these Jonah Jones was given the lion's share of the solo space, although Dizzy Gillespie made the most of a series of short cameos on an instrumental version of "Take the A-Train," with his "horn bursting through for short solo bits," as *DownBeat* put it.[49] But this was almost the last time Dizzy was to be featured on record with Cab. The band made a final visit to the New York studios on September 10, before beginning its fall tour with a long weekend at the State Theatre in Hartford, Connecticut.

During this engagement an event occurred that caused Dizzy to leave the band for good, handing the baton of principal trumpet soloist to Jonah Jones once and for all. Already, the Mills press office was sending out advance publicity that billed Dizzy as providing "the comic relief, both on and off the bandstand," although it qualified this by saying that he was "rated as a truly great trumpeter with further greatness predicted as he matures."[50] The inference to be drawn from this is that Dizzy's clowning had intensified during the six and a half months that Jonah Jones had been in the band. In any event, a combination of Dizzy's clowning and the long weeks spent playing the same show over the summer had led the band to indulge in an uncharacteristic amount of horseplay during Cab's act, including chewing up wads of paper and flicking the resulting spitball onto the stage.

At Hartford, this continued, and on Sunday, September 21, as the small Cab Jivers group was out front, with Cab in the wings, it seemed an ideal opportunity to the brass section, as they sat idle, to see if they could aim a spitball onto the edge of the spotlit area of the stage. Milt Hinton was taking a solo on "Girl of My Dreams," using a few unusual chord substitutions that he and Dizzy had been working on, when he fluffed the notes at the end of his solo. As he finished, Dizzy held his nose, as if to say "You stink!" meanwhile fanning away an imaginary smell with his other hand. At precisely the same time, Jonah Jones propelled a wad of slimy paper onto the stage, where it landed close to Hinton's feet. Cab looking up from the wings to see the cause of the commotion saw Dizzy's waving hand and naturally assumed that the band's inveterate clown had thrown the spitball, although for once in his life Dizzy was innocent.

As the curtain came down at the end of the act, Cab, his temper up, accused Dizzy of throwing the spitball, but Dizzy protested his innocence, saying, "Fess! I didn't do it!" The tough side of Cab—invisible during his shows—came to the fore and he raised his fist against Dizzy, whereupon the young trumpeter drew his knife. Hinton had just put his bass back on the stand when he saw what was happening.

> I tell you, Cab would have been long gone if I hadn't been there. Dizzy was larger than I, but I just interfered with the blow as he was striking Cab with the knife. Cab grabbed Dizzy's wrist and the two of them began to scuffle, and it took the two big pachyderms, Chu Berry and Benny Payne, to pull them apart. When Cab got back to the dressing room, he found his beautiful white suit had red all the way down the pants. When I interfered with the knife I'd stopped it going in his body, but it had gone in his leg. He came back up and told the fellows, "This kid cut me!" and he told Dizzy to get his horn and get out.[51]

Although Dizzy was waiting to meet the band bus when it dropped the cast of the revue off at the Theresa Hotel in Harlem in the small hours of Monday morning, Cab was in no mood for forgiveness. When the band opened at the Strand Theater in Brooklyn on the Tuesday, Shad Collins was back in his old seat in the trumpet section, and Dizzy was no longer part of the organization.

Musically, the casual listener to the band would hardly have noticed the difference between the way the band sounded in Hartford and the way it sounded in Brooklyn. Cab, as ever, was the center of attention with his finely honed act. Dizzy's role had radically diminished since 1940, and Jonah Jones was unquestionably the trumpet star. Chu Berry and Cozy Cole were still the other featured soloists. A report in *DownBeat* confirmed that Cab had taken ten stitches in his posterior, which somewhat curtailed his dancing, but also proffered the opinion that, with Collins back in the brass section, it was "the best band of [Cab's] career."[52] This is borne out by the reviews of the band's shows in the early part of October, as it wound its way through the Midwest.

> Maestro Cab's music is definitely tempoed for jitterbugs and his sendin' jive and barrelhouse boogie had swing addicts bouncing in their seats. It would be unfair to say that Cab is the whole show, but the fact is he seems to be all over the stage, putting his touch on all proceedings and enjoying it as much as anyone. He pours forth his talents as master of ceremonies, singer, actor, and general factotum and contributes much of comedy and music to the show.
>
> Those whose ears are not attuned to barbaric rhythms, the bleatings of hot trumpets and the hammer-like beating of the drums will not relish the show. Alligators and hep-cats however will vote it a "killer diller." The show has freshness, forthrightness and sincerity and there is a certain charm about boogie woogie that has power to please and offers a pleasant change from the more standard brands of swing and sweet music.
>
> New jive numbers and bang up arrangements of old rhythms make up a good share of the show, and there is a vigorous drumming of that old master Cozy Cole and the trumpeting [*sic*] of Chu Berry.[53]

One can forgive a provincial newspaper reporter for mixing up Jonah Jones and Chu Berry, but what comes across from this is a confirmation of *DownBeat*'s assessment, that the band was in top form. Cab's energetic act, his choice of repertoire, and his featured sidemen communicated easily to a general (and multiracial) audience, and he looked set to move into 1942 by consolidating his position as the most popular of all African American big band leaders.

Just two weeks later, all that was under threat. On October 27 the Associated Press wired a report from Conneaut, Ohio, to say that Leon Barry [*sic*] and Andrew Brown, both saxophonists with Cab Calloway, had been injured in a road accident when their car struck a concrete bridge. "Barry, the driver, was taken to hospital with a possible skull fracture, cuts and bruises."[54]

In fact the car was Lammar Wright's and Andy Brown was the driver. Chu Berry was the front-seat passenger. Because this stage of the band tour was by bus, the three of them had elected to use the car as a more convenient and comfortable way to travel, with the chance to stop off and see friends for an hour or two here and there on the way. After leaving Youngstown, where they had played a dance, they were heading for Buffalo, when Brown nodded off at the wheel. The Calloway bus happened on the accident shortly after it occurred and picked up Wright and Brown, shaken but unhurt. But Berry, who had been thrown clear of the car, needed hospital attention.

That night the band played Buffalo with just Foots Thomas on tenor. Cab came into the dressing room at the end of the gig to tell his men that Chu Berry had died in the hospital earlier that evening. It was the tragic demise of one of the greatest saxophone talents in jazz, and also of the man who had been a key element in the gradual reform of the Calloway band, consolidating its position as a genuine jazz orchestra at the highest level.

Chapter 9

Cruisin' with Cab
1941–1948

....

E veryone in the band was devastated by Berry's sudden and unexpected
death. "We were the family," recalled Cab. "His death struck each of us
in a different way. For me it was like losing a brother, someone I had
joked with and hollered at. There was a quiet around the band for weeks."[1]
Berry, with his bulky frame, oddly fitting suits, and his small spectacles perched
on the end of his nose, was a huge character, and his passing left a great void
both musically and socially among his colleagues. Yet in a professional organization like the touring Cotton Club Revue, the show had to go on.

After the Buffalo gig on October 28, the Calloway band was scheduled to
return to New York City for a few days. Although Cab suggests in his autobiography that Chu Berry's chair was left empty, this was not the case for more than
a couple of nights. By November 3, when the band was booked into the recording studio in New York, Teddy McRae had joined from Ella Fitzgerald's band,
where he had been the straw boss during the months following Chick Webb's
death. At the same time, Russell Smith, former lead trumpeter with Fletcher
Henderson and Benny Carter, was also drafted to bolster the trumpets to four
men, taking over the job that Cheatham and Bauzá had previously held, leaving
Jones and Collins free to take the solos, and Wright to balance the section.[2]

McRae was not the caliber of tenor saxophone soloist that Berry had been,
so an immediate consequence was that Cab took the opportunity to reorganize
the Cab Jivers. Danny Barker, Milt Hinton, and Cozy Cole remained, but now

the band became a sextet, with Jonah Jones leading the proceedings on trumpet, with Tyree Glenn doubling on trombone and vibes, as well as providing the occasional vocal, and McRae making up the front line. "They step out on their specialty jam on 'Twelfth Street Rag,'" ran one early report of the new group's feature spot on the revue, "and stir an excited welcome."[3] McRae and Russell Smith were both also on hand when the full band took to the streets in Harlem on November 4, and played at a political rally for Mayor La Guardia at Colonial Park, on Broadhurst Avenue. In front of a crowd of twenty thousand, Cab directed a version of "From the Halls of Montezuma," which was La Guardia's theme song.[4]

Nobody listening to the confident, assured sound of the band from its November 3 recording date would guess that it had suffered a major loss only days before. On Buster Harding's joyous instrumental arrangement of "Tappin' Off," the enlarged brass section makes the most of some stabbing punctuations, made even more brilliant by some neatly executed lip trills, while the reeds, admirably led by Hilton Jefferson, play with perfect precision. Jonah Jones and Cozy Cole indulge in a little phrase swapping before Jones powers upward into an Armstrong-inspired solo complete with some impressive glissandi. Cab himself banters his way through the "Mermaid Song," and produces some impressive cantoral wails on "Nain, Nain." Another recent introduction to the band had been a male voice close-harmony group to back up Cab's singing. The Palmer Brothers had first recorded with him in July 1941, and on this November session they added their sounds to "Who Calls?"

At the end of the year, following a three-week stint at the New Kenmore Theater in New York City, Cab formalized the idea of touring with a male vocal quartet. So from December 1941 the "Cabaliers" became part of his traveling revue and also a regular feature of his record sessions. African American male voice quartets had their roots in the folk music of the nineteenth century. The writer James Weldon Johnson recalled that during his Florida childhood in the 1890s the quartet was ubiquitous in the black population to the extent that he surmised "all male Negro youth in the United States is divided into quartets." Exploring the origins of the sound, he explained, "let one of them sing the melody and others will naturally find the parts."[5] In the 1930s, groups such as the Golden Gate Quartet popularized the close-harmony gospel repertoire, first on a South Carolina radio show, and then nationally after appearing on John Hammond's 1938 Spirituals to Swing concerts. Their secular counterparts, the Mills Brothers and the Ink Spots, were both increasingly commercially successful as the decade went on, the latter group following in Cab's footsteps by achieving a million sales of "If I Didn't Care" in 1939.

By incorporating the Cabaliers into his lineup, Cab was once again connecting to his African American musical heritage, but he was also determinedly pushing the boundaries forward. He was not alone in recognizing the importance of this current vogue, so, for example, in the same 1941–42 touring season Fats Waller took the Deep River Boys out on the road with his big band and into the recording studio. In the case of both Cab and Fats, a strong solo singer could use the quartet to establish backgrounds, to respond to vocal phrases, and to add musical comments over standard lyrics. It is possible to get an impression of the Cabaliers in action with the Calloway band in a series of four "soundies" from early January 1942. These were short pictures made for a kind of visual jukebox—the Mills Panorama—that flourished briefly around that period. In a sense they were the prototype of today's pop video, and they feature Cab, his vocal accompanists, and the band, with its new recruits Collins, Smith, and McRae in place.

In the soundie of "Blues in the Night," the Cabaliers begin by taking a role comparable to a big band reed section. They sing a wordless harmony riff under Cab's first verse, occasionally punctuating the vocal with flares, and adding occasional answering phrases. In the bridge, as Cab sings "Now the rains are falling," the quartet blossoms into full harmony behind his lead. Their harmonic range from falsetto to bass and their "oo-wee" punctuations presage many elements of doo-wop, which would emerge in the following decade, as does Cab's prominent lead vocal.

Three of these four little films were of songs that had been included in the band's recent commercial recordings, namely the aforementioned "Blues in the Night," a remake of "Minnie the Moocher," and "Virginia, Georgia and Caroline." The final soundie is a comic novelty called "The Skunk Song," in which Tyree Glenn joins Cab for some lighthearted vocal joshing. All of the sound tracks were recorded at New York's RCA studios on January 5, and then the movies were filmed to a playback during the following two days, almost certainly at the Eastern Service Studios in Astoria, Long Island.[6] There were two stage sets and two costume designs, a different one used each day. Cab's smart suit, breast pocket handkerchief, and art deco tie are identical in "Blues in the Night" and "Minnie" and the cutaway shots of sections and soloists are similar, against the same bandstand backcloth. It is Shad Collins who takes the growling muted trumpet solo in "Minnie," and—shot at a different angle on a different tree-lined set—plays open horn on "Virginia, Georgia and Caroline." That same verdant set features in the "Skunk Song," and although Collins is once more seen in the close-up shots, the trumpet soloist on the sound track is Jonah Jones.

After dates in Vermont toward the end of 1941 and the traditional New Year in Chicago, Cab's band was on the road for much of 1942, although for the first eight months of the year it generally played long engagements rather than one-nighters. There was a four-week stay in Chicago during April and May, with a return to the Strand Theater in New York for early June, and then the Pullman set off toward California, by way of a short stop in Chicago at the Chicago Theater. On July 9, Cab and the band began a six-week run at the Casa Manana in Culver City.[7]

The United States had joined World War II after the Japanese attack on Pearl Harbor on December 7, 1941. However, in the first few months of 1942, the hostilities had little effect on Cab or the band. He had earlier been turned down by the draft board on the grounds of a slightly enlarged heart, and several of his men were of an age to be outside the first wave of enlistments.[8] But when the entourage reached the West Coast there were noticeable effects of the conflict.

Wartime Los Angeles was a city in overdrive in terms of entertainment. Because of its strategic position in the eastern Pacific, it had become a focal point of U.S. wartime activity. Service personnel and those employed in a mixture of manufacturing industry, naval supply, and military transportation kept the town jumping, notably in the downtown Central Avenue area. The locally based pianist Fletcher Smith recalls that as well as the main theaters and clubs, an entire secondary level of entertainment opened up: "They had so many after hours spots that you could work, man. You'd work up to twelve o'clock and then you'd be off, and the after hours would start at maybe one-thirty or something like that, and they'd work till daylight."[9]

This was the climate into which Cab's band arrived—his men eager to try out the jam-session opportunities of the city as well as to play their nightly shows. Just before this West Coast trip Jerry Blake left the band, the straw boss duties temporarily returning to Foots Thomas, as Irving Brown came in on alto saxophone and clarinet. Meanwhile Teddy McRae left and was replaced by Al Gibson.

During its stay at the Casa Manana, the band recorded four sides in Los Angeles for Columbia, which included one masterpiece, "Ogeechee River Lullaby." Although a saccharine quality hovers around the close-harmony backing vocals, Cab's own beautifully enunciated lyrics and a sparkling trumpet solo by Jonah Jones in his best Armstrong manner are the centerpieces of a fine performance with enduring appeal. This and the other records made on July 27 were to be Cab's last commercial discs to be cut until January 1945, owing to a long-running dispute between the AFM and the record industry that began on August 1, 1942. In pursuit of a levy for musicians to compensate them for the loss of sales incurred through the proliferation of jukeboxes, the union forbade its members to record. The result was an unintentional but seismic shift in the record industry in favor of purely vocal records, because singers were not included in the ban. Frank Sinatra, for example, who had hitherto sung with big band backing, made "I Couldn't Sleep a Wink Last Night" and "A Lovely Way to Spend an Evening," two of his biggest hits of 1943, with the Bobby Tucker Singers. Their vocal harmonies altogether replaced the more familiar sound of accompanying instrumentalists.

Cab, on the road with his huge entourage, selling out theaters, and still able to broadcast with the band over national radio networks, decided to stick with his existing record contract and wait for a settlement. It did not suit him to make purely vocal discs and abandon the show he had built up over so long, and which he was managing to retain more or less intact despite the draft. As things turned out, Columbia (one of Mills's stable of labels) was one of the last firms to settle with the union, and so in 1943–44, apart from a handful of V-Discs made for American troops overseas, the band's only commercial recordings were done for movie sound tracks. This fitted Irving Mills's long-term strategy for Cab, which was to continue to build him into a star who was never dependent on just one form of mass communication. Consequently Mills started the process of introducing him socially to the who's who of Hollywood with the aim of making him a crossover film star, thereby repeating his success with both the white and black public on radio, record, and stage. Columnist Walter Winchell reported:

> In Beverly Hills the other night Irving Mills the music publisher threw a party for many showfolks and musicians. They were all there from Stokowski to Cab Calloway. For the finale all the tooters except Calloway went into a jam session. "Come on Cab," said Mills, "Be sociable." "You forget,"said the swing man. "Me an' Stokowski are stick men!"[10]

By organizing such events, and having them widely reported, Mills was maneuvering to get several of his stable of musicians into the movies in late

1942. In the event, this took a little longer to implement than he would have liked. However, the delay ultimately worked to Cab's benefit because there were changes afoot in the film industry, intended to break down some of the institutional racism that had been such a major factor in *The Singing Kid*. In particular the Office of War Information was pushing to set aside the old racial mores that had so divided the country, in favor of uniting against a common enemy.

The other prime mover was the executive secretary of the National Association for the Advancement of Colored People (NAACP), Walter White, who applied pressure on studio bosses and screenwriters to "use our media to build a world free of racial and religious hatred, a world free of vicious and fictitious notions of the superiority of one race over another."[11] White's goal was integrated movies, in which—much as white and black forces were fighting together against the Japanese and Germans—there would be no on-screen segregation. With the exception of the 1941 *Hellzapoppin'*, in which such African Americans as Slim Gaillard and Slam Stewart appeared alongside the starring comedians Olsen and Johnson, this type of general, informal integration was to take much more than a year or two to achieve. However, what the studios decided to do instead was to throw their energies into making all-black movies and give them mainstream distribution. As a result, both *Cabin in the Sky* and *Stormy Weather* went into production for release in 1943.

Cabin in the Sky was a somewhat old-fashioned musical film tautly directed for MGM by Vincente Minnelli, who had produced Josephine Baker on stage and was reputed to have a talent for working with African Americans. The studio wanted the music to fit the genre of black entertainment established by Cotton Club revues, and so it recruited the experienced team of E. Y. Harburg and Harold Arlen to add new songs to an earlier Broadway score composed by Vernon Duke. There were sensitive consultations during the shooting process with the NAACP, yet in hindsight the result is a quasi-religious fable that reinforces rather than breaks down racial stereotypes. The hero, Joe, played by Eddie Anderson, is an elevator operator and compulsive gambler, wounded in a shooting. He hovers between life and death, and his salvation appears to depend on the good-hearted Petunia (played by Ethel Waters) winning out over the temptress Sweet Georgia Brown (played by Lena Horne). In moral and racial terms there is precious little to distinguish this film from the blunt sermonizing and primitive stereotyping in Dudley Murphy's 1929 "race" movies *St. Louis Blues* (starring Bessie Smith) and

Black and Tan (starring Duke Ellington and Fredi Washington). The consequence was a picture that did well at the box office with both white and black audiences, but failed in its principal objectives. Black critics in general felt that it trivialized "the normal pattern of Negro life" and Walter White averred that overall it was "a disservice to race relations."[12]

The second all black movie of 1943, *Stormy Weather*, had impeccable left-wing credentials, being worked up for Twentieth Century-Fox from an original story, "Thank You, Pal," by the writer Hy Kraft. This was designed to pay tribute both to the African American contribution toward fighting for Uncle Sam and to the essential black ingredients in America's entertainment world. By starting the story with documentary footage of black soldiers who had fought successfully in World War I, and intercutting this with actors representing musical heroes of that age such as James Reese Europe, the two stories would be inextricably mixed, and would offer a plotline in flashback that gave copious opportunities to display almost every distinctive form of black entertainment from ragtime to swing. Bill Robinson was cast as a hoofer and former soldier telling his story to a group of children, and recalling incidents from the jazz age. Kraft got the backing of studio boss Daryl Zanuck to make the film, but his initial ambitions were constantly watered down as shooting went on.

Many of the military exploits Kraft wished to celebrate were dropped. The black composer William Grant Still, who wrote in a symphonic vein, but had also arranged for Ellington at the Cotton Club and more recently composed for Artie Shaw, was commissioned to score the picture and then unceremoniously dumped from the project. Most of the pool of black Hollywood entertainers whom Kraft had in mind, and who had made a profession of playing bit parts in mainstream movies, worked on *Cabin in the Sky*. Fox's executives felt that this precluded them from appearing in their film. Consequently Lena Horne—who had had some notable disagreements with Ethel Waters on the set of *Cabin in the Sky*—was the only high-profile actress to be recruited for both movies. In *Stormy Weather* she was rather improbably cast as the love interest for sixty-five-year-old Robinson. Yet the fortunate result for posterity of being forced to look beyond Los Angeles for black talent was that Fox imported a veritable who's who of black entertainers to create a series of fast-paced acts that pushed the plot into the background and dazzled moviegoers with some spectacular scenes drawn from the worlds of jazz, blues, and revue.

Irving Mills had a direct involvement in assembling the lineup of stars, as the doyenne of Hollywood gossip writers Louella Parsons revealed in the early fall of 1942, using the movie's working title:

> Hot jive dished up in the Duke Ellington—Cab Calloway—Louis Armstrong fashion combined with the haunting beauty of Negro spirituals is planned for "Thank You, Pal." Actually this cavalcade of Negro music is the first movie of its kind. The cast will be composed of Negroes, and the top talents of this race, including Paul Robeson, Ethel Waters, Hattie McDaniels, Rochester, and many others will be sought to lend their luster to this 20th Century musicale, produced by Bill le Baron and Irving Mills.[13]

The final cast list was somewhat different from the lineup announced by Parsons, but in the event, Bill Robinson and Lena Horne were joined by Fats Waller, Ada Brown, Cab Calloway and His Orchestra, the Nicholas Brothers, and Dooley Wilson.

Between the first announcements of the movie in the early fall of 1942 and the band's return to Hollywood in March 1943 in order to film the picture, Cab, his orchestra, and his revue were back on the road.[14] They notched up a great number of miles as they interspersed week-long theater or dance hall bookings with one-nighters at convenient staging posts in between. At the height of World War II, escapist entertainment of the type offered by Cab and his revue was very popular, particularly in large regional centers away from the flourishing entertainment hubs of New York, Chicago, and Washington, D.C. The Calloway show posted record earnings during the first week of November with a weekly take of $17,500 at the Orpheum in Minneapolis,[15] and after spending Thanksgiving week at the Regal in Chicago, it was to continue to earn similarly substantial sums at other provincial venues across the country.

In the buildup to the movie, Irving Mills also placed press pieces that kept Cab in the public eye, while the band was on the road. A typical example was a quite spurious suggestion that Cab might reintroduce the banjo into his orchestra. Cab is reported to have replied:

> Today we are concentrating on tone quality and if there is such a thing as a banjo blackout it is due to the years of experience with an instrument

that has not been able to restrain its rasping tones to fit the smooth mellow notes which [come] from its better-toned sidekick, the guitar.[16]

The article continued by saying, "Here's the payoff, Cab adds that one of his boys tried to pick up a banjo in a second hand store, but the proprietor thought that he had lost his mind."

In fact it was not until after Danny Barker had left Cab that he bought a six-string banjo in 1947 from a pawn shop in the Bowery in order to play revivalist jazz on Rudi Blesh's *This Is Jazz* radio show. In 1942, Barker, the epitome of the hepster big band musician, would have been horrified at the very suggestion of taking up such an uncool instrument. Nevertheless this press story and others like it did much to keep Cab in the minds of his general public at a time when he was not making records and was often off the airwaves while the band played out-of-the-way venues. However, even when it was performing far from home, Cab's band was still making money, and at the start of 1943 he was doing well enough to expand the trombone section to four men. Claude Jones returned briefly to join Keg Johnson, Quentin Jackson, and Tyree Glenn, but during the late spring he was replaced by Fred Robinson. Roger Jones was also a short-lived addition to the trumpets that year, temporarily making the section up to five men.

In the movie *Stormy Weather* itself, Cab's two main featured moments are magnificent, and rank among the finest examples of jazz on film. For his first scene, set in a large nightclub akin to Frank Sebastian's New Cotton Club in Culver City, the camera pans past customers sitting at tables around the hall, and focuses on the stage curtains, from behind which Cab appears wearing an oversize zoot suit and a large floppy fedora. His watch chain stretches to his knees, and his bow tie reaches a fair distance toward his shoulders. As he launches into "Geechy Joe," there's a cameo of his high-note routine with Jonah Jones, as Cab gestures skyward and Jonah makes for the top of his trumpet's range. In front of the band, Cab moves fluently, pointing his fingers to the floor in a hep-cat dance before launching into his blues vocal. Shad Collins plays a muted obbligato behind him, then gives way to Bennie Payne's piano and some punchy band riffs. The high point of Cab's subsequent dance is a slow-motion walk down the "railroad tracks" of the lyric. Here we can see the king of the Zazous in action, in full regalia, and he concludes with some fine wordless scatting, although it is questionable whether any of his dedicated French followers would actually have seen this stellar performance until after the war was over.

The other sequence, "The Jumpin' Jive," is the most dazzling song-and-dance routine in the entire movie. It also offers the chance to focus on some new arrivals in the band's lineup. In place of Cozy Cole, who had not made the trip west from New York, Benny Carter's former drummer J. C. Heard had joined the rhythm section. He is dramatically featured on a snare drum and tom-tom introduction to the song. As the camera pans to the right of him toward Bennie Payne, the band's new tenor saxophonist Illinois Jacquet comes briefly into frame. The most exciting soloist to come into the Calloway band after Chu Berry's death, Jacquet was responsible for this arrangement, which mutates from Cab, singing the "Jumpin' Jive" lyrics and sporting a black tail-coat, to a feature for the similarly attired Nicholas Brothers. They spring from the audience and proceed to dance to a riff based on "Flyin' Home." To start with, the brothers, Fayard and Harold, tap and do the splits all round the band (Fayard's feet narrowly missing Foots Thomas's head), before taking off to dance up and down several sets of stairs, over tables, and across the stage. They finish by leapfrogging over each other's heads down a giant flight of steps, and doing the splits each time they land. Fred Astaire called it the "greatest movie musical number he had ever seen."[17] Looking back on this sequence, Jacquet recalled:

> I joined Cab Calloway in I guess the start of '43, and stayed with him a year. And we made this picture, *Stormy Weather*. The real money I made in that band was when I wrote the music for the Nicholas Brothers in that film, when they did their dance. Twentieth Century-Fox paid me one hundred dollars a bar, for every bar that I wrote for them to dance. Man, I wrote so many bars it would stretch from here to London. In the end they said, "We don't need *that* many bars!"[18]

Sadly, apart from his contribution to this movie, Jacquet's stay with the band is not well documented owing to the AFM recording ban. By all accounts he was an excellent addition to the lineup, being hailed in the press as "a first rate tenor sax player."[19] He was already famous for his barnstorming solo on Lionel Hampton's "Flyin' Home," and he was to go on to become one of the great stars of Norman Granz's Jazz at the Philharmonic concerts, which began the following year in July 1944. The public—and the first jazz disc jockeys—loved his falsetto squeals and baritone honks on Jazz at the Philharmonic's "The Blues Part 2." He later maintained that it was his experience with Cab, learning to involve his listeners and work the crowds, that "got him started" in this outrageously extrovert style.[20] According to Jonah Jones, Jacquet finally left the band in late 1943 after a gig at Dayton, Ohio, for a familiar reason. "He stayed with us for a while, but not too long, because there wasn't enough solos for Jacquet."[21]

Stormy Weather is still widely regarded as the most successful of the all black musical movies of the war years, being praised at the time as "better than *Cabin in the Sky*," through having "enough top notch entertainers to fill three musical pictures, and a repertoire of songs that reads like a cavalcade of American rhythm."[22] This was tragically to be Fats Waller's last film appearance, owing to his death that December, although it confirmed his otherwise unfulfilled potential as a movie performer. It gave Bill Robinson an excellent screen swan song, following his pictures with Shirley Temple in the 1930s. And—despite some rather wooden acting—it made a star out of Lena Horne. A typical review ran, "the highlight of the show is the famed title number 'Stormy Weather,' which Lena Horne sings in her own indomitable style, which has skyrocketed her to fame almost overnight."[23]

Nevertheless it took some considerable nerve on the part of Twentieth Century-Fox to release the movie, because the summer of 1943 saw race riots break out in Harlem and Detroit. These were followed not long before the film's July release by the so-called zoot suit riots which began in Los Angeles at the very end of May. Beginning as scuffles between white U.S. sailors and Latino youths from East Los Angeles, the latter clad in fashionable Calloway-style garb, the Los Angeles unrest escalated rapidly. Within two or three days, thousands of soldiers, sailors, and roughneck civilians were marching through the streets, beating up zoot-suited youths, and in more extreme cases, entering movie theaters and demanding that the house lights be turned on so that they could attack zoot-suited whites, Latinos, or African Americans. A hurriedly issued local ordinance briefly banned zoot suits, and after a week of unruliness all military personnel were confined to their bases until the rioting ended. In these circumstances, releasing an all-black movie in which Cab was prominently garbed in forbidden attire could be seen as provocative. But showing surprising political courage Fox stuck to its guns and *Stormy Weather* was put on general release, although Cab was told not to make public appearances or undertake interviews in support of the film. Within days of its appearance, Walter White sent a note of congratulation to Daryl Zanuck, and described the picture's release as a source of "affirmative prevention" for future social unrest.[24]

Although Cab and the band had spent a large amount of time on the road between their visit to Hollywood in 1942 and returning to make the movie the next spring, the tour's handful of shows in Washington, D.C., triggered a new phase in Cab's personal life. During a week's run at the Howard Theatre, an old friend, Mildred Hughes, introduced Cab to a young and attractive stenographer named Zulme MacNeal, who worked in the local department of housing. A bright, independent college graduate, who had set herself up in her own apartment, and had a circle of middle class intellectual friends outside show business, Zulme—or "Nuffie" as she was universally known—gradually fell in love with Cab. For his part, he found someone who was not after him for his money or his fame, but was genuinely interested in him as a person and what he did for a living. The affair was kindled by letters and occasional visits by Cab to Washington when he was not far from the area. Equally, Nuffie made efforts to travel to hear him and the band when she could. She was soon a familiar figure backstage at the band's gigs.

The stream of other girlfriends dried up as Cab put his considerable energies into getting to know Nuffie better. In 1943, which was also, coincidentally, the year that his mother died, Cab and Nuffie moved in together. When he took her to the set of *Stormy Weather*, he was amazed to discover that she already knew Lena Horne, whom Cab had met years before as a chorus girl at the Cotton Club. It turned out that Lena's uncle, Frank Horne, was the head of the housing department in Washington, D.C., where Nuffie had worked.

Once he and Nuffie had decided to live together, Cab set about obtaining a legal separation from Betty, who, despite having been apart from Cab for almost five years, was in no mood to agree. It took from 1944 until 1949 for Cab to obtain a full divorce, and in the process he parted with several thousand dollars, the house in Riverdale, and a couple of investment properties he had bought in Chicago. The settlement was made in a year when Cab was making the highest earnings of his life in real terms. His gross income in 1944 was $48,000, which was a very substantial amount indeed, equivalent to around $690,000 in 2009.[25] His net annual income after taxes and expenses was estimated at $18,000 and from this he was obliged not only to pay alimony for several decades to come but to make provision for Betty to receive staged cash payments totaling $19,600. At the height of the swing era in 1943–44, such a financial agreement looked attainable. After all, Cab's income had risen steadily every year since he arrived at the Cotton Club, and he was booked ahead for more than a year. Yet within four years of signing the first papers in 1944, he would be forced by changes in fashion and economic circumstances to wind up the big band and scale down to a small group. By the time the final decree was awarded in June 1949,[26] Cab would be paying his former wife a far higher percentage of his annual earnings than anybody envisaged when the settlement was first drafted.

Nuffie had an immediate calming effect on Cab. "She made him a different guy from what he was before," recalled Jonah Jones. One of the first things she suggested Cab do was buy dinner for Jonah once in a while, and the trumpeter was shocked when they were staying in Chicago and Cab, who had never done this in the two years Jonah had been in the band, turned up at his hotel to drive him to work. Jonah continued, "He was a real rough type of guy, but when she got hold of him, he became real nice. He became a wonderful guy."[27]

Cab and Nuffie did not wait until the divorce came through before they started a family of their own. Their first daughter, Chris, was born on September 21, 1945, and her sister Lael followed in 1949, just before Cab and Nuffie finally married. A third daughter, Cabella, was born in 1952. The family set up home at 147 Hazzard Road in Lido Beach, Hempstead, in Nassau County, New York. It was not much more than an hour's drive from downtown Manhattan, but a relatively secluded location for a star with Cab's profile. The select development of houses where they lived nestled between a golf course and the Nassau Beach Park.

However, although Cab, at almost thirty-eight years old in 1945, finally had a home of his own in which he wanted to spend time, the band was his primary family, and he still spent more of his waking hours with them than anyone else. He continued to cut a familiar figure waving his oversized baton in front of his men, but he had considerably modified his act as he reached his mid-thirties. In *Stormy Weather*, we see a more thickset Cab than in his early movie appearances with Betty Boop or in his first short films such as *Cab Calloway's Hi-De-Ho*. In place of the tangled floppy-haired look of the early 1930s, his long locks are neatly slicked down, and rather than the gangly youth of those early pictures, his whole aura is one of older, wiser elegance. Instead of using his whole body to put over a dialogue scene, he acts effectively by using his mouth and eyes. Although there is still a sense of staginess about him, this is less obvious than with Bill Robinson in the same picture. Nevertheless, given his years of experience, Cab's smallest gestures are sufficiently broad to be picked out from a distant stage by members of the audience in the furthermost gallery of a theater. He still dances with great agility, particularly during his handover to the Nicholas Brothers and in his zoot-suited "Geechy Joe." Yet the deliberately frenetic quality of his early 1930s dancing style has been replaced by something more graceful and grounded. The last glimpse on film of the old, frantic, tousle-headed Calloway is to be found in two short sequences from his next movie, *Sensations of 1945*, made in January 1944 by the producer Andrew Stone.

There, in a sequence that shows jitterbugging in the streets, the camera cuts from direct shots of Cab, in his vintage white tie and tails, dancing and waving his baton energetically in front of the band, to a projection of him on a screen above the dancers. In a second, studio-bound scene, he employs similarly exaggerated gestures as he recites sections in song from his *Hepster's Dictionary* to a small top-hatted child who sits in front of the band.

By contrast, the next batch of soundies he made in early 1945 includes some fine footage of Cab in a smart contemporary double-breasted suit and tie, singing "We the Cats Shall Hep You." Apart from some dancing to and fro from one side of the band to the other, some energetic leaps, and a couple of spins, he mainly focuses on singing and pointing his baton. At his cue, another new addition to the band, Ike Quebec contributes a fiery chorus on tenor. Cab is joined by the band's regular vocalist of the time, Dorothy Salters, for "Walkin' with My Honey," and conducts the band behind her, before linking arms with her for the final vocal chorus. A bow-tied Cab, still in a suave lounge suit, dances energetically, but again less wildly than in the '30s, with Rusty Stanford in "Foo a Little Ballyhoo," another soundie from the same series. This new, urbane Cab, still capable of surprisingly agile movement, was typical of the stage persona he adopted for almost all his public appearances from this time on. Even when the white tailcoat was donned again in later life, more measured movements and carefully focused actions became the order of the day.

As well as refining his dance style, now he had adopted a slightly more contemporary mode of dress, Cab also started to rival Duke Ellington for the number of times he changed clothes during a show. Jonah Jones recalled:

Sometimes he'd have on all white, a white tuxedo, with a white shirt, white necktie, white shoes, white socks. And then when the comedians come on, Cab would go off, and his boy would change him. He'd just stand there and the boy would put a whole different uniform on him, perhaps all powder blue, powder blue shirt, powder blue necktie, socks, shoes, and then he'd come back on stage. Next, when the dancers came out, and he didn't have to be out there directing, he'd go off again. Then he'd come back on with an all-tan uniform. And he really looked good in that stuff.[28]

In August 1944, Irving Mills's office sent out a press release to support Cab's appearance in *Sensations of 1945*, which, despite its name, had been released that June. From the document it is possible to get a real sense of how Cab's life was spent with what was arguably the best big band he had so far led.

> When the Cotton Club closed, the Cab Calloway Orchestra went on a tour of the United States. It appeared in such well-known amusement places as the Casa Manana in Hollywood, the Panther Room of the Hotel Sherman in Chicago, and the Lookout House in Cincinnati. In theaters all over the country the Calloway troupe played to standing-room only audiences, returning to New York just long enough to perform at the Strand and Paramount Theaters. $84,200 taken in two weeks at the Paramount was a summer record. . . . In 1943 the Calloway Orchestra accepted an offer from Park Central's Cocoanut Grove in New York where they remained for an extended engagement. From there they went to Frank Dailey's Meadowbrook in New Jersey, and finally back to Broadway for a long stay at the Café Zanzibar, where Calloway heads the Negro group of entertainers.[29]

Cab's residency at the Zanzibar in August and September 1944 was remarkable. Walter Winchell reported that it broke all New York nightclub records, taking $275,000 during the eight-week run.[30]

According to Cab's press releases of the time, it was also the setting for a notable—if slightly mathematically improbable—milestone in his career, as during his run there he was to sing "Minnie the Moocher" for the 100,000th time. In its three recorded versions, the song was also set to pass the one-million-copy mark at the same time. The press reported, "Cab will be presented with the millionth platter which has been pressed in 14 karst [*sic*] gold plate."[31]

There are several extant recordings from that Café Zanzibar engagement that give us a good impression of the band, which, having had numerous changes in personnel, was in the process of severing its final remaining links with the Missourians. It had moved with the times, and could hold its own against any swing orchestra of the mid-1940s, with no hint of anachronism, except in the deliberate revisiting of Cab's earliest hits. Even the perennial—and now gold-plated—"Minnie the Moocher" was being performed in the updated version recorded in 1942, and the early 1930s arrangement was permanently rested.

On the band's new theme tune, Gerald Wilson's modernistic "Cruisin' with Cab," Lammar Wright's high-note work had given way to the stratospheric trumpet register of Paul Webster. Just after his appearance in *Stormy Weather*, Bennie Payne had been drafted, so the rhythm section now featured the light-fingered piano of Dave Rivera. Meanwhile the reeds had the fiery tenor saxophone of Ike Quebec in place of Illinois Jacquet. Foots Thomas had gone to join Don Redman, and for the time being Al Gibson remained on second tenor. Before long Andy Brown was also to leave the reed section. Brown, who had spent virtually all his adult life, almost twenty years, in the band, took it badly. Danny Barker recalls him shaking and screaming periodically after he opened the envelope with his notice. "They took him up and brought him in the dressing room and he sat by the table and cried. Tears was all over the floor—never seen a man cry like that."[32] Brown was replaced initially by Fats Waller's former sideman Rudy Powell. When baritone saxophonist Greely Walton left soon afterward, Powell moved to his chair and Bob Dorsey came in on alto.

Yet again, Cab was judiciously replacing musicians whom he thought were dated or did not fit the image he wished to project, although now he was also having to balance his ambitions against the slow attrition caused by the draft. One other side effect of the wartime conditions was that extraneous members of his revue were also let go. Dorothy Salters had taken the place of the long-serving Avis Andrews, but for the time being Sister Tharpe remained.[33] Otherwise, instead of the usual retinue of comedians, dancers, and singers, the band itself was asked to provide some extra entertainment in the show. Tyree Glenn had long provided additional vocal, and comic, support to Cab, but now other sidemen were tested as possible singers. This had begun with Bennie Payne's attempts at vocals back in early 1943—a "flop" according to *Variety's* reviewer, who concurred with Cab's decision to replace his avuncular pianist as third vocalist with the smoother singing of Quentin Jackson. He was to be regularly featured on "Begin the Beguine."[34] Hilton Jefferson also occasionally took a turn at the mike, singing his feature "Who Can I Turn To?" Meanwhile, the band-within-a-band was adding comedy routines to its sets: "Two of the Cab Jivers (unbilled) pulled good laughs with their appearing and disappearing mike bits. A Donald Duck piece of biz by one of the team laid an egg."[35]

Overall, however, after the vocal and dancing performances of Cab himself, it was the full big band and its exceptional playing that commanded most space in the reviews. At the Zanzibar, critics were full of praise, of which this is a typical example:

> Calloway has whipped a sizeable crew into more than just good shape. He has some great sidemen in the orchestra. People like tenorman Ike Quebec, drummer J. C. Heard, trumpeter Jonah Jones, git man Danny Barker, bassist Milton Hinton, and tram-vibes specialist Tyree Glenn can hold their own with the best musicmakers in the business, and they all provide punch to this group.[36]

In terms of repertoire, the airshots from the club confirm that Cab regularly featured most of the songs he had recorded within the past couple of years, or had sung for his various "soundies." There were a few new ones that had been added to the book but not yet commercially recorded, owing to the AFM ban. The band, by contrast, seemed to be swapping arrangements with all and sundry to make up the sizable proportion of the regular Zanzibar broadcasts that were instrumental numbers. "One O'Clock Jump" and "9:20 Special" came from Basie, "Fiesta in Brass" was associated with Roy Eldridge, "Blue Skies" was similar to the contemporary Ellington arrangement, whereas "And the Angels Sing" was directly comparable to the Goodman chart. But there were also pieces that the band made its own, in addition to the ubiquitous "Cruisin' with Cab." These included "Frantic on the Atlantic," and a feature for the band's now well-established drummer, "Coasting with J. C." Meanwhile, Cab's habitual feature, "St. Louis Blues," was now updated from the 1930s arrangement to a romping swing number that put far greater emphasis on the band. His vocal floated over the pounding guitar of Barker and bass of Hinton, with J. C. Heard's drums adding exciting punctuations. On the broadcast versions, Jonah Jones and Ike Quebec can be heard stretching out on long solos that underlined the band's jazz credentials.

The war provided many big bands with work out on the road away from New York, and Cab's was no exception. Indeed Nuffie recalled that "he did an awful lot of work for army bases, bond drives and that sort of thing."[37] One reason that all swing bands toured, particularly by bus, was that military gigs were exempt from the gasoline ration, so that judiciously placed shows for the army could help stage the band's progress between provincial theaters or clubs, by covering the provision and cost of the all-too-scarce fuel.

The arrival of Ike Quebec into the touring band was the first instance of any of Cab's sidemen being involved with hard drugs. Cab's authority as leader had kept the band clean of such narcotics since he first took it over. Quebec, in later life a remarkably astute talent scout for Blue Note records, was already a heroin addict when he joined although he was discreet about his habit. On one occasion he accidentally left some of his equipment in Jonah Jones's bathroom. So innocent was Jonah's wife that she was more concerned that Mr. Quebec appeared to have forgotten his wallet.[38] Milt Hinton was equally unaware of the warning signs:

> I didn't know what was going on with Ike until much later. I was so naive. Up on the stand night after night, I'd look over and see him with his eyes closed, and I'd think to myself, "This guy better cool it with the ladies, he's been up all night again." I was always amazed how he'd be sound asleep and then suddenly come alive just in time to make his cue.[39]

Cab himself was also largely unaware of the telltale signs of Quebec's addiction. He never worried too much about alcohol, as he liked a drink or two himself, and possessed miracle powers of recovery from even the most massive hangovers. Yet he was hard-headed and disciplinarian with his men if any of them were found using marijuana. This was ironic, because owing to his sequence of drug-related Minnie songs and his zoot suits, *Afro* magazine was to brand Cab as one of the causes of the craze for reefers. In an article headed "Anything for a thrill: Marijuana, Zoot suits, all products of the Jazz Craze," it printed a quarter-page picture of Cab in his *Stormy Weather* attire and captioned it "Cab Calloway sports a zoot suit, a Harlem craze that came in with reefers and jazz fever."[40] The reality could hardly be more different, as Jonah Jones remembered: "He used to go round between shows to the different dressing rooms, to see if he could smell any marijuana. And if he smelled marijuana, he'd fire you right away."[41] The band's senior valet, Rudolph Rivers Jr., was wise to this, and he knew that he had to allocate dressing rooms to the known reefer smokers in the band as far from the stage and from Cab's own dressing room as possible. He also ensured that the smokers had windows in their rooms and good ventilation. Despite Cab's prowling vigilance, none of his men was actually caught and fired for using what Harlem hepsters of the time referred to covertly as "dry."

To enhance his wartime cheerleading role, Cab took on a growing number of charitable and war service duties, including recording a special feature number called "The Führer's Got the Jitters" for the Armed Forces Radio Service. He was photographed many times for the war effort, but in perhaps the most surprising pictures, he was dressed as a chef and seen to be making omelettes, "co-operating enthusiastically with the OPA drive to use up the egg surplus."[42]

One unforeseen consequence of Cab's wartime activities was when questions were asked in the British House of Commons about the growing use of his catch-phrase "hi-de-hi" by U.K. troops serving alongside their American counterparts. H. McKee, a Labour member of Parliament, complained that its use "made officers look ridiculous in the eyes of their men."[43] It is not recorded whether the Mother of Parliaments asked its soldiery to refrain from using the words!

Between the demands of his work to entertain troops and build morale, Cab also found time to drop in on the Garrick State Lounge in Chicago to present J. C. Higginbotham with the 1944 award from *DownBeat* for becoming the year's top trombonist.[44] 1945 saw a very similar round of touring, and another long residency at the Zanzibar, interspersed with photo opportunities and charitable events. His orchestra also became a regular feature on the fund-raising *March of Dimes Cavalcade of Bands*. Yet despite his national celebrity, there was the occasional reminder that, in some parts of the United States, Cab was still a second-class citizen.

On December 22, 1945, Cab and his friend Felix H. Payne, son of a prominent local politician, turned up at the Pla-Mor Ballroom in Kansas City to hear Lionel Hampton and His Orchestra. Hampton had met them earlier at his hotel and invited them to drop by his gig. At around 11 o'clock that evening they bought their tickets and walked through the front entrance when a special police officer named William Todd informed them that "no Negroes were admitted." He offered them a refund. Payne was incensed and lashed out at Todd, whereupon Cab pushed the policeman to the floor. When he regained his balance, Todd "drew his revolver and hit Calloway over the head several times." Cab spent the eve of his thirty-eighth birthday in the General Hospital being treated for severe cuts to the head, and later that day appeared at the municipal court to be charged with intoxication and resisting arrest. At the ballroom, Hampton had stopped his band and walked offstage when he was told what had happened, and fifteen hundred disgruntled patrons got their money back.[45]

Two years later, Cab brought the incident back to court himself, seeking two hundred thousand dollars in damages from the Pla-Mor company for assault, wrongful arrest, and a fractured skull. However, the Circuit Court jury threw out his claim, along with a counterclaim by the Pla-Mor company.[46] Nevertheless, Cab had the satisfaction of seeing Todd's actions widely condemned in the press both at the time of the incident and again when his claim came to court. The following year, in July 1948, the Missouri Supreme Court set aside the previous judgment, and allowed Calloway to sue the Pla-Mor again.[47]

At the end of the war, fashions in popular music began to alter, and tastes shifted away from big bands. Singers such as Frank Sinatra, immeasurably helped by the AFM recording ban on instrumentals, had risen to a position of preeminence. The rising star Louis Jordan with His Tympany Five, a much more economical touring unit than Cab's band and revue, was taking the lion's share of the jump-jive market, and the nascent form of rhythm and blues was beginning to erode the dominance of large swing orchestras. Even in the big band world itself, new groups such as Billy Eckstine's and Dizzy Gillespie's were dividing the audience that remained into those who followed swing and those who sought the newer sounds of bebop.

To start with, booked months ahead, Cab hardly noticed the changes, and apart from his no longer doing war work, 1946 was very much like 1945. The band traveled a similar itinerary around the country, although that year it broke the tradition of opening in Chicago, as it both began the January season and spent the summer months at the Zanzibar in New York, also playing a week at the Harlem Apollo Theatre in September. There had been changes in the rhythm section and Danny Barker, irked by what he considered an unjust fine for being late, left the band to be replaced by former Fats Waller sideman John Smith. Shortly before Barker's departure, Don Redman's erstwhile drummer Buford Oliver took the place of J. C. Heard, yet the band's overall identity remained strong and the same high standards can be heard on its January 1946 airshots as on the previous year's broadcasts. Peacetime also brought with it a return to the traveling revue, and Cab's band was accompanied on tour by the Three Peters Sisters, the Miller Brothers and Lois, and the comedians Moke and Poke.[48]

One unusual interruption to the band's normal itinerary in 1946 was a longer than normal stay in California, during which Cab's eldest daughter,

Camay, who had just dropped out of a program at Hunter College, came out to join the family as a babysitter and nanny for her half-sister, baby Chris. When the long summer season at the Zanzibar began, Camay moved back with the family to the house at Lido Beach, where she lived with her father, stepmother, and half-sister during the fall, as she started a new degree at New York University. A few weeks into term, she and her student friends held a riotous party at the house while Cab and Nuffie were away. The dressing-down she got afterward was so severe she left the house for good, and took a part-time job to finance her studies and student lodgings in Judson Hall. It took two years before Lena Horne brokered a reunion between Cab and his eldest child.

By now, Cab was seasoned at keeping his personal and professional life separate. The public image he projected told little of his family life. Fans could now read his words of wisdom in a new weekly syndicated newspaper column that was sponsored by the Zanzibar. As Walter Winchell reported, he was following in the footsteps of Mayor La Guardia by penning "paid newspaper ads."[49] Again the summer Zanzibar appearance was a great success, bucking the national trend away from the kind of old-fashioned entertainment that had prevailed before the war.

> With the opening of the new summer show at the Zanzibar, this big cafe again rang with "Hi-de-ho" since Cab Calloway and his jumpin' jive bandsmen were back again. Though suffering a bit from first night jitters, Cab was in fine fettle and when he gave out with "Minnie the Moocher," he had the whole packed place singing choruses with him and right lustily too. While Calloway gets top billing and contributed much, he is by no means the whole show. Included in the big cast is Pearl Bailey who since her last Zanzibar appearance has become star of the current Broadway success, "St. Louis Woman."[50]

Yet in 1946 the writing was on the wall for Cab and the Zanzibar. When the band made its final appearances there in September, it was the last time Cab played at what had become an even more successful Manhattan base for him than the Cotton Club. During his absence on the road the following year, it was to close down and be transformed into Bop City, which opened in 1948, playing host to a quite different style of music. His longest summer engagement in New York in 1947 was to be three weeks at the Strand Theater in April, when "hearts brightened by spring wend their merry way to theater windows

and make the cashiers tills ring a merry tune."[51] Dusty Fletcher danced a routine with Cab, the Miller Brothers and Lois were still featured, and the Ravens
vocal group were the "new attraction" added to the *Jumpin' Jive Jubilee* revue.
As a peg on which to hang the title of the new show, Cab marked a somewhat
spurious occasion—the twentieth anniversary of jive talk—which gave rise to
press releases for the ensuing tour with the ring of déjà vu about them:

> If bobbysoxers in your vicinity converse in a language that sounds some-
> thing like tossing a dictionary into an electric fan, you can blame Cal-
> loway. He won't mind—he'll like it. He's so proud of his colorful jive
> jargon that he's set aside the whole month to celebrate the 20th anni-
> versary of jitterbug chatter.[52]

With the end of the first AFM recording ban in November 1944, Cab had
managed to return to the studios in 1945 and made a slow but steady stream
of discs for his old label Columbia. Some of the least long-lived of these were
immensely popular at the time, with a particularly unmemorable ditty called "A
Blue Serge Suit with a Belt at the Back" getting most press attention. Better by
far are his cover version of Joe Liggins's "The Honeydripper" and a piece of hi-
de-hoing called "Hey Now" from May 1946. The most impressive discs the big
band made from this period date from 1947, which was to be its last full year
of operation. Buster Harding's fine arrangement of "The Hi-De-Ho Man That's
Me" was one of the best of Cab's stock-in-trade signature songs, corralling
together into one number many of his trademarks. It begins with a dramatic
cantoral introduction over sustained orchestral chords. Then it turns into a
musical autobiography, plus a jive dialogue, the whole thing interspersed with
intervals of "hi-de-ho" responses, before the cantoral Calloway returns for a
dramatic coda. Cab's beautifully enunciated delivery, the perfect timing of the
call and response, and the latent power of his voice are very well captured on
this disc, and it gives a real impression of how he might have sounded in live
performance at the time. Of the other pieces recorded that year, "Everybody
Eats When They Come to My House" reflects the new domesticated Cab, and
Andy Gibson's storming "Calloway Boogie" is as good as any of the band's flagwavers from the previous seventeen years.

In Cab's autobiography, he gives 1947 as the year in which he called his
men together and told them that he was going to break up the band. Yet it
seems that he actually managed to hold the big band together for a little longer,

although another AFM recording ban meant that its final months went undocumented on record. In July 1948, Cab and the orchestra were at the Roxy Theatre in New York playing opposite the movie *The Street with No Name*, and in August, after Cab appeared on television in a pioneering edition of the Ed Sullivan show, he took the revue to Syracuse, New York, for what appears to have been its last engagement.[53] Jonah Jones recalled what happened next:

> He cut the band down to about seven pieces, me on trumpet, Keg Johnson on trombone, and two saxes, Hilton Jefferson and Sam "The Man" Taylor. There was Dave Rivera on piano, Milt Hinton on bass, and Panama Francis on drums. That lasted for a while. Then he finally cut it down to four pieces and I was the only horn in the band. . . . There were three rhythm, and myself. . . . He was a wonderful director, he loved to direct, so even with the quartet he was directing us. He still changed clothes all night.[54]

The winding up of the band, and in consequence the corporation that owned it, also led to a final parting of the ways with Irving Mills. Ellington had made the break earlier, passing over his management to William Morris in 1939 and then dissolving their other business arrangements in 1943, when he discovered that Mills had been holding back vast sums of record royalties from him.[55]

Cab had kept the connection with Mills going for longer, mainly on account of Hollywood and *Stormy Weather*, but in July 1948 he moved to GAC, the General Artists' Corporation, which was the successor to one of Mills's former rivals, the Rockwell-O'Keefe Agency. By the fall of 1948, for the first time in his life he was leading a small group, he no longer had Mills's inventive stream of publicity behind him, and even with his powerful new agency he was unable to get bookings to play the venues that he had consistently sold out for the best part of two decades. As 1949 began, although he remained the sunniest of onstage personalities, Cab slid into a deep depression.

Chapter 10

Porgy
1949–1970

....

Cab was not alone in facing the problems of maintaining a big band at the end of the 1940s. Of the most famous African American leaders, a few managed to keep their full orchestras afloat by rebalancing their repertoire. Duke Ellington, by subsidizing the band from his royalties, largely avoided such compromises. Lionel Hampton kept a smaller, but still sizable, band going by appealing to a different public. He adopted rhythm and blues techniques of style and presentation, which included Billy Mitchell playing the tenor saxophone on his back and fellow tenorist Gene Morris dropping to his knees during his solos. By contrast, Benny Carter was forced to dissolve his regular band in 1946. Despite the unexpected death of its leader in 1947, the Jimmie Lunceford Orchestra struggled on a bit longer, but folded at the end of the decade following Ed Wilcox's unsuccessful attempts to keep it going. The "Twentieth Century Gabriel," trumpeter Erskine Hawkins, scaled back his big band gradually, ending up with a quartet in 1953.

In January 1950, Count Basie was forced by rising costs and diminishing bookings to cut his regular touring group back to a septet. This small group became an octet when Basie's long-term guitarist, Freddie Green, rehired himself, on the grounds that he'd given so much of his life to the band he was in no mood to be fired. Basie's octet, with Clark Terry, Buddy DeFranco, and Wardell Gray among its members, and Neal Hefti writing the charts, used considerable ingenuity to compensate for the size of the band, and consequently made some of the best music Basie ever recorded. These discs sit interestingly at a stylistic crossroads between those made by his original Kansas City big band and the more forward-looking orchestra he was to lead in the 1950s.

Unlike Basie's, the music that Cab recorded in 1949 is definitely not the most distinguished part of his legacy. It both mirrors his depressed personal state of mind, and also shows him searching for a new role as a popular entertainer. In May his seven-piece band accompanied him in a vocal duet with singer Eugenie Baird in a cover version of "Baby, It's Cold Outside," which Ella Fitzgerald had recorded a few days before in a brilliant version with Louis Jordan. Whereas Fitzgerald and Jordan created a magical rapport, perhaps because they had previously been romantically involved with one another, Cab and Miss Baird simply sound somewhat perfunctory. Theirs is a good professional version of the song, but they fail to spark off each other, their voices lacking the flirtatious sex appeal of Fitzgerald's with Jordan's, subtly backed by the Tympany Five.

On the same session, Cab also made the first of several attempts to capture the sounds of the current vogue for small group rhythm and blues. The roots of this genre can be heard in his earlier big band discs such as "Calloway Boogie," and "The Honeydripper," but here he serves up a lame attempt at "The Huckle Buck." On drums, Panama Francis fails to lift the slow boogie tempo that would have been natural for the backing band of a Kansas City–style blues singer like Big Joe Turner. As a result, the septet sounds generally uncomfortable with the arrangement.

By August 1949, Cab's regular touring group had been cut further back to a quartet. However, he added the trombonist John "Streamline" Ewing and reed players S. A. Stewart and Leon Washington to the lineup for the first of a handful of discs for RCA Victor. A celebration of his long-term friend "Ol' Joe Louis" again tries to fall into the R and B groove, but despite some energetic group shout-backs as Cab celebrates the boxing folk hero, the disc falls short. Its high point is a searing trumpet chorus from Jonah Jones. Even less convincing is a comic routine called "Your Voice" in which Cab berates an uncredited female singer (possibly Eugenie Baird again) for her constant nagging. It is—at best—labored comedy and although it tries to capture the type of wisecracking domestic humor that Moms Mabley was beginning to make her own out on the chitlin circuit, it substantially misses the mark.

The year's final session for Victor, on November 29, makes a stark contrast with the easy, confident swing of the Cafe Zanzibar airshots from just three years before. Whereas those broadcasts showed a slick big band at the top of its game, with Cab comfortably filling a role between his old "hi-de-ho" persona and that of a more mature entertainer, the studio septet from 1949 lacks the relaxed swing of that group and Cab's clear sense of identity. Everything sounds rather forced, particularly on the comic "real dirty blues" of "Roomin' House Boogie," complete with sound effects of a landlady knocking on the wall. Francis's leaden drumming picks up slightly behind a honking tenor solo from Sam "The Man" Taylor, but otherwise the piece lacks movement. Easily the most accomplished of the 1949 small band sides is "I Beeped When I Should Have Bopped." Based on a Dizzy Gillespie piece, Cab directs all the humor in the lyrics to himself, ruefully considering the vogue for bebop. A nicely written chart, played with crisp precision as a consequence of altoist Hilton Jefferson's return to the group, complements Cab's expertly delivered lyrics. Sam Taylor's solo starts at bebop speed but catches the mood of the time by subtly turning into blues honking halfway through.

These records give a glimpse of the start of Cab's lowest period as a performer. All his strengths, the flexibility of his style, his blues authenticity, his interactivity with his fellow musicians and his listening audience, and his sheer panache as a performer, seem to have failed him.

The year also saw eight sides recorded with a studio big band, with temporary personnel added to Cab's quartet of Jones, Rivera, Hinton, and Francis. The results are far more successful than the small band sides, but not exceptional. Among them, the "Duck Trot" is a competently played up-tempo chart with room for Cab to spread his vocal wings with confidence, and "One for My Baby (and One More for the Road)" was to become the template for a song that briefly featured as prominently in Cab's stage act as it did in that of Frank Sinatra. But such an environment was now a rarity for Cab, as he told a reporter in Winnipeg when his quartet played there:

> Big orchestras are out for the time being in the United States according to Cab. Because of the current business situation large groups are too expensive to carry. For the past year Cab has reduced his aggregate to the four musicians who will appear with him at the Casino. These are Jonah Jones, the trumpeter, Panama Francis, the drummer, Milton Hinton on bass and Dave Rivera at the piano. Cab prefers this more intimate arrangement since a large group of musicians tends to detract from the main act.[1]

Although Cab was obliged to cut down his accompaniment, it seems from accounts of his 1949 tour that in several venues his "main act" was still set in a revue that included comedians, singers, and dancers.[2] But the days of such live touring shows, fronted by a single entertainer, were numbered. In the 1950s and 1960s, a few acts such as Johnny Otis, Ray Charles, and James Brown continued to be powerful enough box office draws to maintain a complete traveling revue, but these were exceptions. As the 1950s began, Cab was more often featured as part of a package of "jump jive" stars than as the headliner of his own touring show.

Aware of changing public moods, Cab worked hard behind the scenes to try to create a new career for himself away from the club and theater circuit he had inhabited for so long. When a new television series, updating the prewar radio show *Amos and Andy* was being planned in the summer of 1950, Cab auditioned and screen-tested for the part of the con man George "Kingfish" Stevens. However his athletic and youthful appearance counted against him, and the veteran stage actor Tim Moore landed the part. The controversial show, about two African American men who run a cab company and are frequently duped by Kingfish, ran for sixty-nine episodes, but was damned from the outset by the NAACP for perpetuating outdated stereotypes.[3] Despite yearning for a new start to his career, Cab did well to be out of this particular show.

"After 20 years in rigorous show business, isn't this the first time he's ever been happy over the reason for losing a contract?" asked the radio critic Jack O'Brian, when the news broke of Cab's failure to land the part. The same syndicated column was quick to notice when Cab temporarily disbanded his quartet in the fall of 1950 and went out as a solo cabaret artist. O'Brian speculated, "Isn't Cab Calloway doing a single act for the first time in 20 years because he sees his future as a television entertainer rather than as a bandleader?"[4]

Judging from a set of short television films made for the Snader Transcription Company in 1950, Cab still had much to learn about adapting his stage persona to the small screen. The exaggerated gestures and movements which had worked quite successfully in the cinema looked awkward on television, and one of the lowest points of his entire career is a version of "Calloway Boogie" shot in a fictitious "Cab's Club," with Cab sporting a tartan suit, and leaping energetically in front of his quartet as if it were a big band. Only a carefully staged version of "One for My Baby," in which Cab immerses himself in the role of a barroom drunk, and consequently remains virtually still, shows that he has begun to grasp the minimalist essentials of television performing.

Furthermore, notes that survive among his papers reveal that during this period he was still trying to revive his past experience of success as he looked for ways to transfer his traditional stage revue to the small screen. A draft running order for a putative television show featuring his one-time hit "She's Tall, Tan, and Terrific" suggests a fully formatted variety program built around him. It lists movements for a song and dance troupe of six girls and four boys, details flash dance routines, proposes comedy inserts, and outlines a guest spot for a female vocalist, for whom Cab has sketched in the names of Hazel Scott, Ethel Waters, and Lena Horne. In an alternative format he lists their male counterparts Billy Eckstine, Nat Cole, and the Mills Brothers. "After guest star, direct to musical introduction to Cab Calloway," reads the note, with a list of his possible feature songs including "Minnie the Moocher" and "St. James Infirmary."[5]

Despite his apparently trying to sell this idea to television companies and possible sponsors, it appears that in the early 1950s it remained a pipe dream. Although Cab was to become an occasional guest artist on television, he seldom took center stage as he had done for the last two decades of club revues and traveling shows. When he did make such an appearance, it was as a relic of an earlier age of entertainment. One typical billing ran:

> The Kreisler Bandstand is gonna rock this Wednesday when Cab Calloway books his band in for a one-night stand on the show KGO TV at 8:30. Best remembered by jazz, swing and boogie fans for his famed Cotton Club shows in the plush 20s, Mr. "Hi-de-hi-de-ho" will run through a review of his inimitable song stylings. Sharing bandstand honors on the stage is the sultry sepia songstress Ella Fitzgerald.[6]

Instead of becoming a familiar face on television, Cab reverted to the touring life. Occasionally his quartet was augmented to a larger group by either bringing in New York session players, or local musicians, to play for dancing.[7] For the most part he and his band continued to work what remained of the circuit he had covered for years. But that circuit was shrinking. New forms of domestic entertainment—notably television—were taking over from the dance halls and theaters of the prewar era, which had continued in a kind of suspended animation during the war itself. Gene Lees has written evocatively of the rapidity of the decline in venues, notably on a visit he made to the coal belt of Pennsylvania. At the summer vacation venue of Harvey's Lake, visited some time after its heyday, Lees observed:

> Once upon a time, when you could get here on the inter-urban electric trolley from Wilkes-Barre, there were three dance pavilions round its rim, and two more between the two communities. Five in all. But the trolley was long ago dismantled, the pavilions died, and the sounds of bands no longer drift across the water in the evenings.[8]

What happened so graphically in that description of Harvey's Lake was happening all over the country. Furthermore, there were no more Pullman trains for Cab and his musicians. Instead, the band traveled in a seven-seater Chrysler automobile, with Rudolph the valet and Cab's driver MacNeal. Despite scaling down to a small group to save costs, the material rewards for each man were not much greater than they had been in the mid-1930s. Hinton, Rivera, and Francis were paid $150 a week, and Jonah Jones received $175. Rudolph was paid $125 and the driver $55. Cab paid himself $250 a week.[9] In addition, there were usually modest profits to be made when the theater paid the group a percentage of its receipts, but these were ploughed back into a general band fund that had replaced the old corporation set up under Mills. Nevertheless, on the count-up slips in Cab's files, there are seldom any of the record-breaking audience figures that had been commonplace from the mid-1930s to the mid-1940s. Instead, the most sizable profits were generally in the order of a couple of thousand dollars. Cab's formidable financial commitments to his and Nuffie's young family, and the settlement with Betty made during his highest-earning period, meant that he was no longer a wealthy man.

For what were now far less frequent appearances at the Apollo, or the Strand, in New York, Cab still brought in a female singer to work with his group, to hold the stage during his changes of costume. In 1951, a new recruit, Helen Holmes James, sang with the band, joining during June for a week in Philadelphia, prior to that summer's Apollo engagement. This took place soon after Cab and his quartet had returned from a lengthy first tour of South America.[10] At a time when the band's fortunes were ebbing, this trip was a considerable success, bringing Cab's exuberant style to entirely new audiences. As a result, the following year saw an even more exhaustive tour of South America and the Caribbean.

Starting out in February 1952 in Kingston, Jamaica, where Cab's movies had always been extremely well attended, the band found a large and enthusiastic audience at the Carib Theatre. This included at one end of the social spectrum none other than the governor of the island, Sir Hugh Mackintosh Foot, and at the other, hundreds of ordinary record-buying fans. In Colombia, the unstable political and financial situation led to a few dates being canceled, but the band's newfound popularity in Jamaica was such that these were easily replaced by hastily arranged extra gigs on an unscheduled February return visit to Kingston. During these, the *Daily Gleaner* reported that "their concert tour has taken them to the British West Indian Islands, South America, and the Dutch Antilles. They are now on their way to Haiti, the Dominican Republic, Puerto Rico and the Virgin Islands, after that it is home to New York."[11]

Back in the United States, the perception of Cab in the press was now that he was a fading star rather than a current creator of fashion. Walter Winchell observed that the white tails and zoot suits had been dispensed with, to be replaced by discreet gray pinstripes that were "more Wall than Basin Street."[12] In other reports, Cab himself mourned the passing of the hepster language that he had done so much to popularize, as it was being replaced by beatnik slang:

> Cab Calloway said today it proves if you're old if you can remember way back when a jazz musician was called a hot hepster, and the end of a fast-paced evening left you feeling "real beat." Nowadays an up-to-date cat would say an inspired musician was "the gonest" and indicate fatigue by saying he was "dragged."[13]

In 1952, when Cab was forty-four, despite his South American and Caribbean successes, it seemed that his career was in serious decline. Even so, his new management did not give up on trying to sell him and the band, and he was always welcome in some of the theaters where crowds remembered his heyday. But he was no longer pulling in a mass audience across the country. It was a measure of desperation when stories were placed in the press to suggest he might be the new teen idol:

> Today the teenagers who didn't even exist in those flapper days are suddenly discovering a new star on their entertainment horizon, a guy named Cab Calloway who still has a way with a song and a twinkle.

"I had to face it sooner or later," says Cab with a grin, "I had to realize that a new generation had come along who didn't even know my
name much less my material. I also had to convince a lot of theaters,
bookers and television producers that I could do the hit songs of today."
The hardest job of all was to convince bookers that the modern kids
would rather hear Cab sing "Black Magic" than they would to hear him
sing "Minnie The Moocher." To be sure, Cab must still do his old favor-
ites for the section of the audience which remembers with nostalgia
Cab's wonderful hits like "Minnie," "St. James Infirmary," and so on.
But to win the favor of the teenagers, Cab had to assemble a band that
stacks up with the best of them, and he's putting all the old Calloway
verve into "Jezebel," "Too Young," and other hits of today.[14]

Clearly, despite his depression, Cab had not given up on his ambition to
remain a popular performer, but Nuffie noticed him becoming increasingly
withdrawn, obsessed with the idea that his career was going backward. He
again sought solace at the racetrack whenever band and family commitments
allowed, sometimes betting his entire week's salary or more in an afternoon.
Even this comforting pastime went sour on him during a week's band engagement in Washington, D.C., as he hurried to a race meeting at Charles Town,
West Virginia. Wasting no time in the hope of catching the second of the
afternoon's races, Cab was pulled over for speeding by State Trooper Roy
Smith, as he roared through Leesburg, Virginia, at sixty-five miles per hour.
When he offered the trooper ten dollars to forget about it, Cab was arrested
and charged not only with the speeding offense but with attempting to bribe
a police officer.[15]

Hauled before the judge, who mercifully quashed the bribery charge, Cab
was fined a hundred dollars and obliged to shake the trooper's hand by way of
apology. No races were seen that day, and for a while even Cab's favorite pastime held no attraction for him. After the incident, it quickly became clear to
Nuffie that during his three years of depression, rather than going racing for
fun and a few smallish bets, Cab had gradually developed into a seriously
addicted gambler. She discovered that at some of the tracks he frequented he
owed his bookies so much that they would no longer accept bets from him.
Even if he did not go to the races, he would drop in on his local bookie near
Lido Beach and place a bet most days when he was home. Eventually, with
ever diminishing returns from the band and ever mounting debts, Nuffie put

her foot down. Either she and the children would leave, or he would stop gambling completely. Cab initially protested, but in due course accepted her ultimatum, and for four years he did not place another bet.

Having taken Cab's dissolute behavior in hand, Nuffie also expressed the view that his management was booking him into the "wrong" places, but the fact was that these were often the only places that would take him. In this aspect of Cab's life she was powerless to make a change. Furthermore, the band itself was losing some of its charismatic appeal. In the late spring of 1952, after returning from the Caribbean, Jonah Jones left the quartet as did Milt Hinton, to be replaced by Johnny Letman on trumpet and Aaron Bell on bass.[16]

Cab's repertoire was now a finely balanced combination of his old hits and newer songs that allowed him to keep in touch with current fashions. However, although they were good musicians, Letman and Bell were not the same level of extrovert and entertaining instrumentalists that Jones and Hinton had been. Consequently, to reinforce his act, Cab believed that he needed something different. Harking back to some of the later Cotton Club shows when he had occasionally joined in the revue sketches in costume, he now decided to try the same thing on his touring gigs. Building on the television version of "One for My Baby," where he had convincingly acted the part of a drunk, he decided to step up the acting and costume element of his appearances. The local paper in Reno announced:

> A new and different Cab Calloway opens the New Golden Theatre Restaurant, May 28. The popular "Highness of Hi-de-ho" will be seen as a musical humorist, a romanticist and a philosopher. Many of Calloway's songs will be done in costume and character to fit the song he is singing.[17]

The same report pushes the line that Cab was very happy with his current quartet because it allowed him to explore different moods and atmospheres in his songs, although it also suggests that he still intended to re-form his big band by the end of 1952. This was largely wishful thinking, but after its April shows in Reno, Cab's new act set off to Denver, Colorado, and while there it happened to be seen by the theatrical producer C. Blevins Davis.

Davis was a former schoolteacher from Independence, Missouri. He had long nurtured ambitions to be a theatrical entrepreneur, but before the war his two efforts to mount a Broadway show collapsed. Suave, balding, and well tailored, Davis had nevertheless used his attempts to conquer the Great White Way to become a well-known socialite in New York. In 1946 he married Marguerite Sawyer Hill, some years older than him, and heiress to the railroad entrepreneur James J. Hill. Two years after their wedding, she died, and Davis inherited nine million dollars. "After that," smirked *Time* magazine, "C. Blevins Davis strode forward holding the watering can of wealth."[18]

At the beginning of 1952, Davis had joined forces with the producer and director Robert Breen, who had begun his theatrical endeavors by setting up the Federal Theater in Chicago under the Works Progress Administration. He had recently turned his attention to securing public finding for other worthy artistic ventures on a grand scale. Most recently, in 1950, Breen had cajoled the State Department to underwrite an ambitious European tour by the American Ballet Theater. Now, between them, Davis and Breen cooked up the idea of a full-scale revival of Gershwin's *Porgy and Bess*. Davis's millions would be the cornerstone of setting up the American performances, but once again Breen persuaded the State Department to fund an international tour, with the specific objective that it would "counter Soviet propaganda about the continued enslavement of America's black population."[19]

When C. Blevins Davis saw Cab's new act, complete with costumed and characterful versions of the more current songs, he knew he had found his Sportin' Life. According to Cab in his autobiography, George Gershwin—a regular at the Cotton Club—not only modeled Sportin' Life on Cab's stage persona, but had him in mind for the role when the opera was first cast in April 1935. However, Gershwin's biographer Howard Pollack casts doubt on that, suggesting that John W. "Bubbles" Sublett (half of the song and dance team Buck and Bubbles), who originally played the part, had been the composer's one and only choice.[20]

Whether or not Cab would have been Gershwin's preference, he was ideal for Davis and Breen's new production, convincingly able to bring all his experience of singing about Minnie the Moocher and the opium dens of her Harlem low-life friends to the role of the man who peddles "happy dust" (or cocaine) to Bess. The show was also to star William Warfield as Porgy and Leontyne Price as Bess. Prior to 1952, *Porgy and Bess* had never been given a real extended run, and certainly gave no hint of the exalted status it was to enjoy in the latter part of the twentieth century. The original October 1935 Theater Guild production had lasted a mere 124 performances, and a 1942 revival had managed just over twice that number. Breen was determined that his production would be built to last, and he presented it in a two-act version, which has since become a standard approach, trimming all the action to Catfish Row and Kittiwah Island. A proportion of the sung recitative in the original version was turned into more convincing and contemporary-sounding spoken dialogue. In addition, he used all his directorial skills to fine-tune the show and keep the cast on their toes. Warfield recalled:

> Bobby Breen was a marvelously inventive director. Bouncy and boyish and bursting with fresh ideas, he was always looking for a new highlight to accentuate—and where the libretto lacked them, he made them up. A quirky bit of business, a slang expression that seemed to fit, a gesture or a facial expression that might underline the dialogue—he'd try any-thing on for size and just as easily remove it a few days later as he tried still newer director's tricks.[21]

When Cab was first offered the role, he and Nuffie had deliberated long and hard before he agreed to break up his band and take it on. Were the show not to succeed, he would have destroyed his normal livelihood, so for him, more than for any other member of the cast, joining the show involved decisively turning his back on his present occupation. He had not played as an actor in a stage show since *Hot Chocolates* in 1929, and his few film parts usually involved playing himself. Having taken the resolute step to give up leading a band for the first time since 1930, he got cold feet almost at once. "He felt . . . it was something of a disaster for him," recalled Nuffie. "He was not used to working in relationship to other people on stage."[22]

An added complication, particularly as Breen was such an inventive direc-tor, was that Cab's previously booked band commitments prevented him from joining the cast in time for the premiere in Dallas, on June 9, 1952. For the opening two weeks, Lorenzo Fuller played the part. Cab officially joined the cast when the opera moved to the Civic Opera House in Chicago on June 25. He had a lot of catching up to do to become part of a company that was already several weeks ahead of him in terms of rehearsal and esprit de corps. Breen made it his business to give Cab a crash course in learning how to play as part of an ensemble of actors, rather than as a soloist. Yet he was careful not to smooth out the very distinctive qualities that had made Cab seem ideal for the role in the first place. After almost a month in Chicago, *Porgy and Bess* moved briefly to the Nixon Theatre in Pittsburgh on July 22, before fetching up for a further month at the National Theatre in Washington, D.C., on August 6.[23] By this time, Cab had found his feet in the company, and developed his own distinctive portrayal of the character envisioned by librettist DuBose Heyward as a drug peddler and pimp. The depression that had enveloped Cab since he laid off his big band began to lift as he threw himself into the challenge of the role. For the premiere in the capital, President Truman came alone to see the show, his wife being detained away from Washington. The press reported:

> The president often had a quizzical look on his face at the antics of Cab Calloway, making his stage debut in the role of Sportin' Life. The Negro Orchestra Leader, famed as the "Hi-de-ho King" put into his interpretation the mincing step, facial and body contortions that brought him riches over the past 20 years. He also wore the sporty white suit that has been his trademark. Calloway said people had been after him for 26 years to play the part of Sportin' Life but only recently had the band business become dull enough financially for him to try the legitimate theater.[24]

By and large, the Washington critics liked the new production of *Porgy and Bess*, although some, remembering the show's checkered past, were equivocal about how long it might run. Others felt that Heyward's portrait of the low life of Catfish Row was not quite in keeping with the State Department's aim "to show Europeans that Negroes do have opportunities in the United States." In the end fewer column inches were devoted to the show during the National Theatre run than to the real-life romance that was developing between Warfield and Price in the title roles. As the company set off for Vienna, its first overseas destination, the papers reported: "The center of attention at departure were William Warfield (Porgy) and Leontyne Price (Bess) newlyweds. The young singers, who met when the cast began rehearsing early this summer, were married Saturday in a Harlem, N.Y. church."[25] Aside from his whirlwind romance, Warfield's main memory of this production was the physical torment of playing Porgy. He had talked to previous interpreters of the role, and discovered that playing the crippled hero, wearing a costume that involved the calves and feet being bound to the thighs, had played havoc with their knees. He had a specially padded costume developed and spent long hours each day doing exercises to maintain the suppleness and strength of his legs.

All the cast strode confidently to their airplane at Idlewild (now John F. Kennedy International Airport) and the group was seen off to Europe by a large number of well-wishers. Cab laughed and joked with the crowd, saying how much he was looking forward to seeing Paris again.[26] Before Paris, however, came Vienna, and the cast was apprehensive about playing in a city that was considered the home of so much European opera. How would Austrian audiences react to this African American "folk opera"?

The answer comes from an eyewitness, the writer James Thomas Jackson, later to make his name as a working-class black correspondent, writing about everyday life for the *Los Angeles Sunday Times*. He was serving in the U.S. Army at the time, and he had been posted to a camp some two hundred miles from Vienna, where he negotiated with his commanding officer to allow him to make the round trip to see *Porgy and Bess*. When he arrived, the opening night performance had been sold out, but as he was an African American serviceman in uniform, strings were pulled, and he was found a good seat in the stalls, amid a block reserved for the U.S. State Department and its guests. Fourteen rows from the stage he found the performance completely enthralling. To his— and the cast's—delight so did the Viennese public. Jackson wrote, "At the finale everybody stood and clapped and stomped as all the actors came on stage for a final bow. I counted fourteen curtain calls and still a lot of exuberant applauding and stomping."[27]

Having become a guest of the State Department, Jackson naturally tagged along to the first night party. He recalled:

> The party was a natural ball. Ol' Cab turned them out with his standards "Minnie the Moocher" and "St. James Infirmary," his irrepressible "Hi De Hi De Hi De Ho," and all that splendid jazz from an era long gone. William Warfield sang songs in German, French and English. . . . That was a party that *was* a party! It lasted all night long.[28]

After two weeks in Vienna, where the show was an unequivocal hit, praised for its "life and movement,"[29] the company decamped to Berlin. It is a performance from this period of the tour that has—by lucky accident—been preserved for posterity. For many years it seemed that no live recording of the production survived. However, in 2008, the collector Enno Riekena discovered a privately made tape of a broadcast on German radio of the performance at the Titania Palast in Berlin on September 21, 1952. This was subsequently restored and issued on the Anglo-Swiss Guild label. Overall, the recording reveals a lively, occasionally raucous production, with crowd noises aplenty, considerable onstage banter, and aural evidence of much visual "business." Musically, Warfield is magnificent in "I Got Plenty of Nuttin'," and his duet with Price, "Bess You Is My Woman Now," is wonderfully sung by both principals. Cab's moment of glory comes in act 2, scene 2, where the action has shifted from Catfish Row to a picnic on Kittiwah Island. In "It Ain't Necessarily So," Cab's Sportin' Life migrates easily into the familiar Calloway stage persona. He builds on Gershwin's intended structure for the song by the way he uses his on- (and off-)stage audience to echo his lines, just as he might in his earlier career have encouraged shout-backs from his audience or the band during "Minnie the Moocher."

The short up-tempo scat sequences between verses are vintage Calloway and in the second of these he takes a sly dig at Dizzy Gillespie by incorporating into his scatting the nonsense syllables of Dizzy's song "Ool Ya Koo." Other excellent Calloway moments come in his cadenza to the first stanza, which finds him employing the familiar Jewish cantoral melisma from his "minor moaners," and then we hear him in what was obviously a wild dance routine, accompanied by tom-tom drums at the end of the first run-through of the song. There's a huge burst of applause for this and the heavy-footed sounds of the chorus dancers around him, before he returns to sing the final verse, beginning "Way back in 500 BC . . ."

Cab's other main feature song is "There's a Boat That's Leaving Soon for New York." Here his vocal mannerism of soaring into falsetto for occasional words is initially unsettling, but the sly confidentiality with which he entices Bess (with the aid of some chemical assistance) to come with him is convincing. He is able—in sound alone—to put across the character as roguish and untrustworthy, following which the odd high-pitched word adds to the general slipperiness with which he invests the part.

After a short stay in Paris, the show opened in London on October 9, 1952, for an extended run at the Stoll Theatre on Kingsway. Although members of Cab's family are quoted in his autobiography as staying with him in London "for a year," the show actually clocked up only 142 performances during slightly less than five months in Britain, before returning to New York City in early March 1953, where it settled into the Ziegfeld Theater on Broadway for a further 305 performances. Nevertheless, Nuffie and her daughters did travel over in late November to spend most of the period in London with Cab. The main reason for this was because their third child, Cabella, had been born on October 11, just after the show arrived in the British capital, and Cab was anxious to see the latest addition to the family.

The London run gave rise to some of the most penetrating reviews to have been written about the folk opera. Ronald Duncan, one of the foremost music critics of the period, hated it, describing *Porgy and Bess* as "animalism romanticized, the sordid sentimentalised and finally the mob deified." His objections were principally built around the idea that Gershwin funked the moments of introspective self-examination that are such a strong feature of the European operatic tradition. Why, for example, did we not get an extended number in which Bess reflected on her reasons for following Sportin' Life to New York? Omitting this, pontificated Duncan, "is to avoid writing the opera altogether."[30] Concluding that the work was so flawed as to be "embarrassing, most embarrassing," he dismissed it as a simplistic depiction of external actions, with no attempt to explore the internal conflicts in any of the characters.

His colleague Lord Harewood, writing for the same magazine, *Opera*, took a diametrically opposite view, hailing the production as "wonderful," except that despite Breen's cuts, he felt the piece was still too long. Harewood suggested that even more of the sung recitative could have been thrown out, but he made a strong case for the feel-good element of Gershwin's score, and for the exuberance of the performances. One, in particular was singled out:

> The most outstanding was that of Cab Calloway, who, as the super-spiv Sportin' Life, was playing for the first time a role some of whose aspects were derived from a style of singing he himself had invented. His voice is big, though hardly operatic in quality, his self-confidence and author-ity are boundless, and his personality seemed ubiquitous by the end of the evening. Someone said of him that what he was giving us was not so much a performance on the stage as his backing to the show.[31]

The cavernous Stoll Theatre had been designed and built as the London Opera House for Oscar Hammerstein in 1911. The architect Bertie Crewe produced a vast neoclassical building, complete with rooftop statues and urns, that occu-pied a whole block on the east side of Kingsway, a few steps from the tiny Old

Curiosity Shop made famous by Charles Dickens. The theater housed a vast auditorium, seating almost twenty-five hundred patrons in a rococo master-piece of plasterwork finery, with ornate boxes and steeply raked galleries and balconies. In the 1920s its own company had presented grand opera, but by 1952, as the critic Elizabeth Forbes remembered, its typical offerings were somewhat different:

> The Stoll had all kinds of odd things in those days, like *ad hoc* Italian opera companies. I'd been to see Tito Gobbi in the *Barber of Seville* earlier that autumn. I'd noticed then that *Porgy and Bess* was coming along, but I was rather purist in those days, having just been to Bay-reuth for the first time, and didn't think that the music would amount to much, But then it got a rave review from Lord Harewood in *Opera* magazine, and I decided I ought to sample it. I found it absolutely wonderful. . . . This tour was the first time that Cab Calloway had taken on the role, although very far from the last, as he went on to sing it again in a number of revivals. I think that when you see someone very good in a role in opera or a play, it's usually the best one you see who remains with you, not necessarily the first. It was like that with Laurence Olivier in *Othello*. I can't really remember who else I saw playing it before, only him. In *Porgy and Bess*, Cab made such an impression on me that I can't hear any of the music he sang, such as "It Ain't Necessarily So," without hearing it in Calloway's voice. He was electrifying. If he was on stage, you looked at nobody else, even if he wasn't singing, or speaking or doing anything but just standing there. He had superb diction, too, so that you could hear every single word that he sang.[32]

Such reports of the troupe's British success reached New York, and there was an aura of expectancy about the show when it finally returned to the United States in March 1953. Before that, however, there were some social events in England to be attended to. In particular, during November 1952, the singer Pearl Bailey came to London to marry the jazz drummer Louie Bellson, at Caxton Hall. She was an old friend of Cab's, having appeared with him at the Zanzibar, and also her brother, the dancer Bill Bailey, had been one of Cab's "boys and girls." She and Bellson enjoyed a whirlwind romance, and came to London to wed, as they felt that an interracial marriage would attract less hostile attention from the British press than would have been the case in the United States. The reports, when they did reach America, were—despite somewhat inaccurately describing Bailey as a "Negro blues singer"—respectful and muted, saying: "The twenty guests included Cab Calloway and members of the London cast of *Porgy and Bess*."[33] Fifteen years later, Cab would be starring on stage with Pearl Bailey in another landmark production in the musical theater, *Hello, Dolly!*

For now, however, Cab was glad to have his name in lights again, and to be receiving first-class treatment for himself and his family in Europe. Shortly before he returned to the United States, he was able to do a favor for an old friend. Jonah Jones recalled:

> Cab . . . wrote to me to ask if I would like a job in the pit band when the show came to New York. So I joined the forty-piece pit band in 1953 and stayed with the show for a year. It was okay, but you are playing the same thing night after night and you begin to wonder if you can play jazz any more. I left the show in 1954 when Charles Delauney in Paris fixed up a tour for me in France and Belgium.[34]

When the show did return to America, those who had questioned whether it had been suitable for State Department support were robustly chastised by the doyen of theater critics, Brooks Atkinson, in the *New York Times*. He wrote, "Nothing has done us so much good abroad since Teddy Roosevelt took a bird walk with Lord Grey, Viscount of Fallodon."[35] The reference to the shared interests in ornithology—particularly identifying the songs of native birds—between the one-time British foreign secretary and the former president of the United States may now seem obscure. But Grey's publication of a memoir of their friendship did much to cement Anglo-American relations in the aftermath of World War I. In Atkinson's view, Breen's "magnificent'" production of *Porgy and Bess* had achieved something similar, because of its "Negro artists [who] are the only Americans who can express the wild beauty of an incomparable piece of musical theater. This is one of their finest moments." Virtually all the major critical voices fell into line behind Atkinson, and the production was hailed as a triumph. Only the African American poet and commentator Langston Hughes spoke out forcibly in disagreement—not so much against the production, but the supposed aims of the State Department's sponsorship. Hughes wrote that there would have been little to complain about:

If at the same time . . . it sent abroad other equally effective spectacles in which Negroes were not portrayed solely as childish darkies, crap shooters, dope addicts, ladies of little virtue and quaint purveyors of "You *is*, you *is*, you *is*." . . . Always servants or clowns—and not just clowns or servants but *burlesques* of clowns and servants.[36]

In early 1953, Hughes remained a lone voice, although with hindsight his voice is more in tune with twenty-first century thinking than those of his contemporaries.

By the time of the New York opening, Leslie Scott had taken over from Warfield as Porgy, but the "admirable" Leontyne Price was still singing Bess. Once again praise was heaped upon Cab, whose Sportin' Life "is a memorable figure of evil and revelry—all grace in style, all villainy under the surface."[37] Cab was to settle happily into the role for the following ten months in Manhattan. Headlining in a Broadway show and commuting from the family home in Lido Beach was an unimagined luxury, compared to the anxious years of touring with a quartet, playing ever more insalubrious venues. His status in the show and the value of his name also ensured that he was now able to pay off his gambling debts and meet the continuing costs of his divorce. Before the year was out, Cab and his family could afford to return to their habitual affluent lifestyle.

There was still a strong scent of romance about the show, and although not as high profile as the marriage of Price and Warfield, soon after the return to New York there was another cast wedding. The press reported that "Charles Colman, a chorus singer in the Broadway production of the Negro folk opera *Porgy and Bess* was married to New York stenographer Theda Showell. Cab Calloway who portrays Sportin' Life in the musical was best man."[38]

The long Manhattan run suited Cab. He was able to follow the racing during the day, even though Nuffie now kept him on a strict allowance, and he also enjoyed reunions with many a Harlem crony, as well as discreet liaisons with female friends. But in the early spring of 1954, *Porgy and Bess* again took to the road, this time to play in major theaters across the United States before a return to international touring. To start with, as the company set out for Richmond, Virginia, Cab was enthusiastic, but before long as the tour headed west, he changed his view. For his two major songs in act 2, he was center stage, but although he was both visible and occasionally audible in much of the rest of the action, Sportin' Life was otherwise not the focal point of the plot. Compared to the days when he was headlining his own touring revue, Cab was not always the principal reason people came to see the opera, even though he generally took top billing, now that Price and Warfield had been permanently replaced by less well-known singers.

With his fortunes and his confidence restored, he felt by the summer that the time had come to leave the show, before the company traveled overseas once more. In addition, Nuffie and the girls were miserable. "He was on the road again, and we missed him terribly," she wrote. "The children were getting older and he was getting older and weary of the road."[39] The break came in August 1954, as this press release announced:

> Cab Calloway, the Sportin' Life of the All-Negro show "Porgy and Bess," announced in Los Angeles that he will leave the touring company August 14 to launch a night club act which opens a six week engagement at Las Vegas' plush Sahara Hotel in September. The ex-bandleader said he would be accompanied by a four piece musical group.[40]

By leaving Davis and Breen's touring company, Cab was not—strictly speaking—complying with the wishes of Nuffie and his family and coming off the road. To be sure, he was not setting off for South America or Europe with *Porgy and Bess*, but after the luxury of working for a month and a half until mid-October in a plush Las Vegas hotel, it was not long before he was back on the familiar cabaret and club circuit around the United States. He was barely home for any more time than if he had stayed with the show, not least because he now mainly worked as a solo act, playing a week here and a week there with local backing orchestras.

It is unlikely that this was Cab's original long-term intention in leaving the show. He knew when he gave in his notice that there were two large-scale projects brewing that would—if successful—bring him comparable fame and financial rewards to the previous two years he had spent in the Gershwin folk-opera. First, Breen had plans to make a movie of *Porgy and Bess*, based firmly on his staging of the piece. Louella Parsons, with her ear to the ground for Hollywood gossip, noted Cab's departure, but predicted it would not be long before Cab "catches up with Robert Breen again to recreate his role of Sportin' Life when the film version begins this fall in Munich."[41] Second, the same production team had another big plan, for which they had made discreet behind-the-scenes approaches to Cab. The story broke during Cab's run in Las Vegas.

> An all-Negro production called *Blues Opera* will be premiered in Paris
> early in December by Blevins Davis ad Robert Breen, producers of the
> most recent version of *Porgy and Bess*. Davis and Breen said the opera
> will contain the work of Arna Bontemps, Countee Cullen, Harold
> Arlen and Johnny Mercer, with musical arrangements by Samuel
> Matlowski. If the play is successful, it will open on Broadway in
> September 1955, with a cast of 55 Negro performers, including most
> of the *Porgy* cast.[42]

As it turned out, neither of these projects materialized in ways that could have
been predicted by anyone involved in planning them in 1954. The movie of
Porgy and Bess was to have an extremely checkered production history, and did
not see the light of day until 1959. Sam Goldwyn initially hired the director
Rouben Mamoulian, before firing him and bringing in Otto Preminger, who
had recently made *Carmen Jones*. It then took three years for the project to be
filmed, starring a reluctant Sidney Poitier alongside Dorothy Dandridge. When
the moment finally came to make the movie, Cab turned down the part of
Sportin' Life, which was won—after much brat-pack lobbying—by Sammy
Davis Jr.

Meanwhile, the opposing critical positions adopted over the stage show by
Brooks Atkinson and Langston Hughes mushroomed into a heated and long-
running debate among the intelligentsia about the forthcoming movie, its
content, and the roles of its participants. Cab was immune to this controversy,
having relinquished his interest, but soon after its release the picture was
withdrawn from further public exhibition at the request of the Gershwin estate.
It has seldom been seen since. By contrast, because Sammy Davis Jr.'s recording contract forbade him from appearing on the "original cast" sound track
album, Cab sang the part of Sportin' Life on the record, which was released
and widely available. With orchestrations sensitively developed for the movie
score by André Previn, who also conducted the recording, Cab benefited from
the fracas over the film by making a definitive and exceptionally well-recorded
account of his interpretation of the role. He was also to make frequent television appearances from 1955 onwards, reprising his familiar Sportin' Life songs
from the score, and adding other famous numbers from the show, including
"Summertime."[43]

Harold Arlen's *Blues Opera* was to have an even longer gestation period
than the movie of *Porgy and Bess*. He had been toying with the idea during the

provincial tryouts of his 1954 musical, *House of Flowers,* written with Truman Capote. As that unhappy experience, involving the volatile Pearl Bailey and the experimental British director Peter Brook, was taking its course, Arlen determined to write what the critic Robert Coleman described as "his most ambitious and distinguished project."[44] Based on the 1946 play *St. Louis Woman,* by the Harlem Renaissance writers Arna Bontemps and Countee Cullen, for which Arlen had previously written some incidental music, *Blues Opera* would have a book by Robert Breen and his wife, Wilva. The opera took an age to be written, although Arlen chipped away regularly at the music, nevertheless allowing the project constantly to shift size and shape before his eyes. Every so often a new wave of press releases reassured the public he was on track, so that in mid-1955 it was firmly announced that "Harold Arlen has offered Cab Calloway the role of Ragsdale in his forthcoming *Blues Opera.*"[45]

Then there came a long and ominous period of silence, until in November 1957 André Kostelanetz conducted an orchestral suite at Carnegie Hall arranged by Arlen's amanuensis Samuel Matlowski, and based on the music that was to be included in the *Blues Opera.* The entire work eventually saw the light of day in Amsterdam in 1959, under the title *Free and Easy,* which soon became a byword for one of the biggest disasters in musical theater history. Breen's sure touch was lost owing to a feud with the company manager Stanley Chase. Matlowski's carefully prepared orchestrations for the core of songs originally written as incidental music for *St. Louis Woman* were ditched in favor of new charts by jazz arranger Quincy Jones. Amid organizational chaos, the show died an ignominious death just nine days after it moved to Paris in early 1960. It lost three hundred thousand dollars, and the cast was stranded in Europe. Yet again, although Cab had considered this a plausible career move after *Porgy and Bess,* the time it took to come to fruition, and the many changes Arlen's original idea underwent en route, ruled him out of any participation. As with the television series of *Amos and Andy* or the movie of *Porgy and Bess,* hindsight has shown that he was better off by remaining uninvolved.

Instead, his diary of engagements reads very similarly to that for his early 1950s wilderness years, save that he was no longer carrying the expense of a band. His recent high profile role in *Porgy and Bess* also featured strongly in his press coverage, and ensured that he was usually top of the bill. The new year of 1955 was introduced in style as "'His Highness of Hi-de-ho' Cab Calloway continues to please in the Gold Room of the Hotel Golden-Bank Casino in downtown Reno." Accompanied by the house band, he was in the familiar surroundings of a revue, which also starred comedian Jimmy Ames and the young dancers Lou Mosconi and Camille.[46] Soon afterward he moved to the Mocambo in Hollywood, and as the year went on he toured consistently.[47] While on the road, he continued to make occasional appearances in the gossip columns, not least when *Jet* magazine listed him as "the best known celebrity with full-grown offspring," contrasting his youthful good looks with an excellent picture of his eldest daughter, the twenty-eight-year-old Camay Calloway Brooks, teaching school in Alexandria, Virginia.[48]

In the fall of 1955, just before the birth of his first grandson, Christopher, Cab undertook a solo tour to Great Britain, where he had been such a celebrated member of the cast of *Porgy and Bess*. He was accompanied by a local quartet led by the reed player Vic Ash, which included the pianist Stan Tracey and drummer David "Benny" Goodman. Cab's dejected body language in the photographs from the start of the visit suggest that he had not been received with the hero's welcome he might have expected. "Slumped in a chair with his shirt thrown open," read one caption, "usually dapper singer Cab Calloway rehearses with the Vic Ash quartet for a tour of Great Britain."[49]

Playing Sportin' Life in the plush—if somewhat faded—surroundings of the Stoll Theatre in the West End of London to adoring opera audiences was one thing. It was quite another to be touring the dowdy theaters and run-down music halls of provincial Britain which—although World War II had ended some ten years before—was still recovering from its privations. The English journalist Steve Voce met Cab in 1958, and built up this depressing picture of what happened:

> Cab Calloway spent several weeks in the Autumn of 1955 playing to cheerless and diminutive variety audiences throughout the country. It seems a pity that he couldn't have put his visit forward a couple of years to the present time when he would probably have gained the acclamation that his talents merit. Possessing all the attributes of a great jazz singer—a perfect ear, superb phrasing and timing, and the ability to swing a band with his own voice, it is highly desirable that Cab should be unearthed by somebody like John Hammond or George Avakian and restored to the place in jazz that should be his.[50]

As it turned out, Voce was prophetic in these observations, which were published in June 1958, because Cab was brought back into the recording studio with a big band made up of New York's finest session players at the end of that year. He rerecorded some of his best known songs for Victor, part of a process that many swing era singers and bandleaders undertook at that period, in order to remake their earlier hits in high fidelity stereo sound.

However, on Cab's return home from Britain in the fall of 1955 it was not the jazz world that came a-calling for his services as a recording artist, but that of mainstream popular entertainment. He and his daughter Lael, the middle-born of his marriage to Nuffie, were both featured on a song aimed squarely at the family market called "The Little Child." For a while Nuffie got her wish to spend more time with her husband, while he promoted this new record. As 1956 began, Cab's press coverage was uncharacteristically focused on his home life and particularly his seven-year-old daughter. For her part, although she always pulled herself together on stage when they sang in public, Lael hated the attention, and would "pout and grimace" before every performance, as she was squeezed into her frilly dress and shiny shoes.[51]

The tender song of paternal love was not new. Indeed, Frankie Laine and Jimmy Boyd had recorded it a couple of years before on the flip side of "Tell Me a Story." Commercially, their recording disappeared without trace, except in France, where a cover version was made in French and caught on with the public immediately, through the song's clever mixture of sentimentality, the innocent evocation of childhood, and a touching romanticism. On the back of the song's success in France, it was rerecorded in United States by several artists, of whom the first was Eddie Albert. Then Cab and Lael, not to mention Danny Kaye, also made versions, but it was Cab's that really clicked with the marketplace.[52] Lael sings firmly and clearly but with the endearing innocence of a seven-year-old, and then Cab sings a reply to her questions about whether the world is round and where the "bluebird of happiness" can be found. His voice reveals an intimacy entirely different from much of the hi-de-ho-ing of Cotton Club days. The years in *Porgy and Bess* had given him the opportunity to develop a far richer and more flexible sound, which was to be the hallmark of his mature years, although he still retains the perfect diction and delivery that had marked out his work from the 1930s onward. Even the most seasoned of critics were smitten, a typical example being the disc jockey Bob Foster:

This week when we regularly pick up discs for a record show we conduct on KEEN (Monday 8:30 p.m. to 10) we were handed something called "The Little Child," a French tune, with Lael and Cab Calloway. (Lael is Cab's young daughter.) . . . The words the music and the presentation are all top drawer. Calloway and his daughter sing this one straight with none of the famous Calloway "hi-de-ho" stuff. It's straightforward, shows off Cab's fine baritone voice and has charming lyrics. It's one of those records that everybody will want for his collection, we're sure.[53]

As part of the promotion of the disc, veteran broadcaster Edward Murrow brought his TV show *Person to Person* to Cab's Lido Beach home. This series, which ran from 1953 to 1959, was one of CBS television's most popular shows, and Murrow doorstepped a different personality each week. Much was made of his visit to "rhythm man" Cab Calloway in February 1956.[54]

As it happened, it was one of the last opportunities to film Cab and his family at this particular address, because soon after the show was aired, they moved to a large twelve-room white colonial-style home at 1040 Knollwood Road, in Greenburgh, Westchester County. This house, which had a basement den for Cab and plenty of space for his family, was to be his home until his death, and it is where all three of his daughters from the marriage to Nuffie remember growing up. It was by far the largest, most prestigious home of any African American jazz musician of the time. Although Cab's youngest daughter, Cabella, arranged for it to be sold in the 1990s, Lael Calloway was again living there in 2008, and launched a campaign to save it for the nation as a landmark in musical history.[55]

As 1956 went on, Cab returned to his touring life. There were more guest appearances, both on stage and television, singing the songs from *Porgy and Bess*, but there was also the usual round of clubs and theaters as a solo act. He had now begun to travel with a regular pianist, Cyril "Spider" Haynes, who would work with Cab as sole accompanist, or sit in with the house band, where he would act as musical director, guiding the other musicians through a selection from Cab's library of arrangements. Spider Haynes was born in Panama in 1915, but he had been around in the American jazz world almost as long as Cab, having started out as a teenage prodigy in the early 1930s. Haynes had notched plenty of time with various swing era bands, such as the Savoy Sultans and Noble Sissle's Orchestra. In the late 1940s he had been Lena

Horne's pianist and he established a reputation for reliability while working with her, between spells as the house pianist in various Fifty-second Street clubs. Despite his reputation for always making the gig, on one occasion in mid-1956 in Syracuse, New York, Haynes was unexpectedly taken ill, and unable to play. The call went out for Jay Cole, the pianist brother of Cab's former drummer Cozy, to come across from his regular job nearby, and take over. Cole duly arrived, and remembered, "We used the house band, Cab did all the singing."[56]

Soon Haynes was back in harness, and at the end of the year he joined Cab and singer-songwriter Jimmy Randolph at the Beachcomber club in Miami. This was the first incarnation of what would become another regular Calloway concept in the years to come—turning an existing nightclub into a full-blown recreation of the 1930s Cotton Club. The star female role was taken by Sallie Blair, who was soon to have a (short-lived) success as a singer on the Bethlehem record label. The New York press reported that "Sallie Blair is doing such handsome business at the Boulevard out in Queens that her next assignment will be a real plum. She'll have a starring role, opposite Cab Calloway, in a Miami Beach night club revue patterned after the classic Cotton Club format."[57]

After this idea worked successfully in Miami, the same formula was adopted at nightclubs in several other towns, including Winnipeg and Atlantic City, as the years went on.[58] In such venues, Cab played to a few hundred people in the amiable surroundings of a revue. But at the end of the 1950s, he and Haynes began considering a long-running engagement as the interval entertainment for basketball matches featuring the Harlem Globetrotters. When he was learning his trade in Chicago, Cab had first got to know the team boss Abe Saperstein. Around the time that Cab went out on the road with the Alabamians, Saperstein had taken over the Savoy Big Five—an exhibition basketball team who played before dancing began at the Chicago Savoy Ballroom. Renamed the New York Harlem Globetrotters, by mid-1929 this team was touring the Midwest. Thereby it started a long-running history as one of the most successful basketball teams of all time, and in a sporting equivalent to Cab's own act, it mingled entertainment with winning professionalism.

The two men met again by chance at the end of the 1950s, and Saperstein suggested Cab would be an ideal halftime act. The Globetrotters were currently fielding two teams in professional competitions, one on the

West Coast and one on the East. Ultimately he was to sing for both aggregations, but Cab's first appearances seem to have been at the start of the 1960s in Long Beach, California, with the western team. The local press noted:

> Calloway who appeared here Monday night as emcee for the half-time show of the Harlem Globetrotters at Municipal Auditorium, said, "It's a pity that live entertainment has disappeared the way it has." The leader of the famous band of the 30s is now playing "singles," and is glad to be back with the people. "This job was a challenge because I have to face all of those people alone. When I had my band, the boys gave me a lot of confidence," Calloway said. "I get the impression that people want live entertainment again," he said. "When you can walk out in front of 10,000 persons and you can hear a pin drop, you know you've got their attention."[59]

Cab, backed up only by the solo piano of Spider Haynes, was able to get the huge basketball crowds to sing "Hi-de-ho" along with him. Through what was to become a long association with the Globetrotters during the early 1960s, a new generation experienced his tales of Minnie the Moocher and her friends firsthand. So, too, did Maytime race goers at the Preakness Stakes at Maryland's Pimlico racetrack, where Cab also provided his unique brand of entertainment. He particularly enjoyed the social camaraderie of the Globetrotters, sitting up at night after the games drinking and talking, exactly as he would have done with musicians in earlier times. And the racetrack, where he once more indulged in a little on-track betting, had always been a second home to him as well.

As the 1960s went on, Cab's substantial income from his Globetrotters performances reduced his dependence on the regular circuit of club and theater shows, on which he made fewer appearances. His renewed popularity with a younger audience brought him back occasionally to the television studios. On February 23, 1964, he was a guest on the *Ed Sullivan Show* in an edition which vividly marked the contrast between old and new styles of popular music, as the main featured performers were the Beatles. With a return to his early hit "St. James Infirmary" and a skilled version of "Old Man River," Cab more than held his own against the new sounds of "Please Please Me," and "Twist and Shout." He was the other standout act alongside the Fab Four in a show that also included the singer Gloria Bleezarde, the puppets Pinky and Perky, and the British comedians Morecambe and Wise.

The following year, he took time out for a cameo (and music-free) appearance in the movie *The Cincinnati Kid*. Nevertheless, he was surprised when in 1967 the impresario David Merrick approached him to see if he would consider a return to the musical theater stage. The idea was that he would play the wealthy Horace Vandergelder in what was planned to be an all-black production of Jerry Herman and Michael Stewart's musical *Hello, Dolly!* based on Thornton Wilder's stage play. Merrick was already the producer of a successful Broadway version of the show at the St. James Theatre, starring Carole Channing, which had been running since 1964. Now he planned to extend the run by bringing in his entirely new all-black cast with Pearl Bailey in the role of Mrs. Levi. A widely syndicated story reported:

> Calloway said when he was approached for *Hello Dolly* he wasn't at all sure he wanted to do it. "Then all of a sudden David Merrick made up my mind for me," he said. "We settled a few little things and that was it. I hadn't done a musical in a long time. It was pretty hard to make the transition."[60]

Approaching his sixtieth birthday, Cab had every reason to think of taking things easy. Returning to the rigors of a nightly Broadway show had not been in his plan. But his decision to join the cast was spectacularly vindicated on two grounds. Firstly the play itself was a triumph. Secondly, it achieved something of a landmark in race relations.

It opened during October in Washington at the National Theatre, where President Lyndon Johnson (who adopted the title tune as his theme song) enthusiastically joined in the curtain calls during one performance. It transferred to New York the following month, where it moved into the St. James in place of Merrick's previous production, which went out on tour. The Washington critics were warmly enthusiastic about the show, but nothing had prepared the cast for the marvelous notices they would receive when it arrived in New York. Clive Barnes, observing that Merrick had "show business coming out of his ears," wrote in the *New York Times*:

> Frankly my sensitive white liberal conscience was offended by the idea of a non-integrated Negro show. It sounded too much like *Blackbirds*

of 1967 and all too patronizing for words. But from the first to the last
I was overwhelmed. Maybe Black Power is what some of the other
musicals need. For Miss Bailey, this was a Broadway triumph for the
history books. . . . So far I've done something I never thought I could.
I've overlooked Cab Calloway, but the gorgeous Calloway, as the mean
and respectable Horace Vandergelder, who is Dolly's perfect final
match, amply shared Dolly's triumph. His acting was polished and his
singing was so stylish that right from the start anyone who knew the
show must have been regretting that he had so little to sing.[61]

It was immediately apparent that Merrick had a huge hit on his hands. Other
critics concurred completely with Barnes, who was the most powerful voice
in theatrical criticism in 1967. Adding his enthusiastic approval, Richard
Lebherz, who was used to the world-weary demeanor that Pearl Bailey used in
her cabaret act, wrote:

> I expected to see the familiar tired old Pearl. Cab Calloway I imagined
> would be doing his usual Harlem Cotton Club routine. Instead we got
> a dignified Pearl and an utterly lovable Calloway as Mr. Vendergelder.
> By the way, Mr. Vandergelder in other productions of *Dolly* had a way
> of fading into the background. But in this one there isn't a moment
> when Cab Calloway is on the stage that we don't see him, feel him and
> watch his every move. He is terrific and still has the magic that makes
> him great.[62]

However, it was Lebherz who first observed the other coup that the show's
producer had managed to stage:

> David Merrick has been able to accomplish in his all-Negro production
> of *Hello Dolly* what civil rights hasn't been able to do since it began,
> only in reverse. Merrick has been able to integrate a once all-white
> musical production into an all-Negro musical. The fact is that the pre-
> miere of *Hello Dolly* at the National Theatre in Washington starring
> Pearl Bailey and Cab Calloway is the first musical to treat the Negro as
> a middle class person instead of a Negro in a ghetto. *Porgy and Bess*,
> *St. Louis Woman, House of Flowers*, were all about Negroes involved in
> a typical Negro environment.[63]

Therein lay the key to Merrick's success, which allowed him to extend the 1,600 or so performances the show had already had, before his new cast arrived, to a staggering overall unbroken Broadway run of 2,844.

For Cab there was an additional reason to be proud of his success in this production, because appearing alongside him was his daughter, Chris, now aged twenty-two, in the role of Minnie. As a consequence of her part in the show, Cab enjoyed a little mischief making when he was reunited backstage with Jack Raymond, the *New York Times* Berlin correspondent. He recalled that Cab had been somewhat preoccupied when *Porgy and Bess* had arrived in Germany some fifteen years before, owing to Cabella's imminent arrival. "Was it a boy or a girl?" asked Raymond. Wordlessly, Cab stretched out a hand and introduced him to Chris, implying that she (rather than Cabella) was the daughter who had been born in the course of the European tour of that earlier show.[64]

During the first part of the run of *Hello, Dolly!* father and daughter also appeared as a singing double-act on the *Tonight* show on television, in a week when Victor Borge was the guest presenter. This was a precursor of their frequent work together in the 1980s, when Chris appeared as an additional singer with Cab and the Hi-De-Ho Orchestra, which he formed for international touring in his final years.[65] In her late teens, Chris had dropped out of Boston University, where she had studied acting and drama, but from age nineteen she had started to make a go of being a solo singer with the John Lucien Trio. She auditioned in her own right for *Hello, Dolly!* and was quick to tell the press that nepotism played no part in her casting. "Anyone can open doors for you," she said, "but no one can sing for you or talk for you at an audition or in front of an audience."[66]

Once the all-black *Hello, Dolly!* was well established on Broadway, and she had garnered a good crop of press notices for her performance, Chris Calloway met and fell in love with the South African trumpeter and singer Hugh Masekela, who had left his homeland with the help of the campaigner Father Trevor Huddleston and the English jazz musician John Dankworth, to begin a new career in the United States. At age twenty-nine, formerly married to the charismatic singer Miriam Makeba, he was already remarkably successful, with several crossover jazz-pop records. He was also an immediate hit with the Calloway family when Chris took him home to the house in Greenburgh. He loved sitting in Cab's den, sipping champagne, and talking about the old days of the Cotton Club band that had starred his idols Dizzy Gillespie and

Jonah Jones. Before long, a large-scale wedding was being planned at the house, to fit in around the intensive Broadway schedule of *Hello, Dolly!* Masekela remembered:

> Nuffie marched us through the motions in the gigantic gardens of her estate, briefing us on how the ceremony would go down, from the back porch through the trellises to the gazebo, where the minister would marry us. The guests were going to be the who's who of the entertainment business.[67]

In his autobiography, Masekela is completely candid about his and Chris's use of marijuana, cocaine, brandy, champagne, and barbiturates, which had a cumulatively disastrous effect on Chris. Already having suffered one near breakdown as she dropped out of university, despite her success in the musical, she was dangerously unstable. After taking a cocktail of drugs and alcohol, she set off from New York with Masekela one weekend to see him off at the airport to fly back to his house in Malibu. At JFK, she cajoled her way onto the plane and flew out to California with him. When she got there, she refused to go home.

Cab and David Merrick were furious, but they managed to cast Masekela as the villain of the peace in the resultant publicity. "She wanted to be married at home by the fireplace," ran one report. "Her father wanted her to be married in church. But the prospective bridegroom thought a normal American wedding involved too much publicity."[68]

Masekela's lawyers eventually settled with Merrick for fifty thousand dollars for the breach of Chris's contract. Although the boxes of wedding invitations had been waiting to be mailed, and Nuffie had booked police patrolmen to guard the gates and handle the parking, Chris and Masekela opted for a registry-office wedding in California on May 31, 1968. "We only want Chris to be happy," said a tight-lipped Nuffie. "We will welcome her and her husband. Hugh is well-educated and mannerly, we like him and think he will make a good husband." Cab shrugged his agreement. "What has happened has happened. Eloping with Hugh is what Chris wanted to do and she did it. The theater released her from her contract so she could be with her husband."[69]

Chris followed Masekela around the country as he took part in a nationwide touring package from the Newport Jazz Festival, but her increasingly eccentric behavior drew adverse comments from other musicians and the public alike. Dizzy Gillespie—now long reconciled with Cab and also on the tour—told Masekela that when he and his wife, Lorraine, had occasionally babysat Chris in the late 1940s, she had been crazy. Masekela's friend and business colleague Stewart Levine dismissed claims that Chris's condition had been brought on by the oppressive treatment of her parents. "Cab has always been a happy millionaire," he said. "There's no way Chris could have ever suffered except by her own doing."[70]

Masekela's iron constitution could handle the drink and the drugs. It could handle a punishing tour schedule. Whatever state he was in, through the power of his playing and singing, he could bring the audience to its feet every night with his big hit "Grazin' in the Grass." But he could not handle Chris's erratic moodswings. In August 1968, just three months after the wedding, he arranged a quickie divorce in Mexico. After this, there was some speculation that Chris might return to her role in *Hello, Dolly!* but Merrick and Cab were not prepared to take the risk. "Chris Calloway (Cab's gifted, perky daughter) quit *Hello Dolly* to get married," said one paper, going on to confirm that she "won't return, though her marriage had a short jog."[71]

Chris did, however, throw herself on her father's mercy. Although he would not help her return to the show, in which her former role was being successfully played by Peaches Brewer, Cab did lend his backing to relaunching her solo career. Advertisements for her singing act that appeared that fall carried the strapline "Cab Calloway presents . . ." Meanwhile he continued to star on Broadway, and then in a subsequent national tour, which ran until 1971.[72] Although Cab had long been a friend of Pearl Bailey, had helped launch her career at the Zanzibar, attended her wedding in London, and costarred with her in this show, he was never entirely at ease about her performance. Even on the first night she ad-libbed changes to the title song, and as the tour went on he was increasingly unsure not only of how she would behave but whether she would even show up. She tried to walk out several times but was always coaxed back. The actor Morgan Freeman, whose Broadway debut was as "Rudolph" in the cast, does not remember her ever missing a performance,[73] but Cab experienced over ninety occasions in three and a half years when her understudy was compelled to play the part. In the end, in a bizarre echo of Chris Calloway's behavior, Pearl Bailey simply walked out of the production en route between Houston and Milwaukee.[74] Despite good advance sales, without its costar, the show never opened. Cab's second period in the musical theater was over.

Chapter 11

The Hi-De-Ho Man
1971–1994

....

uring its Broadway run, *Hello, Dolly!* had allowed Cab to return to a
routine very similar to that which he had enjoyed in the course of
Porgy and Bess. He would commute every evening from his home in
Greenburgh to the theater, and spend his free time with his family or at the
racetrack. He could stop off in Harlem to see old friends after the performance, and he could keep up with many of his old colleagues who were working in and around New York. Once the show went on the road, however, he was
back in another equally familiar routine, which he had undertaken for years
with the band, spending a week here and a week there. During the final stages
of its tour in 1971, the musical was presented in some unlikely venues, including the huge sixty-three-hundred-seat Shrine Auditorium in Los Angeles.
Despite the auditorium's having a proscenium stage and being laid out in the
style of a traditional theater, the critics felt that this was one step too far for the
production, so that even Cab and Pearl Bailey, who both resorted to ad libs and
hamming up in the manner of their old revue shows, were floundering in its
cavernous space.[1] Nevertheless, until the tour closed, Cab was back where he
had spent most of his life—on the road.

The debacle over Chris Calloway and her abrupt departure from the Broadway production of the musical had revealed a few cracks beneath the surface
of Cab's long and happy marriage to Nuffie. Chris explained her neurotic
behavior to Hugh Masekela by saying that Nuffie, who had become used to

ruling the roost during Cab's constant absences on tour, was too domineering. When he was at home, Cab avoided confrontation with his wife, being—as Chris put it—"a wimp." Chris had run out on the big wedding at the family house because "it would all have been a show for our neighbors, and not much to do with us."[2] Allowing for a degree of self-justification, it is probable that Chris had a point.

Most of the marriages that came out of the era of the old Calloway band, such as those of Milt and Mona Hinton, Danny and Blue Lu Barker, or Dizzy and Lorraine Gillespie, were similarly long lived, but all of them had a comparable element of tension between the pull of the road (or the studios) and the hearth. Dizzy always longed to be home, but as soon as he had been back in his New Jersey house for a couple of days, he was planning his next escape, because as his road manager Charles Lake put it, "he didn't know what to do with himself when he was at home for any length of time."[3]

Cab was much the same. When the tour of *Hello, Dolly!* finished, against his own wishes, he fulminated against Pearl Bailey for walking out. "I couldn't understand her doing a thing like that," he said. "When I make a commitment to an audience I mean it. A professional performer has a contract that's a lot more than what's on paper."[4] Consequently, once he was back home, but without the comfortable balance between living in his own house and spending part of each day performing in Manhattan, Cab sought opportunities to put himself back on the road as a solo act whenever possible. No longer fronting his own band, he could travel anywhere in the United States, or even abroad, with a box of arrangements of his most famous hits to be used by anything from a backing trio to a local house band. There were some surprises in the box. British saxophonist Alan Barnes, who worked with him in Europe, recalled that "the baritone parts were almost illegible, they were so spattered with generations of musicians' saliva." Altoist Julian Presley found the majority of the music in his pad had been named "Jeff" by Hilton Jefferson, with breathing and fingering marks carefully penciled in. And other arrangements were in the careful hand of Eddie Barefield, whom Cab recruited, years after his time in the ranks of the saxophones, to freshen up some of the charts.[5]

Initially, he was in demand, not least because he had recently acquired a reputation among younger audiences for his cheery appearance as Gabriel in the made-for-television movie *The Littlest Angel.* Shot during the time Cab was on Broadway, and originally broadcast in the Hallmark *Hall of Fame* series in 1969, this featured Johnny Whitaker as a boy who falls fatally from a cliff and ascends into heaven. He is welcomed by Gabriel, played by Cab. Among the other stars with cameo roles, Fred Gwynne (better known as Herman from *The Munsters*) is the boy's guardian angel. This TV movie was shown frequently during 1971, shortly after Cab finished the tour of *Hello, Dolly!*

In 1971 and 1972 Cab appeared at venues from Minnesota to Florida, for charity fund-raisers, for chambers of commerce, and for dances, the common factor being that they got him out of the house. In between, he played hotels and clubs in the Catskills, which were not particularly lucrative, but offered work to an appreciative audience relatively close at hand. In the fall of 1972, he was one of the star turns on the touring Roy Radin Vaudeville Revue, deliberately setting out to recreate old triumphs. As one reviewer noted when the show arrived at the War Memorial Theater in Syracuse, New York:

> Calloway's voice, which with shut eyes, could have been singing on the airwaves of an early radio show, still has that intoxicating, happy quality. After warming the audience with "It Ain't Necessarily So," Calloway turned the Memorial into a singalong, with the room singing "Hi-de-ho" to the refrain of "Minnie The Moocher."[6]

Then Broadway beckoned again. This time the project was a revival of the 1954 Tony Award–winning show *The Pajama Game*, set in the fictional Cedar Rapids factory of Sleep-Tite Pajamas. Cab was cast as Hines, a wily time-and-motion man. Advance interviews with Cab's costar, Barbara McNair, reported that "It's such a great cast. Cab Calloway is going to be wonderful doing the Eddie Foy Jr. part." Prior to the opening, a number of Broadway newshounds turned up at the Riverside Plaza Hotel on West Seventy-third Street, where the cast were being put through their paces in rehearsal by the show's original director, George Abbott, now aged eighty-six, and by the cocomposer and lyricist of the piece, Richard Adler.[7]

From their reports and a general buzz of excitement surrounding the revival, it looked as if Cab might be involved in another long-term Broadway run. After all, the original production had notched over a thousand performances. Before long, however, the less than completely enthusiastic preview notices started coming in, as a result of which the play arrived on Broadway with only a short-term booking at the Lunt-Fontanne Theatre. It opened on December 9, 1973. Adler was hopeful that the show's old magic would be rekindled, and that when the limited run was over, there would be a straightforward transfer to another theater. But he had reckoned without the prevailing market conditions. "This is the worst season to hit Broadway in history," reported critic William E. Sarmento. "Prices are high, shows are generally not worth the price, and no one seems to be going to the theater regularly anymore."[8]

In this context, even a surefire revival needed to be extra special to succeed. Sarmento was noncommittal: *"The Pajama Game* with Cab Calloway, Hal Linden, Barbara McNair and Mary Jo Catlett is quite entertaining if you didn't see the hit twenty years ago."[9] As it happened, judging from all the reviews, the revival was quite good. But just not good enough to ensure a transfer, so that when the curtain was about to fall for the last time at the Lunt-Fontanne, desperate measures were being contemplated by the production team and the cast, as one paper reported:

> Hooray for Cab Calloway and producer Dick Adler! They're looking for $50,000 so *The Pajama Game* starring Barbara McNair and Hal Linden can switch to another musical theater and continue. "I'll work for nothing, I'll pledge $50,000," Cab Calloway shouted during what was supposed to be the last performance. Adler announced, "We're going to fight, We're not closing." The moving cost is for transportation, new marquee, new advertising, new rehearsals with a new crew. Adler hopes to get "co-operation" from theaters. The show must move from the Lunt-Fontanne, Feb. 3rd. Everybody agrees, they need a miracle on 46th Street.[10]

Unfortunately 1974 was not a year of miracles on Broadway, and this production was never to be revived. However, Cab's association with it reinforced the second of two distinct marketing strategies when he resumed his solo career. In both cases he deliberately played the nostalgia card. On the one hand he could continue to hi-de-ho through all his great hits from the 1930s and 1940s, but on the other he was now being booked as a Broadway and musical theater star, singing a selection of songs from the shows. During his run in *Hello, Dolly!* he had taken time out to visit the studios and record an album covering not only the best known songs from that show but those from *Cabaret* and *Mame* as well. The promotion for the disc contained reports of the recording session:

> Fingers snapping, toes tapping, Cab Calloway listened to a record he had just made of "I Will Wait For You" for a new album. . . . "I feel like

I was going on 20," he said. His face is unlined, his brown eyes twinkle under the studio lights and there isn't a gray hair detectable on his head. Most important his voice is as lusty and swinging as ever.[11]

As that record was being sold widely in the nation's record stores, so, too, was a double long-playing album that compiled many of Cab's best-known songs from his big band days. With a cover that featured several poses in the *Stormy Weather* zoot suit, Columbia brought out *The Hi-De-Ho Man* in the spring of 1974, spanning his work for that label from the mid-1930s to 1947.[12]

From 1974 until 1978, Cab maintained a solo career that took in both aspects of his work. He joined forces, for example, with Anita O'Day, Ray Eberle's orchestra, and a jazz group led by Ray McKinley at Pasadena Civic Auditorium, to "recreate the sounds of the '40s." For this type of show, he reverted entirely to his jump-jive hits and got everyone to sing "Minnie the Moocher." He would do the same when he ended sponsored or chamber of commerce gigs, such as one in Naples, Florida, where, after crooning through hits from the shows, he helped them "whoop it up in the wake of the greatest tourist season in Collier County annals."[13]

In between traveling to gigs, and despite his restlessness at being confined to the house between engagements, Cab remained at the center of his family. In 1975—exactly twenty years after her first appearance on record with her father—Lael Calloway relaunched her singing career. This time around, as an adult, rather than a child star, she chose to use her given first name Cecelia as her professional title. According to *Jet* magazine, Cab and "four of his daughters" came along to hear her at the Riverboat.[14] In fact the family party was made up of three of his daughters, Camay, Chris, and Cabella. The "fourth daughter" was Liz Simms Campbell, the child of Cab's old friend and drinking companion cartoonist E. Simms Campbell, who had recently died. Liz was adopted as an honorary Calloway, and often went to social events with the family. At the time of Lael's gig, Liz Campbell's husband, Bryant Rollins, was collaborating with Cab on his autobiography. After many a taped interview and a trawl through the memorabilia that he had amassed on the road, *Of Minnie the Moocher and Me* appeared in 1976.

Lael had not had an easy time of it since her innocent debut on disc with "The Little Child." A teenage pregnancy, an early failed marriage, a tough professional training as a nurse, followed by the death of her second husband from cancer, were all behind her when she opened at the club. She had often felt overwhelmed as a child by the giant personality of her father, but during the mid-1970s she had gotten to know him better as he supported her through her myriad problems. Of all the family, she was the one whom he most liked to take with him to the racetrack or to a ball game. Just as Cab had helped Chris through the aftermath of her romance with Masekela, he now did the same for Lael by supporting her efforts to become a singer in her own right. "I don't want to be a burden on him any more," she wrote of her Riverboat debut. "I'm on my own, Daddy doesn't have to feel obligated to take care of me or support me."[15]

There was family tragedy as well in this period, when in August 1977, John Fortune, or "Papa Jack" as Cab had called him, died. Although he had split up from Cab's mother around fifty years before, he had remained in regular contact with Cab and the family. Fortune had ended up working as the advertising manager for the *Baltimore Afro-American*, the newspaper of which Camay's second husband, John Murphy, was the proprietor. This event briefly reunited Fortune's Calloway stepchildren, Bernice, Elmer, Cab, and Blanche. Apart from Cab, Blanche was still the most high-profile of the other siblings. She gave up the stage during World War II, and at the time of Fortune's death had been living in Miami for twenty years or so, where she raised a stepson. She had become a committed Christian Scientist, yet her devotion to religion did not prevent her hosting a weekly radio show on which she played her favorite jazz and blues music in between news items and interviews. She had also founded her African American cosmetics empire and built it into a very large organization. Consequently Blanche was regularly invited to address conferences and motivational meetings for women in business.[16]

During this period in the 1970s, however, Cab was treading water professionally. He was now being booked for some large international festivals, of the type that had sprung up in the United States and Europe in the wake of the 1948 Nice International Jazz Festival and the slightly younger Newport Jazz Festival in Rhode Island. For example, he appeared in July 1977 at what was then the most sizable European event, the North Sea Jazz Festival in The Hague, Holland. But this was essentially an exercise in nostalgia, reconnecting with fans who recalled his visit there with the Cotton Club Band in the 1930s. In his stage musicals, from *Porgy* through *Hello, Dolly!* and culminating in his short-lived comic acting role in *The Pajama Game*, Cab had been extending his professional range. His voice had developed into a fine musical theater baritone, capable of projecting forcefully into all but the largest theaters, and his abilities as an actor grew at the same time. Now—as he approached his seventies—he was standing still artistically, and reverting to an ever-diminishing repertoire of his own most famous songs, most of which he could probably sing in his sleep.

When he reached the age of seventy, he was fortunate that the growing vogue for African American stage musicals came to his rescue, and found him a new platform for his talents. In 1978 he joined the cast of the touring version of *Bubbling Brown Sugar*. The show was set in various fictitious Harlem nightclubs, and it was crafted by its author, Loften Mitchell, into a pacey sequence of songs, dances, and comic turns in the manner of a Cotton Club revue. Prior to Cab's arrival, the music contained in the show had altered slightly as it ran through 766 performances on Broadway, according to the talents of the available cast. Fundamentally, however, the repertoire was built around songs associated with Cab, Duke Ellington, Count Basie, Fats Waller, and Eubie Blake. The show set off on the road at the very start of 1978, after the final curtain fell at the ANTA Playhouse in New York on New Year's Eve, December 31, 1977. Initially the charismatic dancer Honi Coles starred in the touring version, but Cab took over around the middle of the year. One of the first destinations he played was the city in which he had grown up. *Billboard* reported:

> Cab Calloway had a bang-up time when he returned to his home town of Baltimore. The Hi-de-ho Man, backed by the Madison Street Six, led a crowd of about 300 who were on hand to welcome him, with a round of hi-de-ho. Calloway, who has been in the industry 50 years, was the recipient of a proclamation declaring July "Welcome Home Cab Calloway Month," in honor of his contribution to the country's musical heritage. The presentation was held in Hopkins Plaza, outside the Mechanics Theatre where Cab opened a week-long run in *Bubbling Brown Sugar*.[17]

In the show itself, Cab took the role of John Sage accompanied by Clebert Ford, who played his sidekick, nicknamed "Checkers," and Mabel Lee played his lover, Irene, who never quite manages to get him to the altar. The idea was that two older couples, Calloway and Lee being one of them, showed two younger couples around the bright lights of 1920s Harlem. The reviewers felt that while "Calloway dazzles with his charm and flair, and Clebert Ford delights with his facial pizzaz," poor Miss Lee did not quite manage to hold her own.[18] This seems hardly to have mattered in the light of Cab's "spectacular exultation," which, together with the virtuosity of tap dancer Ronald Stevens, who recreated Bill Robinson's famous up-and-down-stairs routine, carried the show. Cab was to return to this production on and off through into the early 1980s, and most importantly for him it gave him the chance to reprise his talents as both actor and entertainer, and once again to give audiences a flavor of his superlative stagecraft skills, honed by the long months in *Porgy and Bess* and *Hello, Dolly!* Despite his age, he identified with the younger and more rebellious members of the cast. Soul singer Betty LaVette, who played in one of the youthful pairs, recalled, "The people were wonderful, they were. But I found the theater to be very gospel-like, and they always wanted me to hold hands or pray or hug. Honi and I—or when I was doing it with Cab Calloway—we always kind of got away and got drunk."[19]

Working on this touring production of *Bubbling Brown Sugar* was Danny Holgate, the man who had taken over from Spider Haynes as Cab's musical director. He was also the composer of some additional music and linking routines for the original Broadway version, in order to turn an amorphous collection of songs into something resembling a plot. The two men had first met when Holgate was asked to do some arrangements for Lael Calloway's solo show. After Lael's appearance at the Riverboat, Holgate occasionally filled in on Cab's own dates, sometimes providing a trio for club and cabaret evenings, and by the latter years of the 1970s was working with Cab quite frequently. Quite coincidentally, Holgate was asked to work on the touring version of *Bubbling Brown Sugar* at the very time that Cab joined the cast. "We were very close," remembered Holgate, "because before we joined the show, a lot of times when we traveled to engagements it was just the two of us."[20]

For the rest of Cab's life Holgate was to work as his principal musical director, doing fresh arrangements, and leading an occasional big band, which was assembled to back Cab on tour or for long cabaret residencies. They also worked briefly on the traveling version of the Broadway show *Eubie!*, another revue comparable to *Bubbling Brown Sugar*, but almost entirely built around the songs of Eubie Blake. This opened on Broadway in 1978, but Cab joined it on the road a little later. Some elements of this performance can be seen in the 1983 television tribute *Eubie Blake: A Century of Music*. By this time he had also recorded some of the screen performances by which he was to be most remembered by future generations, making guest star appearances with the puppets in the *Sesame Street* children's television show. He appeared three times on the program, twice in 1979 and once in 1980. Suitably togged up in his white tie and tails, he sang and danced "The Jumping Jive" in the show devoted to the letter "j," and was later featured singing "The Hi-De-Ho Man," with scat shout-backs from an amorphous range of Muppets. In a more math-oriented appearance, he sang "I Wanna Count."

Cab came off the road during the course of 1979, spending many an afternoon at the racetrack and enjoying "more leisure time than in several decades,"[21] but toward the end of the year he became involved in a major movie project. When shooting overran its projected October schedule, he was compelled to cancel a couple of theater dates, as a consequence of which he was interviewed for the newspapers about his failure to appear:

> Motion pictures still intrigue the "Hi-de-ho Man." He's just finished shooting in Chicago for *The Blues Brothers*. Its plot is top secret, Calloway reports, but its stars are *Saturday Night Live* graduates John Belushi and Dan Aykroyd. "They're crazy," Calloway says, "but they're the boys." The favorite of the ten films in which he's appeared is *Stormy Weather*, but the star contends "*The Blues Brothers* is the best role I've ever had."[22]

In *The Blues Brothers*, Cab was to play the part of Curtis, the building super who had once worked at the orphanage where Jake and Elwood Blues, played by Dan Aykroyd and John Belushi respectively, had been raised. His theater and concert dates in upstate New York that had been postponed in late 1979 were rescheduled for January 1980, once the movie had been shot and had gone into postproduction.

In the period between filming and the release of the movie in June 1980, Cab and Holgate traveled first to Syracuse, for a "good old days" variety show, which also starred Morey Amsterdam, and then they went on to Rochester to appear with the Philharmonic Orchestra.[23] This was one of a number of concerts that came about because Cab had recently changed his managerial arrangements. Stan Scotland from General Artists' Corporation had been the agency representative sent along to take care of Cab during his booking for *Sesame Street*. Following that first meeting, at Cab's invitation, he had started to take on the job of handling his personal management. He wanted to help

Cab break free of the round of solo appearances for chambers of commerce or low-paying hotels in the Catskills, and take on higher-profile jobs which paid far more satisfactory fees. Scotland suggested the idea of adding symphonic pops concerts to Cab's schedule, in which he would sing a medley of Gershwin tunes and other show songs, but also include an orchestrated version of "Minnie the Moocher." Remembered Holgate:

> We did maybe forty symphony concerts around the country, after Cab was first asked to do a pops concert. He called me one day and asked me to write some string parts for him on "Minnie the Moocher," which was for a concert with the Indianapolis Symphony with Erich Kunzl. That was the start, and I ended up arranging a whole repertoire for him. Later we also did the Barbican Centre in London, maybe three times, with the London Symphony.[24]

For the more prosaic gigs that remained in the diary, or for the basketball and racetrack entertainments that Cab still frequently played, Danny Holgate produced a disco-beat arrangement of "Minnie the Moocher." In an age when his former triumphs were all but forgotten, Cab felt this had more chance of connecting to a contemporary audience than his original "minor moaner." The disco arrangement became the version of the tune that Cab played on all of his solo concerts from 1978 onward, and he announced to *Billboard* that he found it "enjoyable and challenging." Witnessing the septuagenarian's "incredible energy" as he performed the piece generally brought the house down, and it remained his show stopper until the release of *The Blues Brothers* in mid-1980. "It was something the public understood and related to," remembered Holgate.[25] Stan Scotland said:

> All his arrangements of his most famous songs came from the 20s or the early 30s. So Cab liked this disco arrangement, which he recorded for Hologram records. And that's the music he took with him. Sometimes it was a problem. I remember we went to Iceland to do a special show for IBM. In the band were Clark Terry, Bobby Rosengarden, Milt Hinton and so forth. Now it comes to "Minnie the Moocher," which I guess Milt Hinton had played about 10,000 times with Cab, and he just automatically went into the old arrangement. Meanwhile the other musicians are doing the new one. It took Milt a little while to realize

that things had changed, although I don't think the audience noticed. On the bus coming back from the gig, Cab is very quiet. Then suddenly he turns to Milt and says, "Dammit! You've played with me thousands of times, how come you couldn't handle the arrangement of 'Minnie the Moocher'?" The whole bus immediately became quiet. This was his best friend, but Cab had gotten really upset when it came to playing his music wrong, because he himself was so focused on playing it that he'd come out as if it was a new act every night.[26]

The release of *The Blues Brothers* was to put paid to this particular element of Cab's performance. When he turned up on the set, Cab brought the disco arrangement of "Minnie" with him, because he'd been told he was to perform the song in the movie. The director John Landis was horrified, as he had expected the original 1930s chart. Cab put up a spirited resistance, but in the end the scene in the "Palace Hotel Ballroom" in which he sings the song, clad in his familiar white tails, was shot using an earlier style of arrangement.[27]

What we see on screen in the movie is Cab accompanied by the Blues Brothers Band, the small group that Jake and Elwood have spent most of the film trying to reassemble. What we hear on the sound track is the full big band arrangement based on the 1940s version of the chart. One moment Cab is standing in the wings dressed as Curtis in a black coat, hat, and shades. The next minute he is magically transformed into his white-clad persona, and the scene is a brilliant pastiche of the "Let's do the show right here" Hollywood production number, in which there's suddenly a backdrop of Harlem by night, and the stage is also set in white to match Cab's suit. Cab dances between verses, including an updated version of his "moon walk," and we also see Jake and Elwood slinking past outside in similar synchronized steps before sabotaging a fleet of police cars.

Cab's is one of a number of splendid cameo appearances in the film, among others by Aretha Franklin, Ray Charles, and James Brown. In the nineteen years following its release, the movie earned more than $115 million at the box office, in addition to television, video, and DVD revenues. But at the time its $30 million budget was seen as excessive, and the critical establishment rounded on its writers (Landis and Aykroyd) and director (Landis) for perpetuating cinematic racial stereotypes. David Denby in *New York Magazine* fulminated:

The Blues Brothers is a monstrous $30 million expansion of a ramshackle old Hollywood musical revue (like the *Big Broadcast of 1938*), the kind of movie that used to be made for a few hundred thousand dollars. These vaudeville musicals, their unrelated musical numbers stitched together with comedy routines, often featured jazz musicians or black singers and dancers who would never get to star in a movie of their own. Racism was built into the form. Well, things haven't changed that much in 45 years. . . . The great old Cab Calloway, his smile as brilliantly insinuating as ever, sings "Minnie The Moocher" in white tie and tails, in front of a huge audience, killing time for an impatient crowd while the boys are being chased by the police. Calloway's smile—the seal of a great entertainer's joy in giving pleasure—shows up Aykroyd and Belushi's sullen "cool" for the sophomoric thing it is. Yet what an insulting context for Calloway's triumph—as a fill-in![28]

It was one thing for critics, well versed in the history of film, to rail against this picture for repeating the sins of the past. It was quite another for a new, young public to be introduced to the work of Cab, Aretha Franklin, James Brown, and Ray Charles through the comic mayhem inspired by two popular stars of *Saturday Night Live*. The effect on Cab's career was remarkable, and suddenly he was being recognized as a star by a whole new section of the public. At the same time, the disco arrangement of "Minnie" was put to one side once and for all, and the original chart, as performed in the movie, came back into Cab's repertoire, because that was now what his new young audiences clamored to hear. Saxophonist Julian Presley was recruited to a band that Danny Holgate put together to back Cab for a series of shows in Philadelphia during the early 1980s. He recalled:

I was playing with him shortly after his appearance in the *Blues Brothers* movie, and it was incredible the exposure that it got. I believe it did have a big effect on bringing him back to public attention. Dan Aykroyd and John Belushi were hot at that time, and I guess they felt that they should bring Cab Calloway with them into this project. And I also think Cab really made a big difference . . . to the *Blues Brothers* movie.[29]

Immediately after the movie's release Cab briefly returned to the cast of *Bubbling Brown Sugar*.[30] But he and Holgate began to formulate the idea of assembling a regular big band for summer touring, that would gather together the same nucleus of players each year, rather than the somewhat ad hoc lineups they had used in the past. Initially the new group was billed as part of a revue called *Cab Calloway's Cotton Club*, but as the decade went on it shed the additional acts and became known as the Hi-De-Ho Orchestra. Nevertheless, to share the singing burden with Cab, it also frequently included Chris Calloway as an additional vocalist. Her regular features were "This Is My Life" and "Don't Cry Out Loud." Cab was to describe the contribution of his daughter, with whom he was now fully reconciled after the *Hello, Dolly!* incident, as "a very finished performance."[31] Billings for their shows made much of Cab's recent movie success, saying, "Since the movie of *The Blues Brothers* . . . Cab Calloway has revived a brand new audience. A dynamite show for all ages."[32]

When Francis Ford Coppola began work on his film *The Cotton Club* in 1984, there were suggestions that Cab might also appear in that movie. Instead he signed a release in exchange for sixty-five hundred dollars that he might be portrayed by an actor in the picture. But even the interest that this engendered seems to have bolstered what might be termed "the *Blues Brothers* effect" on his career. As a result of the flurry of publicity for Coppola's movie, the press reported that "76-year old Calloway is being swamped with bookings for next year."[33]

By the mid-1980s a new pattern had emerged. Cab and his new band would tour the United States and Europe in the summer festival months, they would take to the road again for short tours in the spring and fall, and he would otherwise pick and choose between individual engagements. Some of these were nostalgic, such as the memorial tribute to Ira Gershwin at the Gershwin Theater in August 1983, in which Cab sang a poignant version of "It Ain't Necessarily So," in memory of *Porgy and Bess*'s lyricist. Others were reunions with old friends, such as the all-star Songwriters' Guild event in January 1984 at the Palace in Manhattan, where Cab starred opposite Peggy Lee.

Another pleasurable gig for Cab was to join forces with his grandson Christopher Calloway Brooks for a 1984 concert in Boston. Camay's son had opted for a musical career, and graduated from New England Conservatory in 1980, where he subsequently joined the faculty as a guitarist and composer. Yet at this early stage in his working life he had chosen a very different area of music from Cab, in the college's Third Stream department, where Gunther Schuller and George Russell headed a team that investigated the interstices between contemporary classical music and jazz. Brooks recorded and toured with Ran Blake, and played regularly in a trio with the clarinetist Joe Maneri, a remarkable improvising musician and composer whose specialty was exploring microtonality. It would have been fascinating to hear Maneri, pianist Gerald Zaritsky, and Brooks playing their free improvisations in one half of the show, before Cab came on to join his grandson for such standards as "Blues in the Night" and "Stormy Weather." At the end of this special addition to the Enchanted Circle series of concerts in the Jordan Hall, New England Conservatory president Lawrence Lesser presented Cab with an award in recognition of his contribution to American music.[34] This was to be one of several events where Cab shared a stage with Brooks, and presaged the point when, in 1998, Brooks would step out as leader and singer in front of his own Cab Calloway Orchestra, featuring several musicians who performed with his late grandfather.

When Cab was on the road in the 1980s and 1990s with his new Hi-De-Ho band, it relatively soon settled into a successful formula, Danny Holgate recalled:

> He put together what can be classified as a club date concert show, in which he did "September Song," "Good Time Charlie," "Stormy Weather," and "It Ain't Necessarily So," in other words all the popular songs from the different points in his life. And that was the show that we did on tour and in Europe. It wasn't until later that I went through an old trunk in his basement and found all this wonderful other material from the original band that we could have been using, but by then it was a done deal, and so we spent years doing that same concert program. We would vary the band numbers from time to time, but basically Cab's part of the concert stayed the same. It was what the public understood and related to. I think if we had used some of the other stuff from the old days, they wouldn't have known what it was. They wouldn't have recognized it, so I don't think the reception would have been as good.[35]

Particularly in Europe, on his summer tours in the 1980s and early 1990s, Cab's reception was terrific. This was not least because he was one of the few really high-profile survivors of the Cotton Club days who was still touring, and audiences hungered for an authentic link with the past. Louis Armstrong had died in 1971, Duke Ellington in 1974, and although Adelaide Hall was still appearing in London, she seldom took to the road or traveled the festival circuit. Cab's former sideman Doc Cheatham was working as a soloist in the United States and Europe, but only at a relatively modest specialist level. With Cab and the Hi-De-Ho Orchestra, mass audiences had a chance to see a genuine link with the glorious past of African American show business. His occasional appearances in Britain with the London Symphony Orchestra, or at the Ritz Hotel in 1986 with a specially convened British band, were extremely entertaining, but to witness Cab once again in front of a regular band of his own was an altogether richer experience. As he had proven in *The Blues Brothers* and on *Sesame Street* his voice had the same power and flexibility it had displayed in the 1930s, and although his movements were a little less frenetic, his dancing was still elegant and light-footed.

The Hi-De-Ho band saxophonist Zane Paul recalled that although "Minnie the Moocher" would be saved for the end of the show, the program that Cab and Danny Holgate had worked out gave him a chance to show his vocal prowess on "St. James Infirmary" and other early hits. Cab was particularly concerned in his latter years that he have the right drummer in his band, who would give him the correct kind of support. Paul remembers him almost coming to blows with some drummers who seemed incapable of providing exactly what Cab required:

> He finally found what he wanted out of this guy called Frank Derek, who was almost the second in command to Danny Holgate, and became the assistant conductor of the band. What Derek gave him was just right, and you could see that in Cab's attitude, he was calm and happy. As a result, Holgate and Derek worked with him till the end of his life.[36]

Another aspect of Cab's touring schedule was that he crossed musical boundaries, in terms of the type of venue he played. Zane Paul had worked with Duke and Mercer Ellington, and with both incarnations of the Ellington band he played mainly jazz clubs and festivals. But he was surprised to find that Cab played a mixture of folk, blues, and jazz events. He was equally surprised that Cab's band might turn up in a small German or French town to play in a huge tent or outdoor venue for several thousand people, and that every time—before the show even started—Cab would be greeted with a lengthy standing ovation. "Even though Duke had the name," Paul remembers, "Cab touched more people."

Cab's visual appearance was no less striking on these latter-day tours than it had been in the heyday of the earlier big band. He told BBC interviewer Russell Davies that he had designed most of the clothes himself, from the details of his white tie and tails to the blue, tan, and green outfits he also wore. When it came to his stage style, he said, "That's my life, that's all it is."[37]

As the 1980s gave way to the 1990s, Cab's voice passed its prime and began to show the first signs of age. In a recording made on the cusp of the new decade to celebrate the long career of his friend and colleague Milt Hinton, issued by Chiaroscuro under the title *Old Man Time*, Cab sang with a group of veterans under the name of "The Survivors." With a lineup that included Doc Cheatham and Eddie Barefield from his own band, plus Basie's tenorist Buddy Tate and drummer Gus Johnson, and Fats Waller's guitarist Al Casey, Cab conducted the recording of Buck Clayton's elegant charts with gusto. In a track of reminiscences which the producer Hank O'Neal included as a bonus on the record, Cab tells tales of the old days with similar enthusiasm. But on the vocal of "Good Time Charlie," Cab definitely sounds a little tarnished round the edges. The range is still there, but the perfect control, the youthful vigor, and the clarity of diction that had always been his hallmarks were all slipping gently out of focus.

Onstage he was still a fine spectacle, and if anything he stepped up his touring schedule, not least when Chris Calloway was diagnosed with breast cancer in the late 1980s and took time out from traveling with him. When Cab played a couple of sold-out concerts at the Hollywood Bowl in the summer of 1990, he professed indifference at the importance of the venue. He was interviewed by the Associated Press:

> It doesn't matter what town he is in any more. Just find a spot and a band and he'll be there. He was in Europe in the spring. He's been all over the United States this summer. "It doesn't mean anything to me, it's just part of the routine" Mr. Calloway said . . . "If I wasn't here I'd be someplace else."[38]

A sense of that life on the road comes across in his 1990 video appearance for Janet Jackson's song "Alright." The plot is built around a dream sequence in which Cab is about to attend the premiere of a movie called *Alright*, and Jackson and two zoot-suited dancers set off to wait for him, ending up in his limo. Later it all seems to have been a dream until Cab finds Jackson on a park bench and presses her watch, which she lost during a dance outside the premiere, into her hand. It was one of his last screen appearances, but it formed a direct link between two show business generations, subtly dominated by the motif of Cab turning up in anytown, anywhere, for a premiere, and being treated automatically as a great star.

Yet gradually the frailties of age prevented him from always fulfilling his lifetime dictum that come what may the show must go on. In some cases this was the result of irascibility. In New Orleans, he was billed to appear in a Cotton Club tribute. On arrival, he was irked to find out that the show was to be hosted by Ray Charles, who had never had anything to do with the famous club. When one of the backstage gophers came up to him, as he was fully togged up in his white suit, and asked him who he was, he took umbrage. He left for home without going onstage. Stan Scotland got the call next morning to retrieve the music from a puzzled band director.[39] Ultimately, with Cab's dignity restored by a suitable apology, he returned to New Orleans to fulfill the rest of the week's engagement.

Not long afterward, Cab and the Hi-De-Ho Orchestra were on tour in Japan. The night before he was due to finish a lengthy run at a club in Tokyo he came out of his dressing room to tell Scotland that he thought he might not be able to complete the show, as he was having stomach problems. At the interval he was too ill to go back on, and as the band played the second half, Cab was whisked into the hospital where he was diagnosed with a blockage. For one of the few times in his life, Cab was unable to complete the final night of the engagement, as he was being flown back to the United States by air ambulance.[40]

Yet even in his eighties, he could still startle his younger musicians with his dedication. Trumpeter Stanton Davis, who was also a regular in the Living Time Orchestra led by composer George Russell, and therefore experienced in a wide range of music, had never met so energetic a touring musician. On the Hi-De-Ho band's final tour to Europe, Cab would always be early on stage, and would be waiting for the bus ahead of his musicians, even if he was suffering from lack of sleep. However jaded he felt before a gig, Cab would tell Davis how the music would "swing me into good health." The most remarkable example of Cab's professionalism on this tour was in Italy. Davis remembered:

Things don't always happen there as you'd expect. We were in this wonderful old theater, but there was no PA. They couldn't get some of the vital parts to make the system work, and we were all wondering how we were going to be able to play there for five days. Cab just said, "We'll do it without mikes." He sang for those five days without a mike, and that's hard, especially with a big band. We were all saying to one another, "He's going to kill himself, he'll lose his voice." But Cab knew how to use the room, how to make the right sound to be heard. This was an operatic hall, and he used the natural sound of the room to project over the band. Of course he was tired, but he did it.[41]

In good and vigorous form, despite recovering from cracked ribs after a fall, Cab saw in the New Year of 1993 with a special show at Club USA, just off Times Square in New York.[42] Then, in the summer of 1993, Cab broke a hip when he fell at his home shortly before he was due to appear at the JVC Jazz Festival in New York. Organizer George Wein had booked Cab to sing on a program that explored the connections between Jewish music and jazz, and it would have been a chance for Cab to reprise "Utt Da Zay" and his other cantoral repertoire. Reluctantly, he was forced to cancel his appearance. Nevertheless by that October Cab had made a considerable recovery, and although he had to attend the event in a wheelchair, he was honored at the White House. President Clinton presented him, along with Ray Charles, movie director Billy Wilder, and playwright Arthur Miller, with the National Medal of the Arts.[43] Danny Holgate remembers that following this award, people began asking Cab whether the time had come to retire.

The truth is, there was just no time to retire, he enjoyed that part of his life so much. He just never stopped. I was with him on his last performance at the Apollo Theatre. It was a dedication and I remember the mayor and the governor were both there, and they brought Cab out in a wheelchair. He performed "Minnie the Moocher" from the wheelchair and that was his last performance.[44]

The following June, he suffered a severe stroke at his home, and was rushed into intensive care in White Plains. Although the press carried reports that he then checked out to "hide away" and recover, he was so severely affected that he had to be confined to a Hokessin, Delaware, nursing home with twenty-four-hour care. He was to die there, with his wife and his eldest and his youngest daughters at his bedside, on November 18, 1994.

The tributes were fulsome, and unlike those for performers who had ceased to tread the boards years before, all of them made much of the fact that Cab had kept performing right up until the last possible moment. "Even in old age, he was a marvel to watch," ran one report. "[He was] a veritable dervish who dashed from one end of the stage to the other, his limbs and his mop of unruly hair flying in all directions as he flashed an enormous smile."[45] The *New York Times* praised his "Cat-like grace on the bandstand [and] a singing style that could be slyly insinuating one minute and wildly exuberant the next."[46]

After his death, his family did their best to keep the legacy of this extraordinary man alive. Chris Calloway, who had recovered from illness to give one-woman theater shows, re-formed the Hi-De-Ho Orchestra and appeared with the band in the mid-1990s. In 2001 she diverted her efforts to celebrate her pioneering aunt Blanche, in a one-woman show called *Clouds of Joy*. Chris lost her battle with cancer in August 2008.

In 1998 Christopher Calloway Brooks donned a zoot suit and fronted the Cab Calloway Orchestra, playing charts which he had lovingly restored from his grandfather's collection of papers in the Boston University Library. Brooks says:

> People say to me, "Why are you 'doing' Cab Calloway?" But I'm really not. I'm expressing who I am as a person. I know his music, arguably as well as anybody else out there, and I love the music. He showed it to me himself, and he was very confident in my doing it, and had trust in wherever I was going to take it. Because I love it and it's an expression of who I am and what I heard as a kid, it's all a very natural thing to me. I love "Minnie the Moocher," but if I stop liking the song, or what it does, then I'll stop doing it. But just the same as him, I think it's a wonderful piece of art.[47]

Spurred by a wide-ranging and affectionate series of "Cab 100" centenary events in 2007, in Brooks's hands the music will live on. At the end of his hundredth anniversary year, Cab was honored with a posthumous Grammy for his lifetime achievement in music. Shortly after his death, a new performing arts school in Wilmington, Delaware, was named for him, and Bill Cosby established a memorial scholarship in Cab's name at the New School of Social Research in Manhattan.

But there is a wider legacy of Cab Calloway. Through his movie appearances in *Stormy Weather* and *The Blues Brothers*, we can see him in his pomp, and in his mature prime. In countless records, we can chart the extraordinary influence he had on jazz singing. With the reissue on CD of virtually all his work, it is possible to appreciate the sheer scale and consistency of his recorded achievement within the world of jazz, let alone his additional musical theater discs of *Porgy and Bess* and *Hello, Dolly!*

At a time when only Louis Armstrong had managed to bridge the gap between African American jazz and popular entertainment, Cab began by following in his footsteps and surpassed him. From the clubs of Baltimore to the cabarets of 1920s Chicago, and on to the mob-run Cotton Club, Cab ultimately transcended racial, class, and national boundaries. His music brought the storytelling traditions of African Americans to a huge public through his tales of Minnie and Smoky Joe, and his catchphrases became familiar the world over to several generations from the 1930s to the 1990s. With his straight hair and light complexion, he might have decided to pass for white, but he was always, uncompromisingly, a black artist.

Not being an instrumentalist like Armstrong, he initially achieved all this primarily as a vocalist, heard across America as he hi-de-hoed from the Cotton Club. His early triumphs like "St. Louis Blues," "St. James Infirmary," "Nagasaki," and "Minnie the Moocher" brought call and response to the forefront of everyday entertainment in the 1930s. But these songs also set a template for the singers who would come afterward, from jump-jive vocalists such as Louis Jordan to more surreal entertainers such as Slim Gaillard, in whose work we find the early seeds of rap and hip-hop. In his films and recordings with the Cabaliers he sowed the seeds for doo-wop, just as pieces like "Calloway Boogie" looked forward to rhythm and blues.

Through his own hepster language, Cab began a linguistic exploration that leads directly to the work of today's MCs. In his choice of dress, and his lithe movements as a dancer, he created an identity that inspired performers from the 1930s right through to Michael Jackson or rappers like Tupac Shakur. It was Shakur who created a hip-hop interpretation of "Minnie the Moocher," which in its video format comes complete with a transformation from grungy clothes to white tie and tuxedo. Equally, Antwan "Big Boi" Patton and André "3000" Benjamin, otherwise known as the rap duo Outkast, were photographed in vintage pinstripes and derby hats, the prime of Cotton Club fashion, to accompany their 2006 release "Mighty O," which takes the "hi-de-ho" section of "Minnie" into new and previously uncharted rap territory. It is not too great a stretch of imagination to say that without Cab, and his particular brand of verbal dexterity, vocal invention, and sartorial style, the early twenty-first century's most dominant form of contemporary urban black culture in the United States, hip-hop, might never have existed.

Suggested Selected Recordings

....

There is currently no comprehensive edition of Cab Calloway's recorded work. However, readers are directed to the following editions:

Cab Calloway and His Orchestra: The Chronological Cab Calloway
Volume 1: The Early Years, 1930–1934
JSP Records JSP CD 908
Four-CD set remastered by the late John R. T. Davies, and the best sound quality reissue of Cab's early work.

Cab Calloway and His Orchestra: The Chronological Cab Calloway
Volume 2: 1935–1940
JSP Records JSP CD 914
Four-CD set remastered by Ted Kendall, keeping up the quality of John R. T. Davies's work.

The French "Chronological Classics" edition has suffered from distribution difficulties and is now hard to obtain in some markets, but it offers a comprehensive set of Calloway material on the following discs:
Cab Calloway and His Orchestra: 1930–1931. Classics 516
Cab Calloway and His Orchestra: 1931–1932. Classics 526
Cab Calloway and His Orchestra: 1932. Classics 537

Cab Calloway and His Orchestra: 1932–1934. Classics 544

Cab Calloway and His Orchestra: 1934–1937. Classics 554

Cab Calloway and His Orchestra: 1937–1938. Classics 568

Cab Calloway and His Orchestra: 1938–1939. Classics 576

Cab Calloway and His Orchestra: 1939–1940. Classics 595

Cab Calloway and His Orchestra: 1940. Classics 614

Cab Calloway and His Orchestra: 1940–1941. Classics 625

Cab Calloway and His Orchestra: 1941–1942. Classics 682

Cab Calloway and His Orchestra: 1942–1947. Classics 996

Cab Calloway and His Orchestra: 1949–1955. Classics 1287

The broadcasts from Club Zanzibar can be found as follows:

Cab Calloway and His Orchestra

AFRS ONS 356 and 405 (September 8 and 22, 1944). Magnetic (Lux) MRCD 123.

Cab Calloway and His Orchestra

AFRS ONS 773 and 690 (July 9 and 15, 1945). Magnetic (Lux) MRCD 132.

Cab's most significant musical performances are on:

Gershwin: *Porgy and Bess* (September 1952): William Warfield, Leontyne Price, Cab Calloway, Berlin RIAS Symphony Orchestra/Smallens. Audite 23405.

Gershwin: *Porgy and Bess* (Film soundtrack 1959): Robert McFerrin, Pearl Bailey, Cab Calloway. Arr. and cond. André Previn. Back Biter 555220.

Hello, Dolly! (1967 Broadway Cast) Pearl Bailey, Cab Calloway. RCA 58584.

Notes

Chapter 1

1. Calloway and Rollins, *Of Minnie the Moocher and Me*, 8. In the twelfth census of the United States, 1900, Baltimore Ward 13, Baltimore City, Md., roll T623 613, p. 18A, Cabell Calloway (born May 1878) is listed as working in real estate.

2. Thirteenth census of the United States, 1910, Rochester Ward 14, Monroe, N.Y., roll T624 991, p. 9A, enumeration district 138, image, 998. The census actually lists the family's address as Henrietta Avenue, but since the adjacent streets to be enumerated all intersect with the present-day Henrietta Street, it is a safe assumption that this was the Calloway household's address.

3. Fourteenth census of the United States, 1920, Baltimore Ward 14, Baltimore, Md., roll T625 663, p. 7B, enumeration district 238, image 1024. This shows that Elmer was aged eight in 1920, and contradicts the assertion in Calloway and Rollins that the boy was born in 1916.

4. Author's interview with Camay Calloway Murphy, September 25, 2005.

5. Calloway and Rollins, *Of Minnie the Moocher and Me*, 13.

6. Baltimore Register of Deaths, Cabell Calloway, October 15, 1913. I am grateful to Jean-François Pitet, the Hi-De-Ho Blog, and members of www.genealogue. com for research into the sequence of death dates of Cabell I and Cabell II.

7. Ages and address from fourteenth census.

8. Baltimore Register of Deaths, Cabell Calloway, May 8, 1919.

9. Calloway and Rollins, *Of Minnie the Moocher and Me*, 12.

10. Author's interview with Stan Scotland, September 25, 2005.

11. Steve Voce, "The Marquis of Harlem," *Jazz Journal*, vol. 9, no. 6 (June 1958), 9.

12. "Grace Choir Gives Recital," *Baltimore Afro-American*, April 11, 1919.

13. Peterson, *Century of Musicals in Black and White*, 322; "Opening at Grand Theater, Chicago, of Whitney and Tutt's Smarter Set Company," *Chicago Defender*, December 3, 1921.

14. William E. Clarke, "Up and Down Going Big at the Lafayette," *New York Age*, March 25, 1922.

15. Dance, *World of Earl Hines*, 49–50.

16. Gilbert Gaster, "Clyde Bernhardt," *Storyville*, no. 44 (December 1972), 58.

17. Peterson, *Century of Musicals In Black and White*; "Buzzin' Around," *New York Age*, May 27, 1922; Bradford, *Born with the Blues*, 144; "Grand Theater, Chicago: Ramblin' Round, with an All-Star Cast of Principals including Emmet Anthony, Late Star of 'Liza,' Ollie Powers, the Popular Tenor, Blanche Calloway, Late of 'Shuffle Along,'" *Chicago Defender*, July 7, 1923.

18. "Chicago's Classiest Cabaret: Blanche Calloway, Late Star of 'Shuffle Along,' and a Cast of 20 Sparkling Personalities," *Chicago Defender*, September 13, 1924; *Chicago Defender*, September 20, 1924.

19. McCarthy, *Big Band Jazz*, 27.

20. Floyd G. Snelson Jr., "Sunset Vanities at Chicago Cafe," *Pittsburgh Courier*, September 27, 1924.

21. Dates of foundation of the school from the program for the East Brandywine Township Sesquicentennial Celebration, May 14, 1994. The Industrial and Agricultural School continued until it became insolvent in 1993, and Delaware County Community College now stands on the site.

22. Wilson, *Teddy Wilson Talks Jazz*, 2.

23. Wright, *The Negro in Pennsylvania*, 139.

24. Calloway and Rollins, *Of Minnie the Moocher and Me*, 28.

25. Ibid., 35.

26. Interview with Murphy.

27. Calloway and Rollins, *Of Minnie the Moocher and Me*, 41. Kuska, *Hot Potato*, 93–95.

28. Kuska, *Hot Potato*, 93–95; "Wilberforce University Court Team . . . ," *Xenia (Ohio) Evening Gazette*, January 26, 1926; "Basketball between Leading Colored Organizations in the Country . . . ," *Xenia (Ohio) Evening Gazette*, February 2, 1926.

29. Calloway and Rollins, *Of Minnie the Moocher and Me*, 36ff.

30. "Only and Original Plantation Days: Lafayette, NYC," *New York Age*, February 14, 1927. According to the report this starred "Blanche Calloway" [*sic*].

31. Empress Theatre, Decatur, Ill., December 5, 1924; Columbia Theater, Davenport, Iowa, December 12, 1924; "Plantation Days," including Jones and Jones, Four Crackerjacks, Farrell Chadwick, and beauty chorus, split the week between Orpheum, Des Moines, Iowa, and Palace, St. Paul, Minn., December 20, 1924; Majestic, Milwaukee, January 3, 1925; Palace Theatre, Flint, Mich., February

28, 1925. All dates from *Pittsburgh Courier.* "Plantation Days en Route to Detroit," *Elyria (Ohio) Chronicle-Telegram,* April 11, 1925; Pantages, Toronto, April 25, 1925; Chateau Theatre, Chicago, May 9, 1925; Pantages Theatre, Calgary, June 27, 1925; Pantages, Seattle, July 11, 1925; Pantages Theatre, Tacoma, Wash., July 25, 1925; Pantages, Ogden, Utah, September 26, 1925. All dates from *Pittsburgh Courier.*

32. "Negro Revue at Columbia," *Davenport (Iowa) Democrat and Leader,* December 12, 1924.

33. "Plantation Days," *Mansfield (Ohio) News,* June 19, 1924.

34. *Chicago Defender,* November 17, 1925.

35. *Baltimore Afro-American,* April 17, 1926.

36. Calloway and Rollins, *Of Minnie the Moocher and Me,* 51; "Willard Theater, 31st and Calumet Avenue, Chicago. The Only Original Plantation Days, with Ada Brown, Dave & Tressie, Green Grass Mason & Lee Bailey, The Three Browns, Blanche Calloway, Roger Mathew, Hollywood Four, Baby Theda Davis, and the Original Pepper Chorus," *Chicago Defender,* October 16, 1926.

37. *Chicago Defender,* April 30, 1927.

38. "I have now looked through the entire yearbook, and did not find any mention of anyone named Calloway, a very disappointing result. I really hoped to find him there, perhaps on an athletic team or in a band. The yearbook has listings and individual pictures for the graduating class, and group or individual pictures of some other students who were involved in various extracurricular activities." Letter to the author from Robert Helfer, Chicago alumnus, December 29, 2008.

Chapter 2

1. Details from the City of Chicago landmarks website, www.ci.chi.il.us/ Landmarks/S/SunsetCafe.html (accessed March 21, 2009).

2. Dance, *World of Earl Hines,* 49–50.

3. Calloway and Rollins, *Of Minnie the Moocher and Me,* 58; "Metropolitan Theater, Chicago, Anniversary Week," *Chicago Defender,* June 11, 1927 (Hall is billed as "Adele Hall"); "Blanche Calloway Was the Attraction at the Vendome Last Week with Tate's Magnificent Orchestra," *Pittsburgh Courier,* May 7, 1927.

4. Author's interview with Christopher Calloway Brooks, September 25, 2005.

5. Oliver, *Savannah Syncopators,* 58.

6. Riis, *More Than Just Minstrel Shows,* 6.

7. Brooks, *Bodies in Dissent,* 262.

8. Riis, *More Than Just Minstrel Shows,* 47.

9. Riis, *The Music and Scripts of "In Dahomey,"* xliii.

10. Riis, *More Than Just Minstrel Shows,* 54.

11. Dance, *World of Earl Hines,* 49–50.

12. David Griffiths, "Take a Bow . . . Roger Boyd," *Storyville,* no. 85 (October/ November 1979), 25ff.

13. *Chicago Defender*, July, 2, 1927; ibid., July 23, 1927; Cameron Williams, *Underneath a Harlem Moon*, 111.

14. Steve Voce, "The Marquis of Harlem," *Jazz Journal*, vol. 9, no. 6 (June 1958), 9.

15. Dance, *World of Earl Hines*, 49–50. Calloway family information from author's interviews with Christopher Calloway Brooks and Camay Calloway Murphy, January 22, 2009.

16. Ray Boyce, "Cab Calloway: No One Can Escape His Spell," *Syracuse Post-Standard*, January 11, 1980. Joe Glaser confirmed these figures: "Cab Calloway started for me at thirty-five a week, while his sister Blanche was making two or three hundred." Shapiro and Hentoff, *Hear Me Talkin' to Ya*, 113.

17. Collier, *Louis Armstrong*, 163.

18. Calloway and Rollins, *Of Minnie the Moocher and Me*, 58. Author's interview with Christopher Calloway Brooks for BBC Radio 3, September 15, 2007.

19. Ned E. Washington, "His Hi-De-Highness of Ho-De-Ho," *Ho-De-Ho* (New York, Mills Artists Inc., 1934) (official Irving Mills press pack for Cab Calloway).

20. Calloway and Rollins, *Of Minnie the Moocher and Me*, 59.

21. Gilbert Gaster, "Clyde Bernhardt," *Storyville*, no. 44 (December 1972), 58.

22. "Elmer Snowden," *Storyville*, no. 18 (August/September 1968), 5.

23. "Footlight Personals," *Baltimore Afro-American*, October 6, 1928.

24. Calloway and Rollins, *Of Minnie the Moocher and Me*, 60ff.

25. Dave Peyton, "The Musical Bunch," *Chicago Defender*, December 31, 1927.

26. Personnel from American Federation of Musicians [hereafter AFM] records from *International Musician* and Rust, *Jazz Records*.

27. Calloway and Rollins, *Of Minnie the Moocher and Me*, 63.

28. McCarthy, *Big Band Jazz*, 48.

29. Boyd Atkins advertised at the Sunset in *Chicago Defender*, May 18, 1929.

30. Alabamian tour venues confirmed by *International Musician* records of AFM transfers and Calloway and Rollins, *Of Minnie the Moocher and Me*, 68.

31. "Local Elks to Give Dance Thursday Evening," *Moberly (Missouri) Monitor-Index*, June 4, 1929. Copy for this announcement is included on Mike Meddings's Jelly Roll Morton homepage, www.doctorjazz.co.uk, and includes the somewhat inaccurate description of the band as "The original Alabamians, an eleven piece band and Victor recording artists who were formerly with Jelly Roll Morton."

32. Basie, *Good Morning Blues*, 119.

33. McCarthy, *Big Band Jazz*, 210.

34. Voce, "The Marquis of Harlem," 9.

35. *International Musician* AFM transfer records. Cab was still billed in some advertisements for the band as its director, for example at the Danceland Ballroom in Davenport on Sunday, December 22, but he was appearing in *Hot Chocolates* by then, and could not have been with the Alabamians. The advertisement is to be found on http://www.kazoolips.com/PHIL_PAGE_26.html (accessed July 22, 2009).

36. Singer, *Black and Blue*, 222.

37. Chorus line details from Wells, *The Night People*; *New York Age*, June 1, 1929.

38. *New York Age*, February 8, 1930.

39. *Pittsburgh Courier*, May 10, 1930; *Baltimore Afro-American* June 7, 1930; Stratemann, *Duke Ellington*, 26. The *Courier* article suggests that Cab may already have been with the Missourians by this time, but the other documentary evidence seems to contradict this.

40. Voce, "The Marquis of Harlem," 9.

Chapter 3

1. Author's interview with Jesse Stone, March 9, 1997.

2. Dial, *All This Jazz about Jazz* , 20; Jeff Hopkins, "The Missourians, 1925–1930," liner note to Vintage Music Productions CD VMP 0212, 2007; "Good Programs on WHN," *New York Age*, December 10, 1924.

3. "Cotton Club, Harlem, Bars Colored Couple, Accompanied by White Friends," *New York Age*, July 9, 1927.

4. Calloway and Rollins, *Of Minnie the Moocher and Me*, 88.

5. Opening night flier for *Breezy Moments in Harlem*, July 13, 1927. Program for *Dan Healy's Blushing Browns* (undated) from Jimmy McHugh scrapbooks, McHugh family archive, Los Angeles, with "Special restricted music by Jimmy McHugh." The cast included Aida Ward, Leitha Hill, Leonard Ruffin, Brown & McGraw, and Shirley Jordan. The band is listed as the "Cotton Club Orchestra, starting their third year here," which is consistent with Andy Preer and the Missourians having arrived at the club under that name in 1925.

The 1928–29 tour dates are from union transfers in *International Musician*, and include (in chronological order): Cleveland, Columbus, Pittsburgh, Milwaukee, St. Louis, Chicago, Terre Haute, Ind., Peoria, Ill., St. Paul, Minn., Bloomington, Ill., Chicago, Terre Haute, Ind., Galesburg, Ill., Waterbury, Conn., finishing in April 1929.

6. Most discographies, following the lead of Popa, *Cab Calloway Discography*, have listed the banjo player for the Missourians' February 17, 1930, date as Charlie Stamps; however, Morris White is noted in all the AFM transfers for the band from mid-1928 onward, so he had clearly replaced Stamps by the time of the band's Victor recordings of 1929–30.

7. McCarthy, *Big Band Jazz*, 211.

8. Joop Visser, "This Is Hep: Cab Calloway and His Orchestra," liner notes to *This Is Hep*, Properbox 141, 2008; Whitburn, *Pop Memories 1890–1954*, 72.

9. Details of AFM transfers from *International Musician*, August 1930.

10. David Griffiths, "Those Were the Days—Earle Nappy Howard's Life Story," *Storyville*, no. 88 (April/May 1980), 146.

11. Calloway and Rollins, *Of Minnie the Moocher and Me*, 84.

12. "Night Club Is Raided," *Olean (N.Y.) Evening Times*, January 17, 1930.

13. "Arrests Near in Nightclub Man's Slaying," *Syracuse Herald*, May 1, 1930.

14. Bruce Allen Hardy, "Charlie Davis, Copenhagen and the Musical Culture of the 20s," *Storyville*, no. 62 (December 1975/January 1976), 63.

15. Calloway and Rollins, *Of Minnie the Moocher and Me*, 85.

16. For details of comparable recordings, see Oliver, *Songsters and Saints*.

17. Griffiths, "Those Were the Days," 146.

18. "Cab Calloway and His Missourians," *Baltimore Afro-American*, February 7, 1931.

19. "Chicago and New York Clubs," *Chicago Defender*, March 21, 1931.

20. Lawrence, *Duke Ellington and His World*, 157. In Calloway and Rollins, *Of Minnie the Moocher and Me*, 110, Cab suggests that he owned 50 percent of his band, with Mills, Ellington, and other parties owning the other half. Lawrence's research suggests this was hubris, and so I have followed the more pessimistic percentages in his text.

21. Stratemann, *Duke Ellington*, 48; *Variety*, June 30, 1931.

22. Shipton, *I Feel a Song Coming On*, 56.

23. Washington, *Ho-De-Ho*.

24. Ibid.

25. The sales figures were computed in the era predating reliable charts, but the million mark was reached, according to Whitburn, *Pop Memories 1890–1954*. The 1978 figure comes from Molaire, Jones, and Tanksley, *African-American Who's Who*, 67.

26. Cab Calloway interviewed by Russell Davies for the BBC film *The Cotton Club Comes to the Ritz*, 1985.

27. Schuller, *The Swing Era*, 332.

28. Author's interview with Milt Hinton, March 23, 1993; "Cab Calloway from Cotton Club on NBC Red (KBC) Network, 9:30 (Central)," *Chicago Defender*, June 30, 1931 (this season of broadcasts apparently ran from May to July).

29. Author's interview with Camay Calloway Murphy, September 25, 2005.

30. Author's interview with Christopher Calloway Brooks, September 25, 2005.

31. Author's interview with Alan Cohen, June 7, 1995.

32. Ibid.

33. Interview with Murphy.

34. *Syracuse Herald*, May 1, 1930. This lists "beer, nightclubs, slot machines and politics," not to mention "women" and "the fight racket." The paper also notes that Madden and his associate Bill Duffy were being investigated regarding their protégé, the Italian fighter Primo Carnera, "using weapons not fists to win fights."

Chapter 4

1. Barker, *A Life in Jazz*, 154.

2. Author's conversation with Snub Mosley, during UK tour in 1979.

3. "New Acts," *Variety*, October 6, 1931.

4. Calloway and Rollins, *Of Minnie the Moocher and Me*, 110.

5. Steve Voce, "The Marquis of Harlem" *Jazz Journal*, vol. 9, no. 6 (June 1958), 9.

6. "Cab Calloway (in person) and his Cotton Club Orchestra, direct from the Cotton Club, New York City, at the Casino, Bemus Point, Saturday July 25th. Dancing 8.30–12.30 EST. $1.50 a person. Cab Calloway's First Appearance on Tour." *Dunkirk (N.Y.) Evening Observer*, July 22, 1931.

7. David Griffiths, "Those Were the Days—Earle Nappy Howard's Life Story," *Storyville*, no. 88 (April/May 1980), 146. Howard is almost certainly referring to Shamokin, Pa., a sizable coal-mining town.

8. "Cab Calloway and Crew," *Wisconsin State Journal*, February 9, 1931; *Variety*, April 1, 1931; "Hectic Helmut Makes Many Friends While on Radio Tour of This Country," unattributed clipping from Jimmy McHugh archive for 1931; Walter Winchell, "On Broadway," *Port Arthur (Tex.) News*, August 17, 1931.

9. *Brownsville (Tex.) Herald*, October 12, 1931.

10. Shipton, *I Feel a Song Coming On*, 107.

11. Jablonski, *Harold Arlen*, 41ff.

12. Calloway and Rollins, *Of Minnie the Moocher and Me*, 93.

13. *"Rhythmania"* dates courtesy of Jean-François Pitet, the Hi-De-Ho Blog; sales figures from Joop Visser, "This Is Hep: Cab Calloway and His Orchestra," liner notes to *This Is Hep*, Properbox 141, 2008.

14. Details of Cotton Club revues from Suskin, *Show Tunes*.

15. "Cab Calloway and Band at Oriental," *Chicago Daily Herald*, February 12, 1932.

16. "Cab Calloway on NBC Red at 11 (Central)," *New York Age*, November 13, 1931.

17. "Cab Calloway Talkartoon," *Athens (Ohio) Messenger*, December 6, 1931.

18. Lehman, *The Colored Cartoon*, 31; Edward Rodriguez, "Rotoscope," *Computer Graphic Artist*, Global Media, Delhi, 2007.

19. "Band Is heard in Big Broadcast of Radio Stars," *Benton Harbor (Mich.) News-Palladium*, October 24, 1932.

20. "Fletcher, Noble, Cab, Edwards Follow," *Pittsburgh Courier*, October 31, 1931.

21. "Poll of Bands of the Year," *Pittsburgh Courier*, December 31, 1931. Results: 1. Ellington (50,000); 2. McKinney (42,000): 3. Sissle (39,000): 4. Mills Blue Rhythm Band (38,500); 5. Calloway (32,500); 6. Blanche Calloway (32,000); 7. Louis Armstrong (30,000).

22. "Her Circuit—Jazz to Cosmetics," *Fresno Bee*, March 25, 1970.

23. Russ Shor, "Charlie Gaines," *Storyville*, no. 68 (December 1976/January 1977), 44.

24. Kirk, *Twenty Years on Wheels*, 103.

25. Büchmann-Møller, *Someone to Watch over Me*, 17.

26. David Griffiths, "Take a Bow . . . Roger Boyd," *Storyville*, no. 85 (October/November 1979), 25–27.

27. Calloway and Rollins, *Of Minnie the Moocher and Me*, 112.

28. *Piqua (Ohio) Daily Call*, May 18, 1932; Floyd G. Snelson, "Newsy Newsettes: Blanche Calloway and Her Orchestra Are at the Pearl, Philly This Week, to Be Followed by the Palace on Broadway," *Pittsbugh Courier*, April 2, 1932.

29. *Centralia (Wash.) Daily Chronicle*, August 1, 1932.

30. "Blanche Calloway Meadowbrook Ballroom," *North Adams (Mass.) Transcript*, August 29, 1932.

31. Ralph Matthews, "Looking at the Stars—Family Stuff," *Baltimore Afro-American*, March 12, 1932.

32. Interviews with Camay Calloway Murphy and Christopher Calloway Brooks, September 25, 2005; "Public Dances at Armory Every Friday," *Appleton (Wisc.) Post-Crescent*, September 9, 1932.

33. Shipton, *I Feel a Song Coming On*, 113.

34. Analysis of *International Musician* transfer deposits kindly supplied by Howard Rye and Josephine Beaton.

35. "Harriett Calloway Band Here Tuesday," *Greely (Colo.) Tribune-Republican*, July 23, 1933.

36. Eric Townley, "Eddie Barefield, Hitting the Road," *Storyville*, no. 76 (April/May 1978), 149–50.

37. Cheatham, *I Guess I'll Get the Papers and Go Home*, 34.

38. Ibid.

39. Gilbert Swan, "In New York," *Indiana Evening Gazette*, February 8, 1932.

40. "Cab Calloway Another Week at the Oriental," *Chicago Daily Herald*, February 19, 1932.

41. Snelson, "Newsy Newsettes."

42. Tour itineraries from Howard Rye and Josephine Beaton's research into *International Musician*. Calloway and Rollins, *Of Minnie the Moocher and Me*, 125.

43. Cheatham, *Guess I'll Get the Papers*.

44. "Irving Mills," *Orchestra World*, May 1936, 3.

45. Washington, *Ho-de-Ho*.

Chapter 5

1. Hennessey, *From Jazz to Swing*, 123ff.; Magee, *The Uncrowned King of Swing*, 169.

2. Schuller, *The Swing Era*, 326.

3. *Melody Maker*, July 22, 1933.

4. Spike Hughes quoted in Tucker, *The Duke Ellington Reader*, 67.

5. Wilder Hobson, "Introducing Duke Ellington" (1933), in Tucker, *Duke Ellington Reader*, 96.

6. Schuller, *The Swing Era*, 326–29.

7. Ibid., 331–32.

8. The signed membership card of Jack Jarvis of Philadelphia was auctioned on eBay in July 2009. Details from photographs reproduced during the online auction.

9. Eric Townley, "Eddie Barefield, Hitting the Road," *Storyville*, no. 76 (April/May 1978), 149–50.

10. Howard Rye, "Visiting Firemen: Cab Calloway and His Cotton Club Orchestra," *Storyville*, no. 91 (October/November 1980), 30. Details updated by Rye in a letter to the author, December 19, 2008.

11. *Melody Maker* review quoted in Godbolt, *History of Jazz in Britain*, 116.

12. Rye, "Visiting Firemen," 30–31.

13. The commercial version of Hudson's arrangement of "Moon Glow," as played on the tour, was published in the May 1936 edition of *Orchestra World*, in an issue devoted to Mills Artists.

14. Calloway and Rollins, *Of Minnie the Moocher and Me*, 137.

15. "Cab Calloway," *Jazz Tango Dancing*, April 1934, reproduced on the Hi-De-Ho Blog, http:www/thehidehoblog.com/index.php?sujet_id=8179 (accessed July 20, 2009), translated by author.

16. Cheatham, *Guess I'll Get the Papers*, 47.

17. "Cab Calloway," *Jazz Tango Dancing*, March 1934; *idem*, April 1934, Hi-De-Ho Blog site.

18. Cab Calloway, "Notes from My London Diary," *Tune Times*, April 1934, 363.

19. Leslie Thompson, interviewed by Olga and Kevin Wright, "My Face Is My Fortune," *Storyville*, no. 83 (June/July 1979), 187.

20. Calloway and Rollins, *Of Minnie the Moocher and Me*, 137.

21. Calloway, "Notes," 369.

22. Ibid.

23. *De Jazzwereld*, May 1934; Allard Möller, letter, *Storyville*, no. 92 (December 1980/January 1981), 68.

24. "Cab Calloway," *Jazz Tango Dancing*, April 1934.

25. Handbill reproduced in Tournés, *New Orleans sur Seine*, 32.

26. Panassié, *Hot Jazz*, 248.

27. Corinne Grenouillet, "L'univers sonore des Communistes: Chansons et références musicales," in Aptel-Muller, *Recherches croisées*, 145.

28. Zwerin quoted in Shapiro, *Turn the Beat Around*, 15.

29. Fishman, *The Battle for Children*, 67.

30. Calloway and Rollins, *Of Minnie the Moocher and Me*, 137.

31. Ibid., 136.

32. Cheatham, *Guess I'll Get the Papers*, 47.

Chapter 6

1. *New York Amsterdam News*, October 19, 1935; Cameron Williams, *Underneath a Harlem Moon*, 301.

2. Knight, *Disintegrating the Musical*, 223–24.

3. "Irving Mills," *Orchestra World*, May 1936, 3.

4. Tour venues from union transfers in *International Musician*.

5. "Among Our Colored Citizens," *Chester (Pa.) Times*, May 5, 1934.

6. Swayze's death date and details from Chilton, *Who's Who of Jazz*, 324, and Kernfeld, "Ed Swayze." For band personnel, most current discographies follow Popa, *Cab Calloway Discography*, but although his pioneering work did much to set out the Calloway oeuvre in great detail, he incorrectly brings Thornton Blue back to the lineup in 1935, fails to notice that Keg Johnson replaces Harry White, and keeps Ed Swayze alive after his untimely death! Howard Rye and Josephine Beaton have collated AFM transfers in *International Musician* that chart the membership of the band in detail.

7. "Cotton Club Players Offer Midnight Show," *San Antonio Express*, September 29, 1934.

8. George Ross, "In New York," *Ironwood (Mich.) Daily Globe*, September 28, 1936.

9. "Cab Calloway, 'Goose' Goslin in Detroit," *New York Age*, October 19, 1935; "Calloway at M'Fadden's," *Oakland Tribune*, November 14, 1935.

10. Panassié, *Hot Jazz*, 248.

11. "Jolson Takes Unusual Pains Making Film," *Ames (Iowa) Daily Tribune*, April 4, 1936.

12. "Theater News," *Wisconsin State Journal*, April 26, 1936.

13. Popa, *Cab Calloway Discography*, 12.

14. Büchmann-Møller, *Someone to Watch over Me*, 40.

15. "The Singing Kid," *Oakland Tribune*, April 8, 1936.

16. Büchmann-Møller, *Someone to Watch over Me*, 40.

17. Eric Townley, "The Judge: An Interview with Milt Hinton," *Storyville*, no. 89 (June/July 1980), 168.

18. Shipton, *Fats Waller*, 101; Nat Hentoff, "Morgan—Riverboat Bass," *Jazz Record*, February 1946, 11ff.

19. "First Theater Date for the Band Will Be Indianapolis," in "Calloway East," *Variety*, January 29, 1936.

20. Townley, "The Judge," 168.

21. Hinton and Berger, *Bass Line*, 68.

22. Bushell, *Jazz from the Beginning*, 89.

23. "Cab Calloway Sings," *Ogden (Utah) Standard-Examiner*, September 20, 1935.

24. Barker, *Buddy Bolden*, 127.

25. Author's interview with Milt Hinton for BBC Radio 3, March 23, 1993.

26. Cheatham, *Guess I'll Get the Papers*, 44.

27. Bushell, *Jazz from the Beginning*, 90.

28. Dizzy Gillespie interview with Roy Plomley for BBC Radio, January 19, 1980, quoted in Shipton, *Groovin' High*, 57.

29. Bushell, *Jazz from the Beginning*, 88.

30. "Ether Chatter," *Lowell (Mass.) Sun*, February 21, 1934.

31. Bushell, *Jazz from the Beginning*, plate section.

32. Hinton and Berger, *Bass Line*, 72.

33. Cab Calloway, *The New Hepster's Dictionary*, 251.

34. "Bama State Collegians and Avis Andrews Head New Bill at the Apollo," *New York Age*, July 25, 1936; Ross, "In New York."

35. Shipton, *I Feel A Song Coming On*, 129.

36. Haskins,*The Cotton Club*, 114.

37. Ross, "In New York."

38. Calloway and Rollins, *Of Minnie the Moocher and Me*, 134.

39. Some discographers suggest that Doc Cheatham briefly left the band at this time to be replaced in the short term by Shad Collins. Union records indicate that Cheatham remained in the lineup throughout, so I have attributed the trumpet solo in "Copper Colored Gal" to Randolph, as it is clearly not Cheatham or Wright.

40. Hinton's 208 card is still shown in transfers from October 1936 in *International Musician*, but thereafter he is listed as a member of 802. Hinton and Berger, *Bass Line*, 76. Broadcast times from "Cab Calloway on the Ether Waves," *Baltimore Afro-American*, October 17, 1936, 13.

41. Author's interview with Camay Calloway Murphy, September 25, 2005.

42. Ibid.

43. AFM deposit with local 38, Richmond, listed in *International Musician*.

44. Cheatham, *Guess I'll Get the Papers*, 35.

45. Ibid., 41–42; Bushell, *Jazz from the Beginning*, 91.

46. "Cab's Rooster Teaches Him Dance Craze 'Peckin,'" *Chicago Defender*, July 3, 1937.

47. Bushell, *Jazz from the Beginning*, 99; Haughton's details from AFM transfers in *International Musician*.

48. James Gentry, "Bronzeville," *Chicago Defender*, July 31, 1937.

Chapter 7

1. Author's interview with Milt Hinton for BBC Radio 3, March 23, 1993.

2. Ibid.

3. Bushell, *Jazz from the Beginning*, 88.

4. Interview with Hinton.

5. Hinton and Berger, *Bass Line*, 88.

6. Charles G. Sampas, "N. Y.—Hollywood," *Lowell (Mass.) Sun*, November 12, 1937; "Mills Salaried Exec. of American Record Co," *Variety*, March 3, 1937.

7. Calloway and Rollins, *Of Minnie the Moocher and Me*, 174.

8. Barker, *Life in Jazz*, 171.

9. Ibid. 156.

10. George Ross, "This New York," *Charleston (W. Va.) Daily Mail*, March 7, 1938.

11. "Cotton Club, N.Y.," *Variety*, March 23, 1938.

12. Barker, *Life in Jazz*, 168.

13. Damon Runyon, "The Brighter Side," *Syracuse Journal*, February 3, 1938.

14. Ibid.

15. Erenberg, *Swingin' the Dream*, 71.

16. "New Tunes in Arcadia Film," *Portsmouth (N.H.) Herald*, February 19, 1938.

17. "Reviewer Lavishly Lauds New Republic Production" *Cullman (Ala.) Banner*, February 11, 1938.

18. George Ross, "In New York," *Chester (Pa.) Times*, June 14, 1938.

19. George Tucker, "Man about Manhattan," *Hagerstown (Md.) Daily Mail*, July 2, 1938.

20. Dale Harrison, "New York," *Reno (Nev.) Evening Gazette*, June 27, 1938.

21. Ross, "In New York"; Joop Visser, "This Is Hep," liner notes to *This Is Hep*, Properbox 141; "Cab Calloway—Review of the Year 1945," unattributed clipping in Calloway scrapbooks in Calloway Collection at Boston University.

22. Tommy Dorsey, guest columnist, "Walter Winchell on Broadway," *Logansport (Ind.) Pharos-Tribune*, July 7, 1938.

23. "Cab Calloway Brings Cotton Club Revue to Majestic," *San Antonio Express*, July 8, 1938.

24. According to the 1930 census (Nashville, Davidson, Tennessee, roll 2239, p. 1B, enumeration district 112), Blake's father was Cuban and his mother from Indiana, where he was born. He had been adopted by the widowed Alice Blake. Cheatham, *Guess I'll Get the Papers*, 25.

25. Hinton and Berger, *Bass Line*, 70.

26. Lees, *You Can't Steal a Gift*, 56.

27. Author's interview with Jonah Jones, May 25, 1995.

28. Dinerstein, *Swinging the Machine*, 161.

29. The lyric is entirely about Arturo Toscanini, recently appointed as founding conductor of the NBC Symphony Orchestra, but the title was changed as a precautionary measure by Vocalion, who first issued the record, in order not to offend the famously irascible Italian-born conductor.

30. "Cab Calloway," *East Side News*, July 8, 1939.

31. Haskins, *The Cotton Club*, 133ff.

32. George Ross, "In New York," *Bluefield (W. Va.) Daily Telegraph*, September 20, 1938.

33. *New York Times*, April 2, 1939.

34. Cheatham, *Guess I'll Get the Papers*, 51.

35. Popa, *Cab Calloway Discography*, 15, suggests Collins was in Calloway's band in 1937. Some editions of discographies by Brian Rust, Walter Bruyninckx, and Thomas Lord initially followed this view. AFM transfer records show that Cheatham remained in the band throughout 1937 and 1938. Collins was with Hill in 1937 according to AFM records, during which year he is on the passenger lists for the band's European tour, and he is listed in Hill personnel in a March 1938

transfer listing from Baltimore. John Chilton has suggested he briefly joined Don Redman before returning to New York.

36. Author's interview with Jonah Jones, May 25, 1995.

37. Cheatham, *Guess I'll Get the Papers*, 46.

38. Gillespie, *To Be or Not to Bop*, 132.

39. Cheatham, *Guess I'll Get the Papers*, 46.

Chapter 8

1. Calloway and Rollins, *Of Minnie the Moocher and Me*, 190.

2. Ibid., 156.

3. *Baltimore Afro-American*, March 4, 1939.

4. Barker, *Life in Jazz*, 168.

5. "New York's Tracks to Install Mutuels for Racing in 1940," *Syracuse Herald-Journal*, November 10, 1939, 84.

6. Author's interview with Stan Scotland, September 25, 2005.

7. Calloway and Rollins, *Of Minnie the Moocher and Me*, 152.

8. Author's interview with Christopher Calloway Brooks, January 23, 2009.

9. Calloway and Rollins, *Of Minnie the Moocher and Me*, 150, 159.

10. Hinton and Berger, *Bass Line*, 110.

11. Barker, *Life in Jazz*, 168.

12. Voorhuis, *Negro Masonry in the United States*, 46.

13. Hinton and Berger, *Bass Line*, 110. Also see the Hi-De-Ho Blog, www.thehidehoblog.com/index.php?sujet_id=3648 (accessed August 14, 2009).

14. Hi-De-Ho Blog.

15. Robert Francis, "Cab Calloway," *Brooklyn Eagle*, September 29, 1939.

16. *Brooklyn Eagle*, October 4, 1939.

17. Gillespie, *To Be or Not to Bop*, 109.

18. Ibid., 110.

19. Hinton and Berger, *Bass Line*, 93.

20. Barker, *Life in Jazz*, 164.

21. Author's interview with Clark Terry, October 8, 2000.

22. Calloway and Rollins, *Of Minnie the Moocher and Me*, 160.

23. Shipton, *Groovin' High*, 63.

24. Joop Visser, "This Is Hep," liner notes to *This Is Hep*, Properbox 141.

25. Hankus Netsky, "Cab Calloway: On the Yiddish Side of the Street," article posted on the *Secular Culture and Ideas* section of the online Jewish book community site www.jbooks.com (accessed August 16, 2009); Jaffee, *The End of Jewish Radar*, 42.

26. Author's interview with Camay Calloway Murphy, September 25, 2005.

27. Sublette, *Cuba and Its Music*, 461.

28. Unattributed cutting from 1939 scrapbook in Cab Calloway Collection, Boston University.

29. *Brooklyn Eagle*, October 4, 1939. Barker's song went on to be a rhythm and blues hit for Wanda Jackson in 1956. Tour publicity reproduced in Vail, *Dizzy Gillespie*, 11.

30. Vail, *Dizzy Gillespie*, 12.

31. *New York Age*, September 30, 1939.

32. Gillespie, *To Be or Not to Bop,* 167.

33. Author's interview with Milt Hinton for BBC Radio 3, March 23, 1993.

34. Barker, *Life in Jazz*, 164.

35. Ibid., 165.

36. Danny Barker, quoted in Shapiro and Hentoff, *Hear Me Talkin' to Ya*, 333.

37. Hinton and Berger, *Bass Line*, 88.

38. "Feather Signed Up," *New York Amsterdam News*, January 6, 1940.

39. Dave Dexter, *DownBeat*, October 15, 1940.

40. Hinton and Berger, *Bass Line*, 88.

41. "Cab Calloway Eyes Symphony: He'll Do One in Swing Time for Carnegie Hall," *New York Amsterdam News*, April 27, 1940.

42. *DownBeat*, September 15, 1940.

43. "Cab on Coast: Booked for Long Run at Roost," *New York Amsterdam News*, March 1, 1941.

44. Eric Townley, "Muted Jazz: An Interview with Jonah Jones," *Storyville*, no. 85 (October/November 1979), 7.

45. Author's interview with Jonah Jones, May 25, 1995.

46. Ibid.

47. Ibid.

48. Vail, *Dizzy Gillespie*, 16–17.

49. *DownBeat*, September 1, 1941.

50. *Lima (Ohio) News*, October 5, 1941.

51. Interview with Hinton.

52. *DownBeat*, October 15, 1941.

53. Sterling Sorensen, "Drama, Stage and Screen, in Madison," *Madison (Wisc.) Capital Times*, October 16, 1941.

54. Associated Press wire, October 27, 1941.

Chapter 9

1. Calloway and Rollins, *Of Minnie the Moocher and Me*, 174.

2. *New York Amsterdam News*, November 15, 1941.

3. *Variety*, December 10, 1941.

4. *New York Amsterdam News*, November 4, 1941.

5. James Weldon Johnson, "The Origins of the 'Barber Chord,'" *Mentor*, February 1929, 53.

6. I am grateful to film historian and archivist Mark Cantor for confirming these dates, in a letter of August 24, 2009.

7. Tour dates courtesy of Howard Rye, in a letter of August 24, 2009.

8. Calloway and Rollins, *Of Minnie the Moocher and Me*, 198.

9. Bryant et al., *Central Avenue Sounds*, 84.

10. Walter Winchell, "On Broadway," *Brownsville (Tex.) Herald*, October 20, 1942.

11. Green, *Memphis and the Black Freedom Struggle*, 152.

12. Cripps, *Making Movies Black*, 83ff.

13. Louella O. Parsons, "Paging the Stars," *Lowell (Mass.) Sun*, October 22, 1942.

14. Various dates have been proposed for the shooting of Cab's sequences for *Stormy Weather.* Popa, *Cab Calloway Discography*, suggests January 1943, and Joop Visser in the liner notes to *The Illinois Jacquet Story*, Properbox 49, 2002, proposes April/May. According to *International Musician*, the band was finishing its road tour in January 1943, working in New Jersey in February, then appearing at the Sherman Hotel Chicago for a long engagement in April and at the Strand in New York for three weeks in May. The movie opened on July 21 in Manhattan. A March shooting date, when there was a four-week gap in the band's touring and theater schedule, suits the editing and release timetable for a picture of this complexity.

15. "Stage Shows," *International Musician*, December 1942, 16. On its way to Hollywood in February 1943, the band grossed $19,500 at the Adams Theater in Newark, N.J., according to the same column in February 1943, 11. Chicago dates from Al Monroe, "Swinging the News," *Chicago Defender*, November 14, 1942.

16. "Cab Not So Hot on Resurrecting Banjo," *Baltimore Afro-American*, May 2, 1942.

17. "Dancer Fayard Nicholas Dies at 91," *USA Today*, January 25, 2006.

18. Author's interview with Illinois Jacquet for BBC Radio 3, July 1992.

19. *Columbus Citizen*, November 3, 1943.

20. Interview with Jacquet.

21. Author's interview with Jonah Jones, May 25, 1995.

22. *Brownsville (Tex.) Herald*, January 14, 1944; "Stormy Weather," *Sheboygan (Wisc.) Press*, October 23, 1943.

23. "Film Musical Now Showing," *Galveston News*, September 3, 1943.

24. Cripps, *Making Movies Black*, 85.

25. Calloway and Rollins, *Of Minnie the Moocher and Me*, 191. Currency values rounded from www.thepeoplehistory.com/1940s.html (accessed December 2009).

26. "The Cab Calloway Marriage Is Legally Hi-De-Hover," Walter Winchell, "On Broadway," *San Antonio Light*, June 9, 1949.

27. Interview with Jones, 1995.

28. Ibid.

29. "Cab Calloway—Review of the Year 1945," Irving Mills press release, clipping in scrapbook in Cab Calloway Collection, Boston University.

30. "Walter Winchell," *Port Arthur (Tex.) News*, September 22, 1944.

31. *New York Amsterdam News*, June 2, 1944.

32. Barker, *Life in Jazz*, 173.

33. Salters's presence confirmed in Popa, *Cab Calloway Discography*, 25; "Sister Tharpe Is Featured Artist with Cab Calloway on the Present Tour," Al Monroe, "Swinging The News," *Chicago Defender*, April 7, 1945.

34. Undated clipping from *Variety* in Calloway scrapbook, Cab Calloway Collection, Boston University; *Columbus Citizen*, November 3, 1943.

35. "Strand Theatre, New York," *Billboard*, July 3, 1944.

36. *Orchestra World*, September 1944.

37. Calloway and Rollins, *Of Minnie the Moocher and Me*, 198.

38. Author's interview with Jonah Jones, May 16, 1997.

39. Hinton and Berger, *Bass Line*, 111.

40. *Afro Magazine*, February 22, 1947.

41. Interview with Jones, 1997.

42. *Portsmouth (N.H.) Herald*, June 17, 1944.

43. *Chicago News*, April 10, 1943.

44. *DownBeat*, February 15, 1944.

45. *Benton Harbor (Mich.) News-Palladium*, December 24, 1945.

46. *Amarillo (Tex.) Daily News*, May 21, 1947; "Cab Calloway Denied Damages in Suit," *Oakland Tribune*, May 22, 1947.

47. "New Trial Ordered for Cab Calloway," *Portland (Me.) Press Herald*, July 13, 1948.

48. "Cab Calloway," *New York Age*, September 28, 1946.

49. "Walter Winchell," *Brownsville (Tex.) Herald*, July 12, 1946.

50. L. L. Stevenson, "Gadabout Notes around Manhattan," *Bluefield (W. Va.) Daily Telegraph*, July 13, 1946.

51. "Cab Calloway's Revue at Broadway Strand," *Pittsburgh Courier*, April 12, 1947.

52. L. L. Stevenson, "Cab Calloway Marks 20th Anniversary of Jive Talk," *Bluefield (W. Va.) Daily Telegraph*, November 4, 1947.

53. "In Person, the Famous Cab Calloway, His Orchestra and Show Direct from His Engagement at the Roxy Theatre," *Syracuse Post Standard*, August 8, 1948; *Syracuse Herald-Journal*, July 31, 1948.

54. Interview with Jones, 1995.

55. Gottschild, *Waltzing in the Dark*, 91.

Chapter 10

1. Marjorie Burden, "Jive Talking Cab Calloway Comes to City," *Winnipeg Free Press*, July 28, 1949.

2. "Coming May 31 for One Week, Cab Calloway and His All Colored Revue," *Syracuse Post Standard*, May 25, 1949.

3. Hawes, *Filmed Television Drama*, 72.

4. Jack O'Brian, "Radio Round Up," *Cumberland (Md.) Evening Times*, August 31, 1950; ibid., September 26, 1950.

5. Draft running order in Cab Calloway Collection, Boston University.

6. Bob Franklin, "Show Time," *Independent Journal (Marin, Calif.)*, April 7, 1951.

7. *Winnipeg Free Press*, November 20, 1950, details a "Hi-De-Ho Formal Ball" on November 25 with Cab and a sixteen-piece orchestra.

8. Lees, *Arranging the Score*, 149.

9. Band payment records in Cab Calloway Collection, Boston University.

10. "To Appear in New York," *Monessen (Pa.) Daily Independent*, June 14, 1951; "Cab Calloway Orchestra to Play Here Aug. 29," *Charleston (W. Va.) Gazette,* August 10, 1951, which reports, "Recently the band director returned from an extensive engagement in South America and Havana."

11. "Governor Gives Patronage to Cab's Performance," *Daily Gleaner (Kingston, Jamaica)*, January 17, 1952; "Cab Calloway Calls," *Daily Gleaner,* February 29, 1952.

12. Walter Winchell, "On Broadway," *Eureka (Calif.) Humboldt Standard*, January 12, 1952.

13. Jay Breen, "No More Hepsters, Jive Talk Now Changed, Cab Calloway Mourns," *Corpus Christi (Tex.) Caller-Times*, December 2, 1951.

14. Joey Sasso, "New Star for Teen Clientele," *Brainerd (Minn.) Daily Dispatch*, January 19, 1952.

15. "Cab Calloway Famed Negro Bandleader Is Arrested," *Frederick (Md.) Post*, March 21, 1952; Calloway and Rollins, *Of Minnie the Moocher and Me*, 207.

16. Calloway and Rollins, *Of Minnie the Moocher and Me*, 204; "City Jive Cats Get Hep with a Hi-De-Ho Plus!" *Winnipeg Free Press*, April 5, 1952.

17. "New, Different Calloway Opens First Show," *Reno Evening Gazette*, May 27, 1952.

18. "Manners and Morals, the Beau from Mo," *Time*, September 10, 1951.

19. Stephanie Strom, "Robert Breen, 80, Arts Executive and Theatrical Producer Is Dead," *New York Times*, April 2, 1990; Rimler, *George Gershwin: An Intimate Portrait*, 171.

20. Pollack, *George Gershwin: His Life and Work*, 593.

21. Warfield, *My Music and My Life*, 132.

22. Calloway and Rollins, *Of Minnie the Moocher and Me*, 205.

23. Carnovale, *George Gershwin: A Bio-Bibliography*, 66.

24. "President Treats Self to Theater without Missus," *Lumberton (N.C.) Robesonian*, August 6, 1952.

25. "Folk Opera Cast Leaves by Plane for Europe Tour," *Bradford (Pa.) Era*, September 2, 1952.

26. Ibid.

27. Jackson, *Waiting in Line at the Drugstore*, 70.

28. Ibid.

29. Max Graf, "Porgy and Bess Begins European Tour in Vienna," *Musical America*, vol. 72, no. 12 (October 1952), 9. This is a condensed version of Graf's review for *Weltpresse*, September 9, 1952.

30. Ronald Duncan, "Porgy and Bess: The Work and Its Conception," *Opera*, December 1952, 711.

31. Lord Harewood, "Porgy and Bess: The Work and Its Performance," *Opera*, December 1952, 718.

32. Author's interview with Elizabeth Forbes, June 7, 1995.

33. "Negro Blues Singer Married to White Musician in London," *Lubbock (Tex.) Morning Avalanche*, November 20, 1952.

34. Eric Townley, "Muted Jazz: An Interview with Jonah Jones," *Storyville*, no. 85 (October/November 1979), 8.

35. Brooks Atkinson, "Return of a Classic," *New York Times*, March 15, 1953.

36. Hughes, *Collected Works of Langston Hughes*, 451.

37. Atkinson, "Return of a Classic."

38. "Porgy Singer Weds Court Stenographer," *Jet*, July 16, 1953.

39. Calloway and Rollins, *Of Minnie the Moocher and Me*, 205.

40. "Cab Calloway Quits 'Porgy' for Night Club Act," *Jet*, August 19, 1954.

41. Louella O. Parsons, "Hollywood," *Lowell (Mass.) Sun*, July 27, 1954.

42. "All Negro 'Blues Opera' Set for Paris Premiere," *Jet*, September 23, 1954.

43. "TV Previews," *Syracuse Herald-Journal*, August 16, 1955; "Sings of Porgy and Bess," *Mason City (Iowa) Globe-Gazette*, May 11, 1956.

44. Robert Coleman, column, *New York Daily News*, February 27, 1955.

45. Dorothy Kilgallen, "Hollywood Bulletin Board," *Lowell (Mass.) Sun*, July 29, 1955.

46. "Golden Show Has Variety of Talent," *Reno Evening Gazette*, January 8, 1955.

47. Loella O. Parsons, "Hollywood," *Lowell (Mass.) Sun*, January 17, 1955.

48. *Jet*, August 11, 1955.

49. "Cab Readies for English Cats," *Jet*, October 6, 1955; "Daughter of Cab Calloway, Camay Calloway Brooks Has Cab's First Grandson," *Jet*, October 20, 1955.

50. Steve Voce, "The Marquis of Harlem" *Jazz Journal*, vol. 9, no. 6 (June 1958), 9.

51. Calloway and Rollins, *Of Minnie the Moocher and Me*, 195.

52. Erskine Johnstone, "In Hollywood," *Portsmouth (N.H.) Herald*, February 24, 1956.

53. Bob Foster, "Cab Calloway Hits with Unusual Disc," *San Mateo (Calif.) Times*, February 7, 1956.

54. "Program Notes," *Cedar Rapids Gazette*, February 26, 1956.

55. Juli S. Charkes, "Struggling to Preserve Cab Calloway's Home," *New York Times*, September 16, 2008.

56. Peter Carr, "Jay Cole," *Storyville*, no. 61 (October/November 1975), 10.

57. "Voice of Broadway," *Anderson (Ind.) Daily Bulletin*, November 1, 1956; Earl Wilson, "It Happened Last Night," *Petersburg—Colonial Heights (Va.) Progress-Index*, October 11, 1956.

58. "Cab's like Fine Wine, He Mellows with Age," *Winnipeg Free Press*, April 11, 1959, review of show at Rancho Don Carlos; "Jean Sampson . . . May Head East for Atlantic City When Cab Calloway Opens His Cotton Club Revue," *Jet*, April 30, 1959.

59. Bill W. Dunlevy, "Cab Playing 'One-Nighters,' Loves 'Em," *Long Beach (Calif.) Independent*, January 31, 1961.

60. "Cab Calloway Swings at 60," *Madison (Wisc.) Capital Times*, December 26, 1967.

61. Clive Barnes, "Pearl Bailey Stops the Show," *New York Times*, November 16, 1967.

62. Richard Lebherz, "Hello Dolly," *Frederick (Md.) News*, October 16, 1967.

63. Ibid.

64. Leonard Lyons, "Lyons Den," *Syracuse Post-Standard*, November 20, 1967.

65. "TV Highlights," *Nashua (N.H.) Telegraph*, December 29, 1967.

66. Jane Margold, "Stardom Takes More Than a Name," *Oakland Tribune*, April 28, 1968.

67. Masekela and Cheers, *Still Grazin'*, 201.

68. "Chris Calloway 'Disappoints' Family; Elopes," *Jet*, July 11, 1968.

69. Ibid.

70. Masekela and Cheers, *Still Grazin'*, 209.

71. Jack O'Brian, "Spray Net Not Mace for Rowdy Hippies," *Logansport (Ind.) Pharos-Tribune and Press*, September 23, 1968.

72. Performance details from Peterson, *Century of Musicals in Black and White*, 166.

73. Gill, *No Surrender! No Retreat!* 140.

74. Calloway and Rollins, *Of Minnie the Moocher and Me*, 187.

Chapter 11

1. *Long Beach (Calif.) Independent*, July 9, 1971.

2. Masekela and Cheers, *Still Grazin'*, 205.

3. Author's interview with Charles Lake, June 12, 1994.

4. Calloway and Rollins, *Of Minnie the Moocher and Me*, 187, 188.

5. Author's interview with Alan Barnes, June 7, 1995; author's interview with Julian Presley, September 25, 2005; comment about Barefield from author's interview with Alan Cohen, June 7, 1995.

6. "Calloway, Kingston Trio, Vaudeville Returns," *Syracuse Post-Standard*, October 21, 1972.

7. "It Happened Last Night," *Dover (Ohio) Times Reporter*, October 27, 1973.

8. William E. Sarmento, "Broadway Season Is Off to Worst Season in History," *Lowell (Mass.) Sun*, December 23, 1973.

9. Ibid.

10. Earl Wilson, "On the Town," *Uniontown (Pa.) Morning Herald*, January 29, 1974.

11. "Cab Calloway Swings at 60," *Madison (Wisc.) Capital Times*, December 26, 1967.

12. William D. Laffler, "Record Reviews," *Bennington (Vt.) Banner*, May 1, 1974.

13. "Cab Calloway Makes with Sound of 40s," *Pasadena (Calif.) Star News* October 27, 1974; Tony Wetzel, "Cab Calloway to Hi-de-Ho for Chamber," *Naples (Fla.) Daily News*, April 20, 1975.

14. "New York Beat," *Jet*, October 16, 1975.

15. Calloway and Rollins, *Of Minnie the Moocher and Me*, 218.

16. "Her Circuit—Jazz to Cosmetics," *Fresno Bee*, March 25, 1970; "John Fortune Sr." *Annapolis (Md.) Evening Capital*, August 19, 1977.

17. *Billboard*, August 12, 1978.

18. Ed Campbell, "Calloway Cavorts 'Brown Sugar' to Sizzling New Blaze," *Frederick (Md.) News-Post*, August 1, 1978.

19. Freeland, *Ladies of Soul*, 93.

20. Author's interview with Danny Holgate, September 25, 2005.

21. Joan E. Vadeboncoeur, "Few Mountains Left: Landmark Guest Calloway Reviews Career," *Syracuse Herald Journal*, January 6, 1980.

22. Ibid.

23. Boyce, Ray, "Cab Calloway: No One Can Escape His Spell," *Syracuse Post-Standard*, January 11, 1980

24. Author's interview with Danny Holgate, September 25, 2005.

25. Ibid.; Radcliffe Joe, "It's Calloway and 'Minnie' Again," *Billboard*, September 16, 1978, 14.

26. Author's interview with Stan Scotland, September 25, 2005.

27. Author's interview with Christopher Calloway Brooks, September 25, 2005; Pratt, *Doug Pratt's DVD*, 176.

28. David Denby, "Two-Faced Blues," *New York Magazine*, June 30, 1980.

29. Interview with Presley.

30. "Bubbling Brown Sugar," *Frederick (Md.) Post*, July 3, 1980; "Bubbling Brown Sugar," *Elyria (Ohio) Chronicle Telegram*, July 18, 1980.

31. "Cab Calloway to Revisit Legendary Cotton Club," *Syracuse Herald-Journal*, September 26, 1985.

32. *Logansport (Ind.) Pharos-Tribune*, September 29, 1985.

33. Marilyn Beck, "Hollywood," *Santa Fe New Mexican*, October 3, 1984.

34. Ernie Santosuosso, "Cab Calloway to Join Grandson Brooks in Free Concert," *Boston Globe*, October 5, 1984.

35. Interview with Holgate.

36. Author's interview with Zane Paul, September 25, 2005.

37. Cab Calloway interviewed by Russell Davies for BBC Television, "Cotton Club Comes to the Ritz," 1986.

38. John Rogers, "At 82, Cab Calloway Is Still 'Hi-De-Ho-ing'," *Frederick (Md.) News-Post*, August 30, 1990.

39. Interview with Scotland.

40. Ibid.

41. Author's interview with Stanton Davis, September 25, 2005.

42. "Performer Cab Calloway Shares a Laugh," *Pacific Stars and Stripes*, January 4, 1993.

43. "Clinton Presents Awards to Artists," *Doylestown (Pa.) Intelligencer*, October 8, 1993.

44. Interview with Holgate.

45. "Cab Calloway, 'Hi-De-Ho' Bandleader Dead," *Frederick (Md.) News*, November 19, 1994.

46. John S. Wilson, "Cab Calloway Is Dead at 86," *New York Times*, November 20, 1994.

47. Interview with Brooks.

Bibliography

Aptel-Muller, Michel. *Recherches croisées Aragon/Elsa Triolet*. Besançon: Presses Universitaires de Franche-Comté, 2001.

Barker, Danny. *A Life in Jazz*. Ed. Alyn Shipton. New York: Oxford University Press, 1986.

————. *Buddy Bolden and the Last Days of Storyville*. Ed. Alyn Shipton. New York: Continuum, 2000.

Basie, Count. *Good Morning Blues—As Told to Albert Murray*. London: Heinemann, 1986.

Bradford, Perry. *Born with the Blues*. New York: Oak Publications, 1965.

Brooks, Daphne A. *Bodies in Dissent: Spectacular Performances of Race and Freedom, 1850–1910*. Durham, N.C.: Duke University Press, 2006.

Bryant, Clora, et al. *Central Avenue Sounds*. Berkeley: University of California Press, 1998.

Büchmann-Møller, Frank. *Someone to Watch over Me: The Life and Music of Ben Webster*. Ann Arbor: University of Michigan Press, 2006.

Bushell, Garvin, as told to Mark Tucker. *Jazz from the Beginning*. Oxford, U.K.: Bayou Press, 1988.

Calloway, Cab. *The New Hepster's Dictionary*. 4th ed. New York: Cab Calloway Inc., 1944.

Calloway, Cab, and Bryant Rollins. *Of Minnie the Moocher and Me*. New York: Crowell, 1976.

Cameron Williams, Iain. *Underneath a Harlem Moon*. London: Continuum, 2002.

Carnovale, Norbert. *George Gershwin: A Bio-Bibliography.* Santa Barbara, Calif.: Greenwood Press, 2000.

Cheatham, Adolphus "Doc." *I Guess I'll Get the Papers and Go Home*. Ed. Alyn Shipton. London: Cassell, 1996.

Chilton, John. *Who's Who of Jazz*. 4th ed. New York: Da Capo, 1985.

Collier, James Lincoln. *Louis Armstrong*. London: Michael Joseph, 1984.

Coueroy, André, and Schaeffner, André. *Le jazz*. Paris: C. Aveline, 1926.

Cripps, Thomas. *Making Movies Black: The Hollywood Message from World War II to the Civil Rights Era*. New York: Oxford University Press, 1993.

Dance, Stanley. *The World of Earl Hines*. New York: Scribner, 1977.

Dial, Harry. *All This Jazz about Jazz*. Chigwell, U.K.: Storyville, 1984.

Dinerstein, Joel. *Swinging the Machine*. Amherst: University of Massachusetts Press, 2003.

Erenberg, Lewis A. *Swingin' the Dream*. Chicago: University of Chicago Press, 1998.

Fishman, Sarah. *The Battle for Children: World War II, Youth Crime and Juvenile Justice in Twentieth Century France*. Cambridge, Mass.: Harvard University Press, 2002.

Freeland, David. *Ladies of Soul*. Jackson: University Press of Mississippi, 2001.

Gill, Glenda Eloise. *No Surrender! No Retreat!* London: Palgrave Macmillan, 2000.

Gillespie, Dizzy, with Al Fraser. *To Be or Not to Bop*. Minneapolis: University of Minneapolis Press, 2009.

Godbolt, Jim. *A History of Jazz in Britain, 1919–50*. London: Quartet, 1984.

Gottschild, Brenda Dixon. *Waltzing in the Dark: African American Vaudeville and Race Politics in the Swing Era*. New York: Palgrave Macmillan, 2002.

Green, Laurie Bush. *Memphis and the Black Freedom Struggle*. Chapel Hill: University of North Carolina Press, 2007.

Haskins, Jim. *The Cotton Club*. London: Robson, 1985.

Hawes, William. *Filmed Television Drama, 1952–1958*. Jefferson, N.C.: McFarland, 2002.

Hennessey, Thomas J. *From Jazz to Swing—African-American Jazz Musicians and Their Music, 1890–1935*. Detroit, Mich.: Wayne State University Press, 1994.

Hinton, Milt, and David G. Berger. *Bass Line—The Stories and Photographs of Milt Hinton*. Philadelphia: Temple University Press, 1988.

Hughes, Langston. *The Collected Works of Langston Hughes*. Vol. 9. *Essays on Art, Race, Politics, and World Affairs*. Ed. Christopher C. De Santis. Columbia: University of Missouri Press, 2002.

Jablonski, Edward. *Harold Arlen—Rhythm, Rainbows and Blues*. Boston: Northeastern University Press, 1998.

Jackson, James Thomas. *Waiting in Line at the Drugstore and Other Writings of James Thomas Jackson*. Ed. June Acosta. Denton: University of North Texas Press, 1993.

Jaffee, Martin S. *The End of Jewish Radar: Snapshots of a Post-Ethnic American Judaism*. Bloomington, Ind.: iUniverse.com, 2009.

Kernfeld, Barry, ed. *The New Grove Dictionary of Jazz*. London: Macmillan, 1988.

Kirk, Andy, as told to Amy Lee. *Twenty Years on Wheels*. Oxford, U.K.: Bayou Press, 1988.

Knight, Arthur. *Disintegrating the Musical*. Durham, N.C.: Duke University Press, 2002.

Kuska, Bob. *Hot Potato—How Washington and New York Gave Birth to Black Basketball and Changed America's Game Forever*. Charlottesville: University of Virginia Press, 2004.

Lawrence, A. H. *Duke Ellington and His World*. New York: Routledge, 2001.

Lees, Gene. *Arranging the Score*. London: Cassell, 2000.

———. *You Can't Steal a Gift—Dizzy, Clark, Milt and Nat* . Lincoln: University of Nebraska Press, 2004.

Lehman, Christopher P. *The Colored Cartoon—Black Representation in American Animated Short Films*. Amherst: University of Massachusetts Press, 2008.

Magee, Jeffrey. *The Uncrowned King of Swing: Fletcher Henderson and Big Band Jazz*. New York: Oxford University Press, 2005.

Masekela, Hugh, and D. Michael Cheers. *Still Grazin': The Musical Journey of Hugh Masekela*. New York: Three Rivers Press, 2004.

McCarthy, Albert. *Big Band Jazz*. London: Barrie and Jenkins, 1983.

Molaire, Mike, F., Jones, Marsha, and Tanksley, Fred. *African-American Who's Who, Past and Present Greater Rochester Area*. Rochester, N.Y.: Norex, 1998.

Oliver, Paul. *Savannah Syncopators, African Retentions in the Blues.* London: Studio Vista, 1970.

———. *Songsters and Saints: Vocal Traditions on Race Records.* Cambridge, U.K.: Cambridge University Press, 1984.

Panassié, Hugues. *Hot Jazz—The Guide to Swing Music.* New York: Witmark, 1936. (Eng. trans. of *Le Jazz Hot,* Paris: Correa, 1934.)

Peterson, Bernard L. *A Century of Musicals in Black and White: An Encyclopedia of Musical Stage Works by, about, or involving African Americans.* Santa Barbara, Calif.: Greenwood Press, 1993.

Pollack, Howard. *George Gershwin: His Life and Work.* Berkeley: University of California Press, 2007.

Popa, James. *A Cab Calloway Discography.* 2nd ed. Zephyr Hills, Fla.: Joyce, 1987.

Pratt, Douglas. *Doug Pratt's DVD: Movies, Television, Music, Art, Adult and More.* Vol. 2. New York: Harbor Electronic Publishing, 2004.

Riis, Thomas L. *More Than Just Minstrel Shows: The Rise of Black Musical Theatre at the Turn of the Century.* Brooklyn, N.Y.: Institute for Studies in American Music, 1992.

———. *The Music and Scripts of "In Dahomey."* Madison, Wisc.: A-R Editions, 1996.

Rimler, Walter. *George Gershwin: An Intimate Portrait.* Urbana-Champaign: Illinois University Press, 2009.

Rust, Brian. *Jazz Records.* 5th ed. Chigwell, U.K.: Storyville, 1983.

Schuller, Gunther. *The Swing Era.* New York: Oxford University Press, 1989.

Shapiro, Peter. *Turn the Beat Around.* London: Macmillan, 2006.

Shapiro, Nat, and Nat Hentoff. *Hear Me Talkin' to Ya.* Harmondsworth, U.K.: Penguin, 1962.

Shipton, Alyn. *Fats Waller—The Cheerful Little Earful.* 2nd ed. New York: Continuum, 2002.

———. *Groovin' High: The Life of Dizzy Gillespie.* New York: Oxford University Press, 1999.

———. *I Feel a Song Coming On: The Life of Jimmy McHugh.* Urbana-Champaign: University of Illinois Press, 2009.

Singer, Barry. *Black and Blue—The Life and Lyrics of Andy Razaf.* New York: Schirmer, 1992.

Stratemann, Klaus. *Duke Ellington Day by Day, Film by Film.* Copenhagen: JazzMedia, 1992.

Sublette, Ned. *Cuba and Its Music, from the First Drums to the Mambo.* Chicago: Chicago Review Press, 2007.

Suskin, Steven. *Show Tunes, the Songs, the Shows and Careers of Broadway's Major Composers.* Rev. ed. New York: Oxford University Press, 1999.

Tournés, Ludovic. *New Orleans sur Seine: Histoire du Jazz en France.* Paris: Fayard, 1999.

Tucker, Mark. *The Duke Ellington Reader.* New York: Oxford University Press, 1995.

Vail, Ken. *Dizzy Gillespie: The Bebop Years, 1937–52.* Cambridge, U.K.: Vail, 2000.

Voorhuis, Harold Van Buren. *Negro Masonry in the United States.* Reprint, Whitefish, Mont.: Kessinger, 1995.

Warfield, William, with Alton Miller. *My Music and My Life.* Champaign, Ill.: Sagamore, 1991.

Washington, Ned E. *Ho-De-Ho.* New York: Mills Artists Inc., 1934.

Wells, Dicky. *The Night People.* Boston: Crescendo, 1971.

Whitburn, Joel. *Pop Memories 1890–1954.* Menomonee Falls, Wisc.: Record Research Inc., 1992.

Wilson, Teddy, with Arie Ligthart and Humphrey Van Loo. *Teddy Wilson Talks Jazz.* London: Cassell, 1996.

Wright, Richard R. *The Negro in Pennsylvania: A Study in Economic History, 1912.* Whitefish, Mont.: Kessinger, 2000.